ENTROPOLOGY

ENTROPOLOGY

LOUIS ARMAND

A∅P
ANTI-OEDIPUS PRESS

Entropology

Copyright © 2022 by Louis Armand

ISBN: 978-0-99-915357-4

Library of Congress Number: 2023940701

First Anti-Oedipal Hardcover Edition, September 2023

RAW DOG SCREAMING PRESS

www.rawdogscreaming.com

Cover Design by Interior Ministry

www.alienistmanifesto.wordpress.com

Interior Design by D. Harlan Wilson

www.dharlanwilson.com

Anti-Oedipus Press

Grand Rapids, MI

@AntiOedipusP
@antioedipuspress

www.anti-oedipuspress.com

SF SCHIZ FLOW

BOOKS BY LOUIS ARMAND

FICTION

Glitchhead
Descartes' Dog
Hotel Palenque
Vampyr
The Garden
Gagarin
GlassHouse
The Combinations
Abacus
Cairo
Canicule
Breakfast at Midnight
Clair Obscur

THEORY

Feasts of Unrule
Videology
Helixtrolysis
The Organ-Grinder's Monkey
Event States
Literate Technologies
Solicitations
Incendiary Devices
Techne

EDITED

Avant-Post
Language Systems
Contemporary Poetics
Technicity (with Arthur Bradley)
City Primeval (with Robert Carrithers)
Pornotopias (with Jane Lewty & Andrew Mitchell)

ACKNOWLEDGEMENTS

Culture is both a discourse of power & a locus of complexity (strange attractor), both ideological & logistic, determinate & emergent.

While the present volume continues an investigation of complex systems, entropy, de-evolution, cybernetics & the discourse of power that dates back to the mid-1990s, it is also a response to Wolfgang Iser's 2008 Prague lecture, "Culture, a Recursive Process," shaped by a series of discussions at Konstanz University on the subject of "Culture & Crisis." As the line of argument developed in *Entropology* should make abundantly clear, our positions remained fundamentally divergent despite some points of agreement.

For Iser, cultural theory, while naming its object, had been unable to define it, to say *what it is*. Iser considered this anomalous: a discourse confounded by/ with its object. It represented an utter failure of epistemology, engendered by the dilemma posed by entropy to anthropology (Lévi-Strauss). Attempting to rectify this, Iser turned towards cybernetic models of dynamic systems, recursivity & chaos.

In Iser's last work, a certain project of recuperation became evident: to situate "culture" as the episteme of a discourse that both deconstructed & re-founded epistemological thought. It was obviously doubtful that any attempt at incorporating complexity & indeterminacy into a formal epistemological framework could resolve the problem of the "whatness" of culture & its definitional "crisis" – a problem that was itself the product of such a hermeneutic.

The question of culture, being in some sense exemplary of this problematic, was then re-orientated from a *relation of crisis* to a *condition of crisis* (the crisis of epistemology). Culture was not supposed to become thinkable merely in terms of some reduced, abstracted form, as an artefact of power (Balibar, Luhman), but rather as a "dynamic structuration": form as active emergence & not as a passive backdrop of social history (Lefebvre). Crisis would be that dynamic tension through which emergence "occurred"; catastrophe would be its evolutionary engine, propagated by resonance, patterned by interference.

Yet such emergence could only occur at the very limits of knowledge – of the unknowable. Moreover, its conditions would be universal: an apparent paradox, in which the status of culture (*technē*) would become indistinguishable from that of a general ecology (*physis, poiēsis*). This rapport between the so-called living & non-living was determined by an underlying entropement or *différance* (Derrida), arising spontaneously & continuously just as fluctuations in the quantum field amplify into a quasi-infinite array of dissipative structures: the work of entropy. The internal logistics of this array – & the signifying (intelligent) environments that co-evolve with it – are the domain of "culture."

In addition to the dialogue with the late Wolfgang Iser, the author also wishes to thank David Vichnar, Vít Bohal, Dustin Breitling, Diffractions Collective, Interior Ministry, Guillaume Collett, Germán Sierra, Márk Horváth, Adam Lovasz, Bogna Konior, Amy Ireland, Robin Mackay, Michael Uhall, Martin Procházka & D. Harlan Wilson for their critical interactions.

Sections of this book originally appeared in *AI & Society*, *La Deleuziana*, *Litteraria Pragensia*, *Alienist*, *Sci Phi Journal*, *CounterText*, *Diffractions Collective*, *The Palgrave Handbook of Critical Posthumanism*, *Trans*Migrations*, *Technicity* & *Speculative Ecologies: Plotting through the Mesh*.

Research for this book was supported by the European Regional Development Fund-Project "Creativity & Adaptability as Conditions of the Success of Europe in an Interrelated World."

CONTENTS

1

[ENTRE/POLITY]

All systems are ideological.

A system is defined by a set of operations that produce or maintain a type of pragmatic fiction called a "state" (i.e., a form or identification). A state defines a set of permitted operational/discursive bounds. Beyond these bounds, the system either breaks down or evolves into something else. The dynamics of a system are thus valorised with regard to such constraints. What cybernetics calls *positive feedback* promotes the idea of sustainability or growth of a system. *Negative feedback* causes it to decohere. But these are *metaphors*. To speak of "positive feedback" is ultimately as nonsensical as speaking of "positive evolu- tion" – it imports an ideological element under the guise of system dynamics. "Decoherence" produces "growth" & vice versa. In so doing, these apparently homeostatic interactions affect within the system an idea-of-itself so that it isn't solely metaphorical to say that a system possesses a degree of self-conscious- ness. Produced by the relation of the system-in-abstract to the collective effect of its operations, such a self-consciousness is also a *political* economy.

The complexity of a system evolves in relation to the elasticity of its constraints & its "generative" capacity for self-contradiction. What determines the "ideolog- ical tendency" for systems to emerge in the first place is entropy. Coherence isn't the antithesis of entropy. It is the systematisation of entropy's capacity to increase, to maintain a dynamic interval or difference, to affect a leading edge by which *expenditure predicates productivity* & *circulation predicates value* – even in the apparently fantastical form of the *perpetuum mobile* or *eternal return* (a time crystal for example doesn't *violate* entropy, it is a "phase" of matter correlating to the operations of entropy "itself," a phase *out-of-equilibrium* that nonetheless is both stable & evolutionary – whereas blockchains can be defined as syntropic or *entropy traps*). The formal expression of these "self-contradictory" relations is *ideology*. Likewise, the entropological conception of *form* is not a species of fixed capital, but *technē* (i.e., generative constraint). Entropy is *technopoiēsis*.

When an existing system is overstressed, new systems of dissipation (i.e., expenditure) emerge. The "self-expression" of a given system can equally bring about a crisis in its apparent singularity, the fact being that its form isn't merely relative but is a product of relativity. It is just as meaningless to speak of "fixed capital" as it is to speak of a "crisis of overproduction." By definition, every system overproduces itself, & every system exists in a state of inchoate crisis. In this respect, the self-consciousness of a system corresponds to its self-identity in nomenclature only: all systems that do not decohere can be said to *evolve into themselves* ("the narcissism," as Freud said, "of small differences"). There is no such thing as a *conservation of value*. Whatever identities become attached to a given system – be they informatic, biological, social, economic, or political – are historically nominal (& thus anomalous) terms, designating what is an event-state or state-in-flux. The ideological nexus of cognition, capital & culture is also their respective "content."

If entropy defines a "balance of power" (e.g., the relation of a system to a *motive force*: that-which-makes-possible as much as that-which-permits), it is to the extent that it is simultaneously the remittance of power (not seduced, but *constituted*, by its own decadence). This is what Bataille called "the accursèd share": that which, within a *system* of identity, of self-conscious *reason*, would correspond to the occluded episteme, both the unknowable & unthinkable, in effect *the impossible*. The balance-of-power only appears to be the inverse of that tipping point where possibility emerges into a system. This isn't equivalent to "reason's necessary self-contradictoriness" evaluated dialectically as a "special capacity to transcend the limits of a kind of thought which fails to rise above the level of the understanding," as Gadamer has said of Kant. Entropy doesn't precomprehend reason. It produces the possibility of reason out of an irreducible difference.

The horizon of transcendence is the spectre haunting every totalising movement. Behind reason's "special capacity" is the libidinal force of entropy. Bataille called it *expenditure without reserve*; Kant called it *the sublime*. Entropy nevertheless ends up devolving upon an image, an *aesthetics* of the impossible. The greater its dissipative potential, the more a system dreams of autonomous action: the reduction of entropy. In its dream of transcendence, doesn't entropy achieve self-consciousness? By way of chance & complexity, the very "thing" that evolves isn't the apparent proliferation of forms or systems, but an "originary difference" (Derrida) for which all these are in effect the vehicle, so to speak, without conveying anything as such. In this movement of self-maximisation, what is entropy's accursèd share? At what critical point does its own movement decohere & *break time-translation symmetry*? In what medium resides its apparent *irrecuperability*? What medium transmits its *force*?

Beyond the confines of one specialist discourse or another, the central question here is what is named by the term "entropy"? What, in this work or action of naming, is entroped by & within the very *phenomenon* that the term "entropy" presumes to designate – as if this phenomenon, objectified & abstracted from a universal condition, were not the opening-of-possibility of designation *in the first place* & of the *form of the question*?

Prague, August 2021

2

CATASTROPHE PRAXIS

"Nietzsche's account of the eternal return presupposes a critique of the terminal or equilibrium state. Nietzsche says that if the universe had an equilibrium position, if becoming had an end or final state, it would already have been attained. But the present moment, as the passing moment, proves that it is not attained & that therefore an equilibrium of forces is not possible."
– Gilles Deleuze, *Nietzsche & Philosophy*

Precognitions. There are certain things as if *known in advance*: "the world will end," "death is inevitable," "nothing lasts (forever)," etc. Yet all of these are posed against a background of absolute nonknowledge: the meaning of "forever," of "endlessness," of "nothing," of "death" & therefore of "life." They are, in effect, figures of speech, if not metaphors: the constructed verism of the profoundly unknowable, lying somewhere upon the further shore of a present bounded by catastrophe. But catastrophe is a black box in which the rationality of the knowable, the predictable, the modellable breaks down. What good is it to confront ecological collapse armed with a survivalist handbook if the climate patterns that have so far defined the idea of a biosphere cease to exist? What use is an immunological corporate-state enterprise when the accelerated form, force & frequency of viral pandemics reduces its system of control to an epistemological precariat? And what type of theoretical fictions do we inhabit when we pretend that catastrophe itself will permit a transitional phase of human social re-becoming (*homo catastrophicus*)? What do we do when it behaves as nothing more than a dialectical "figure" beholden to the rules of a critical discourse that is infatuated with the idea of its own futurity? At a time when the language of "revolution" has undergone an almost complete rehabilitation, the thought that travels abroad under its name nevertheless does so in the pay of a radical conservatism: from the conservation of the planet, to the conservation of the human, to the conservation of a culture of consumption, capital & crisis. (Though the world is moribund, the spectacle of its end has never been more productive. Conservation is nothing if not a mode of perpetuated ending, of an ending-in-abeyance or in-abyss.) Yet none of this violates the fundamental logic of these discourses, which have secretly *known this all along* & which exist to *conserve* this secret: not the secret of any *thing*, nor a conspiracy among things kept from the "world," but the knowledge assiduously kept from itself – its "unknown-known." Broadly speaking, the discourse of humanism (including all the forms of anti- & post-humanism) isn't the *consciousness* of this catastrophism, but the contrary.

Covidology. From the moment COVID-19 entered the western consciousness, it became a *phenomenon*. This phenomenon was characterised by two dominant modes: PANIC (that the virus posed an existential threat to the existing "world order") & DENIAL (that the virus didn't really exist at all). But there is also a more subtle characteristic, which has largely gone unacknowledged, between the *instantaneously known*, the *unknown*, the *unknowable* & the *unavowable*. There has been no shortage of observations to the effect that COVID is as much a product of "late capital" as it is a "force of nature," that it is ideological as much as it is biological, & that it is anthropocenic *par excellence*. Like "the Anthropocene" – a term meant to designate both an "objective" geological register & the accumulation of capital effects into an "autonomous" geo-technology – the phenomenon of COVID marks a confusion between the idea of an "objectifiable thing" (virus) & an "alien force" (pandemic) capable of bringing about a kind of *automatic revolution* independent of (yet parasitic upon) collective human agency. Like "the Anthropocene," the phenomenon of COVID-19 has renewed a certain apocalyptic tone in contemporary discourse, which sees in it an instrument of radical upheaval, a catalyst of world-transformation, an irresistible acceleration of THE END of the status quo, of the regime of global capital & (as always) of history. The purview of this "End of History" has produced a vertiginous anachronism at the heart of all these covidologies. No sooner had COVID presented itself as a *fait accompli* than it availed itself of a compulsive *historicisation*. Before virtually anything at all was really known about the novel coronavirus spreading across the planet, mouthpieces everywhere simultaneously proclaimed the "return" to a New Normal & the "advent" of a post-catastrophe World Order *unlike any that had gone before*.

Omega Men. Viewed retrospectively, the timeline in which the first major financial stimulus packages were announced (to assist economies in their *recovery* from the COVID-19 crisis or mitigate its impact) appears to have been a phenomenon in itself, occupying a temporality both *after the fact* & hyperstitionally *in advance of it*. It wasn't simply that governments & financial institutions sought to shore up their own futures by treating the pandemic as ostensibly over before it had really begun (& thus purchasing the political-economic conditions for the continuation of the status quo). Nor was it that this convulsive routine of economic stimulus was a kind of primal reflex in the face of potentially catastrophic uncertainty (& not merely a routine formalism). Rather, what this temporality of responses brings into view are the operations of a certain *regime of anachronism* at work in the control of "reality," the end of which is *always-already* its beginning (the dialectics of power). Within two months of introducing financial stimulus into their economies, beginning in March 2020, it is estimated that world governments collectively spent more on COVID – over $10 trillion USD – than during the entire 2008 Global Financial Crisis, driving global debt to unprecedented levels (in the first nine months of 2020, global debt rose by $19.3 trillion). These are not simply ritualistic gestures to conjure a virus out of existence, but a ruthless struggle on the part of capital to foreclose on the possibility of its own "end" & erase the idea of that possibility. How is it that this *revolutionary struggle* is largely invisible within a critical discourse that is instead preoccupied with transcendental utopias & street protests with no prospect of a "seizure of power"?

Fetish. On 11 March, the Director General of the World Health Organisation declared COVID-19 a "global pandemic." On the 24th of the same month, Slavoj Žižek, ever ready to preach from the mount, published a book entitled *Pandemic!: COVID-19 Shakes the World*.[1] A month earlier, in the course of Europe's inaugural (& most intensive) lockdown, Giorgio Agamben published the first of many denunciations of the "new dictatorship of telematics" entitled "The Invention of an Epidemic."[2] In it, he lamented the reduction of social existence to "bare life" under a biopolitical "state of exception." Armed with a reactionary non-knowledge, Agamben's instant humanist sentimentality isn't the discipline of a *defence* of life, but its subsumption into an act of liberal self-gratification. The denunciations that followed (e.g., "Requiem for the Students"[3]) are all the more remarkable for the fact that their primary motivation stems from a threat to academic *lifestyle*. The Socratic system of political education in which Agamben's privileged position had been assured – even in the twenty-first century – was yet again being harassed by that most Platonic of nemeses: *technē* (in the by-now trivial form of a digital interface). The relative folly of Žižek & Agamben's interventions exposes the extent to which the production of critical fetish objects has come to manifest the same cultural & economic forms as those it pretends to "critique." What Žižek & Agamben have not been willing to examine is, to rephrase Bourdieu, "the entire set of social mechanisms that make possible" the figure of the "public intellectual" – even, or especially, in these apparently anti-intellectual times – as the producer of that fetish called *critique*.[4] In other words, while claiming a unique cultural authority to direct the way the COVID pandemic is being critically *thought* & thereby *known*, they elide the constitution of the a field that serves as the *locus where the belief in the value of critique is produced & reproduced* in the first place. In this field, the *critical exception* to "technological mediation" is bound up with a *human exception* (e.g., with the "authoritarianism" of a coordinated epidemiological response).

Automatic Revolution. COVID has produced an industry of response, including intellectual industries, caught between two replay loops: 1. the anticipatory replay in which the ever-prescient mouthpieces of the coming apocalypse have found their readymade occasion, & 2. the temporal replay of the so-called second & third waves in which these same industries find their occasion exhausted. Žižek's *Pandemic!* & its sequels (*Pandemic! 2: Chronicles of a Lost Time* & *Heaven in Disorder*), along with Agamben's collected interventions (*Where Are We Now? The Epidemic as Politics*), are only the most conspicuous examples. In particular, Žižek amplifies a tendency to propose an entire social-theoretical project in lieu of a "concrete analysis" – not as a *mode of action* but as a *prerequisite* for action: Žižek's "new communism," Agamben's new humanism, Latour's "Gaia hypothesis," etc. This pathological retreat into (grandiose) New Myths – as a proxy for the task of direct intervention – seems paradoxically geared towards the *conservation* of a cultural status quo (the same litany of issues, the same litany of responses), rather than a practical instrumentalising of the pandemic for the purpose of deconstructing the prevailing culture that gave rise to it. In the end, we've been left with ideological theatre, mechanically repeating an exhausted histrionics, punctuated by eruptions of "protest" & a mesmeric belief in something that might be called *automatic revolution*: that COVID will do the work of direct social/institutional *critique* all by itself, bringing about the end of global capital *as if by magic*. In effect, COVID has become the "objective correlative" of the old discredited idea of a *withering away of the state*. And what it has revealed is again a willingness among the philosophers of the self-styled "left" to herald the arrival of a new tyrant in order to dispense with the existing one.

Spectres. The spectre of history hangs over the present situation, yet it isn't the one they'd been anticipating. In 1848, there arose an expectation of worldwide social-democratic revolution: the accelerated decadence of the old world order, the impulse to emancipation of an industrial proletariat, the inevitability of progress forged through the industry of capitalism. The social-democratic revolution failed. The bourgeoisie triumphed, but that triumph did not produce a politically emancipative effect. Between 1917 & 1918, even under conditions of a catastrophic world war & the global "Spanish Flu" pandemic, coinciding with the final collapse of the imperial order, expectations of a world-wide socialist revolution didn't eventuate. The Bolshevik Revolution barely succeeded against the forces of an international counterrevolutionary effort – everywhere outside the Soviet Union, reaction triumphed. In 1968, etc., etc.: the corporate state triumphed. Blinded by the expectation of *an automatic social revolution*, the mouthpieces of history could not see the actual revolution taking place before their eyes. They believed that capitalism was an historical phase (or a mere instrument) on the path to revolution; they did not grasp that *it was the revolution*.

At every stage, capitalism has revolutionised itself in its material, logistical & broadly "cybernetic" (or, as we will see, *entropological*) forms. Today, the gaze of "theory" drifts once more from its object onto the horizon of Expectation, unwilling or unable to perceive that the revolution taking place *does not belong to it*. Similarly, the primary error in Deleuze & Guattari's post-1968 lament, *Anti-Oedipus*, was assuming that capitalism is a force of inertia set *against* the flow of liberated "schizes" that capitalism had incidentally produced; instead, it was the moral *arrière-garde* of a failed "revolutionary ideology" seemingly determined to re-Oedipalise the spectacle of capital's totalisation while romanticising the emancipatory potential of its sacrificial straw man. In subverting the system of diagnostics (social medicine) even as it insisted that capital lay within its epistemological grasp, deleuzoguattarianism evoked a radical "schizoanalysis" capable of producing existential catastrophe within the system, yet unmindful of the possibility that, in doing so, nothing had been produced but a description of capital's own evolutionary movement. This inverse symptomatology has passed down to the present situation.

M'aidez. *Mayday! Mayday! We're going to crash!* What happens when the nominal addressee of this emergency broadcast is the *agent* of catastrophe? Is it a call to arms or merely a verbalised rage, a cry of defeat? *Mayday! This is the End! We're fucked!* At least since the turn of the millennium, anti-globalisation & anti-authoritarian movements have arisen & spread like minor pandemics in waves of protest & increasingly radicalised "discontent" around the world. From global capital to climate catastrophe & COVID, an accelerated cycle of such phenomena have fed the spectacle of the corporate state's seemingly endless demise. On the level of civil disobedience, each of these has tended to exhibit both a strange credulity towards the idea of protest & a simultaneous incredulity towards social master narratives. Each has likewise occasioned the question of whether or not, *as protest*, such forms of direct action fall victim to the desire for a benevolent, paternalistic corporate state – even if this benevolence extends only to the state being a good or rational adversary with a conscience available to appeal. In this desire, too, is reflected the idea of a rational society directed by collective self-interest, which it is ultimately prepared to delegate to the care of the state so that the *Mayday!* reflex may be said to be an expression of the deep-rooted paradox that traverses all hegemonic structures: the seeking of aid from the very thing that has caused harm & which must be opposed, subverted, overcome, or destroyed *before it's too late*. (Such is its hysterical condition that protest is always prepared to exhaust itself in symbolic forms of parricide as if to avert the real catastrophe. In this instance, the catastrophe isn't globalisation, climate change or COVID, but an open admission that the *social contract* has in fact long ceased to exist. Furthermore, the objective reality bearing upon the world isn't any pseudo "natural disaster." It is the real void of political subjectivity.) And if only those protests that have "descended" into riots & have evolved into quasi-insurrection – as in Chile, Guatemala, France & Hong Kong – have given any appearance of putting the corporate state to the question, on every occasion their insufficiency has (as if by necessity) fuelled a decisive & ever-more-virulent *reaction*: an actual "dictatorship of telematics," like the "cybernetic revolutions" that preceded it (as if on a permanent schedule at least since 1968). In this respect, the admiration some have shown for the Chinese & Korean responses to COVID is not merely a kind of sympathy for the devil, as has often been supposed. Instead, we see yet another symptom of the appeal of the New Myths – foremost among them, the myth of the unassailable adversary & the myth of the hyperrational corporate state. There is nothing more irrational than a belief in the rationality of the corporate state ... unless, perhaps, it is a belief in the rationality of social relations.

Procurement. The New Myths do not merely repeat those of the recent past (the late-twentieth century had no shortage of them): the myth of No Future mirrored in that of the coming Extinction; the myth of Unfettered Growth, of Inexhaustible Resources mirrored in that of a *post*-Anthropocene, *post*-COVID reconstructionism; the mythic dimension of global capital mirrored in that of revolutionary despair; & so on. On the contrary, the New Myths are a dialectical ensemble of overabundant crises, of renewable apocalypse. It achieves its apotheosis in the ongoing spectacle of the disintegration & reconstitution of the spectacle itself – under the gravitational sway of the Myth of the Impossible (the impossibility of an end of capitalism, the impossibility of revolution, the final impossibility of an *after*-life, etc.). The domain of the political is fully inscribed within this "new" convulsive movement of forethrow & recapitulation, between a humanistic ideal & a recursive technicity that does not contradict but *produces it* in all its desiring insufficiency. Where Rousseau's social contract had promised universal rights universally, the provision of rights (i.e., the collective rights of the individual) under covidocracy becomes a procurement problem. In short, the New Myths arisen under "pandemic conditions" are seemingly not ideological but logistical. Or rather, the ideological has ceased to be distinguishable from the logistical. In just the same way, political abstractions like "emancipation" have come to present an insurmountable *procurement burden*. In January 2020, the World Health Organization issued the statement that wearing "medical masks when not indicated may cause unnecessary cost, procurement burden & create a false sense of security that can lead to neglecting other essential measures such as hand hygiene practices. Furthermore, using a mask incorrectly may hamper its effectiveness to reduce the risk of transmission."[5] Of which Zuzana Holečková has written:

> The declaration is a neatly formulated, perfect example of political correctness because what is hidden behind the words "may cause unnecessary cost, procurement burden" is the fact, which the WHO was well aware of, that there is not sufficient quantity of masks available. And it is nobody's fault because it is not possible, practical & desirable to maintain a universal stock of protective equipment; no emergency plan in the world has ever been designed to do so ... The problem is the masses: How to manage

the relatively rich, educated, healthy & thus long-living masses; how to feed, tame & console them, literally, politically & culturally, if God is dead & so-called democracy shoreless? How to give them the illusion of "free will" (& equal access to universal health care, because what is more sacred than human life?) & not to expose the fact that something like "free will" is an insurmountable procurement burden? This is our current modernity.[6]

Yet if the capacity to maintain the *promise of emancipation* – in place of its actual (impossible) realisation – remains a measure of the viability of any given system of (mythic) power, this isn't because "emancipation" is impossible *as such* (sheer romanticism). It isn't even that the idea that "emancipation" contradicts the *raison d'être* of the system of power it belongs to. It's that *the logistics of its procurement* in any sense other than being *for the system itself* renders it fatal.[7] Emancipation without subjection to a correlative system of power has no meaning. Such is the *pharmakon* of all social palliatives that procure for themselves, we might say, the pandemic they best deserve.

Sur/vival. Talk of *survivalism* looks forward to a residual world in which all the dirty work of social re-terraforming has been done, leaving the politico-economic equivalent of *Jurassic Park* in its wake. From the point of view of a certain primitivism, this readymade catastrophe presents itself as a benevolent "force of nature," an automatic revolution. Were this a Hollywood movie, there would be a guerrilla army of social-engineers-in-waiting whose mission is to establish the perimeter of a New Darwinism: a terrain of self-sufficiencies, an institutional wilderness where the Law is a dark continent & power is a buried temple at which only the intrepid future ape may worship. Contesting the rule of these primitivists would be all those refugee neo-Huxleyites, armed with a UN one-worldism of the *we-shall-rebuild* variety familiar from endless "disaster" fictions. There would be the inevitable happy ending; reason & a new modernity would ultimately prevail (such films should simply self-destruct, like the messages in *Mission Impossible*, taking the viewer with them). These two visions of survival are symbiotic: the terraforming aspirations of the one are reborn within the primitivist aspirations of the other. They are, in fact, the same impulse, driven by the same evangelism. To each, the world is a zero sum. They are truly the children of the juggernaut, the quasi-divine *force majeure*, prepared to carve out the future in flesh & blood – but only after the fact. Such fictions are as heroic as they are absurd, like a tale told of little Oedipuses whose mamapapas have been stolen from them by an "act of God": one wants to rebuild their father's house, the other wants to run free in the orchard. Something is too perfect; the sheer horror of human existence seems to have gone up in smoke with the death of parental tyranny. It's a purely *allegorical* world & nothing could possibly breathe there. Only madness could save them – the madness of repetition, "civilised man" at war with "natural man," modernism or barbary, etc. – to determine who shall be the unique source of Gaia's pleasure. At least this way a future is guaranteed: the eternal return of the same. Blanqui contra Nietzsche.

Potlatch. Is there such a thing as a political economy of "exit"? At every point, the ruthlessness of the virus has been posed against the imperative of an ethics of social response between those who would *make live* & those who would *let die*. And at every point, this inordinate project of conservation (to save the planet, to save humanity, to save the future, etc.) has run up against the fact that the only real project of conservation in the offing is that of power itself; the rest are chattels, the spoils of victory. When Agamben complains about the "state of exception," he is acknowledging that "bare life" isn't what is left when the procurement of individual or collective liberties is withdrawn – "bare life" is the fictional existence in which these things are imagined to be real in the first place. Under conditions of so-called "late capitalism," bare life is the one you pay for on credit in lieu of the one alienated within the Panopticon. In this relation, it is the individual that is the true "state of exception," & it is for this reason that its *action* is always instead a *reaction* to the agenda of the corporate state (e.g., a stone thrown at the shield of a riot cop, a lament about the loss of human contact in the classroom, even Virginia Woolf wanted to burn down the universities – what has happened?). For its part, the corporate state would like either to outsource COVID or transform it into a tradable commodity or financial instrument (monetisable "futures," like carbon credits), as if it were some kind of objective correlative of "market adjustment,"whereas COVID pre-empts & even threatens to usurp capitalism's position & function at every turn, proliferating, accelerating, & expropriating the means of production to its own processes of insatiable consumption. Correspondingly, global capital, in the guise of neoliberalism, had until now been able to parasitise infrastructure everywhere while opting-out of any real liability for it, banking on a future that would always, as if by magic, be recapitalised (e.g., by "individual tax-payers" who've been seduced by this myth into believing that they, too, can *opt out*). Thus the parasitic function of global capital finds itself both in direct alignment & direct competition with the parasitism of COVID. The question that arises isn't how to affect an *exception* from the ongoing "crisis," as if one or other of its elements (COVID or capitalism "itself") might simply be detached from the global equation, but the contrary: How can a direct political relation be re-established within it that isn't a "residue" of an expenditure-without-reserve, of potlatch?

Global Minimum. Inevitable as it may appear in retrospect, the cybernetic revolution that Harvey Wheeler proclaimed in 1968 was by no means an obvious outcome of the reaction against the events of that year. It was the product of a loosely confederated opportunism that wildly misconstrued cybernetics simply as an instrument of social control & of increased production unfettered by the pressures of industrial labour. By the 1970s, however, the cybernetic revolution had brought about the conditions for the abolition of the bourgeois state (as conceived up to that point) & the advent of neoliberalism (as an ideological & economic force whose direct consequence would, following the dissolution of many Cold War geopolitical boundaries, produce the forms of global capital still operative today in which the dominant "class" is nominally techno-oligarchic while in substance being the evolved system of information management). A subsequent iteration – the "digital revolution" of the 1990s – completed the task of abstraction & automation initiated by the industrial revolution at the end of the eighteenth century (overlapping with another revolutionary period), permitting the rise of a dominant new economic & political force. This abstract, diffuse, often unacknowledged force has, to a greater or lesser extent, redefined the political domain across swathes of the planet via the mass-automation of logistics & a radical realignment of mass-mediatised social reality into increasingly integrated forms of social media & datocracy. Just as between the invention of Mercator's cylindrical map projection in 1569 & the launch of the GPS radionavigational satellite network in 1973, the *global* came into view not as a self-contained unicum but as a geodesic system of coordinate *interlocutions*: a distributed individuality where every "position" in geolocational spacetime is in communication with every other & propagates via a web of aggregated *differences*. Building on this idea, in 1960, internet pioneer Ted Nelson proposed a globally integrated information system to be called Xanadu. Described as a "unique symmetrical connective system," it would employ profuse, fine-grained, deep linkage & stabilised media to construct a prototypical *worldwide web*.[8] In their recent proposals for an information theory of individuality, David Krakauer, Nils Bertschinger & Eckehard Olbrich complete this picture by positioning the "individual" as a cybernated evolutionary aggregate "that propagate[s] information from the past to the future & [has] temporal integrity."[9] This movement of propagation may be likened to a *between two interlocutors* – in other words, a *difference* integral to itself – even if we must insist that its temporal vector will be nothing if not recursive in the predicative time of a transmission to which an *anachronistic present* stands in a relation of *decoherence*. (The authenticity of the present isn't what stands obscured by this observer paradox: it is its consequence, built of its fabric.)

Entropocene. At the very end of his 1955 memoir, *Tristes Tropiques*, Lévi-Strauss calls for a critical project of *dissipative anthropology*, to which he alludes under the term "entropology," yet which he does not in fact realise in any of his subsequent major texts (*Anthropologie structurale* [1958], *La pensée sauvage* [1962], *Mythologiques* I-IV [1964-71]): "Every verbal exchange, every line printed, establishes a communication *between two interlocutors*, thus creating an evenness of level, where before there was an information gap & consequently a greater degree of organisation. Anthropology could with advantage be changed into 'entropology,' as the name of the discipline concerned with the study of the highest manifestations of this process of disintegration."[10]

In his coinage of the term "entropology," Lévi-Strauss affects a definition of *integration by hierarchisation* as the principal characteristic of social organisation. Integration also takes place on the level of relations (*"une communication entre les deux interlocuteurs"*), which may be hierarchically indeterminate. Here a contradiction will later emerge in the attempt to recuperate this dissipative anthropology for a general *neganthropology*.[11] As yet only implicit is the realisation (via Claude Shannon) that entropy doesn't describe a mere *dissipation of energy through work*, but rather (like Boltzmann, who defined entropy as the number of unobservable configurations of a system) that it corresponds to an *information potential* transmitted from a signaller to a receiver (i.e., between interlocutors).[12] Nevertheless, Lévi-Strauss persists in identifying entropy with an inevitable tendency towards (social) dis-integration whereby the study of human society (microstate) is bound up with the apparent "destiny" of the universe (macrostate).

In the face of this movement towards systemic homogeneity, Lévi-Strauss envisages a counter movement: a ceaselessly accelerated production of "bifurcations" & "difference" (complexification) describing a (positive) negentropic feedback spiral capable (like Maxwell's demon) of recuperating the (negative) movement of entropy as a (positive) object of knowledge (i.e., "entropology"). This amounts to a kind of hermeneutic recycling of *potential*. Such a project, *as both a critique & reconstruction of anthropology*, could neither exist within the framework of Lévi-Strauss' structuralism nor survive outside it. "Entropology," in the sense given, is the solicitation from within of an impossible "deconstruction." A more explicit theorising of this entropic turn in the "human sciences" has had to wait several decades for a "posthumanist" turn in the wake of (& more often than not in reaction against) "deconstruction." It is a turn that – by no means paradoxical – has at the same time entailed a *return of anthropology* ("a new humanism"[13]) & a reinstatement of structuralism's "universal problematic"[14] under the guise of a discourse of what has all too readily been subsumed into "the Anthropocene."

The acme of a Lévi-Straussian "entropology" arrives with Stiegler's misreading of Schrödinger in *Neganthropocene* (2018). The former acolyte of Derrida casts neoliberalism as an entropic doomsday device whose proliferating systems of (negative) feedback are driving the world along a teleology of extinction. Stiegler grasps onto the concept of negentropy as a redemption of the world's loss by converting "negative" into "positive" feedback, providing life ever after for productive circuits of harmonious growth. (It seems not to matter that such a productivism always amounts to little more than a conceptual Ponzi scheme.) This rather conventional binary describes a mirror-effect around the dream of perpetual growth, a paradise regained in which entropy lurks like the proverbial serpent with designs to bring about the Fall, unless it is productively curbed so as to observe the harmonious laws of this changeless realm. Such nostalgia is a dream of death: the idealised death of a pristine state of being brought low by the ravages of entropy. Yet if entropy corresponds to what Freud called *Todes-trieb* or *death drive*, this is because it describes the "death" at the origin of life: no entropy, no being.

Thing. A correspondence establishes itself between Lévi-Strauss' putative entro-pology & the project of re-reading Marx's *Capital* embarked upon during the succeeding decade by Louis Althusser, Jacques Rancière & others. In his contri-bution on commodity fetishism, Rancière makes this observation: "What is lost in fetishism is the structural implication that founds the distance of the thing from itself, a distance which is precisely the site at which economic relations are at play."[15] The "thing" (i.e., the *form* of the commodity) is thus firstly the site *between two interlocutors* wherein economic relations (the communication of value) mirror social relations & each can be characterised as *in-formation*. What appears to "pass into the thing" in the work of production is neither an *alien entity* nor *alienated subjectivity* "but a relation."[16] This relation permits it to function as a site of (more than) symbolic exchange & the circulation of value, which is also to say of an *entropology*: both "entropement" & "entropy." And, as in Lévi-Strauss, what is first *information potential* inscribes a matrix of *dis-integration* & *alienation* since, in its signifying subjection, "it is the form which becomes alien to the relation it supports &, in becoming alien to it, becomes a [mere/inert] thing & leads to the materialisation of relations."[17] Likewise, Stiegler's "negentropy" is limited to a *redistribution* of the *production of entropy*, ignoring the operation of entropy "as productive force" in & of "itself" (i.e., as the encompassment of production, its anteriority, so to speak – the condition of the productivity of pro-duction & not anything that can be *brought under the rule of production*). Like the "thing" defined as a *relation*, entropy maintains a *minimum of self-separation* against Rancière's *materialisation* (disintegration into *mere* thingness), a kind of Planck constant of *différance*. In this manner, Krakauer & co. provide parallels between the idea of an "individual" as a mode of propagation & the "parasitic" operation of a virus. "Viruses," they argue,

> constitute obligate translational parasites, incapable of completing their life cycles without first appropriating the protein synthesis machinery of a host cell. The viral capsid contains a largely *inert* genome responsible for encoding only a small fraction of the proteins required for synthesizing a new virus genome & the capsid required for egressing from the infected cell. *The virus exists only within the larger dynamical, regulatory network of the cell*. Hence, the virus – understood as the active parasitic agent – is comprised largely of host encoded factors. And yet it can replicate, adapt, & has a persistent identity that distinguishes it from its "host" environ-ment – despite the fact it relies on its "host" environment for replicating.[18]

Extrapolation reveals how the cell here can also stand for a frame-of-reference wherein the inert & dynamic are shown to interact, & by means of which "dissipation" presents as productive propagation (the viral *logos*), while at the same time – & by the same gesture – soliciting the deconstruction of this binary. It is necessary, therefore, to speak of entropology as the relation of entropy not only to its *logos* but to the operations of *technē* that bring into constellation the terms of its signifying production. In the structuralist arrangement, entropy remains an aftereffect, a decoherence, a degradation, rather than a *condition of possibility* of any system whatsoever (just as the COVID *pandemic* is treated as a *product* of capitalism rather than as the *mode of production* of capitalist re-evolution). This hierarchy repeats itself in Stiegler's adoption of the term; disintegration remains a *product*, not a *production* of the Anthropocene (or what he thereby renames the *Entropocene*[19]). Here, again, the distinction remains one between evolution & its *artefacts*, between the entropic condition of all production & the *reification of production*.

Crisis Epidemic. As if propagated from the future onto a consciousness of the present, the acceleration of crises defined as the Anthropocene will have appeared to bring prophetically into view nothing short of the End of Global Capital. This will happen on the naïve assumption that what has so far been called "capitalism" has already met its limits.[20] All that has really come to pass is the end of an epistemological regime by which both the capitalist "object" & the limits of its possibility have been "measured." As with all such regimes, the terms under which capitalism's *ends* are situated are only discoverable at the point said regime is no longer able to maintain even the appearance of functioning (the "end of capitalism" is first & foremost contained within the terminal crisis of its "objective critique"). The limits that have been met in the foreclosure of the present (yet still approaching) catastrophe are those of an entropo-epistemology that believed itself capable of accounting for the totality of a global means of evolution. This is more than simply the disillusionment of a delusion of grandeur. Nor is it merely the reprise of a tragic view of history. Unlike critique, which has always secretly clung to the dream of revolution *in its own image*,[21] there is nothing sentimental about capital, having no greater attachment to any particular constellation of forms beyond the advantage they present at any given juncture. Likewise, all evolution is, in its major convulsions, *catastrophic*.

Entropophagy. In the Nietzschean *Wiederkehr*, the "will to power" is entropy. To the question, then: What is entropy? A further reply comes in the shape of this apparently abstract formula: Entropy = the self-metabolising of *différance* (spatiotemporalisation à la Derrida). The tendency for entropy to increase is thus contiguous with the tendency of *différance* to propagate a "repetition compulsion" (*Wiederholungszwang*).

Neither entropy nor *différance* are conditions that befall the universe; they name operations intrinsic to it – operations bound up with the possibility of structure & therefore of existence (even an apparent absence of structure is a structural phenomenon).

Three propositions:

1. Every state is a *form* of metabolism.
2. Every state metabolises some other state.
3. Every "end state" or *metabolic rift* mirrors an "initial state" of *différance* produced by random intrinsic noise.

The idea of entropy has so far remained under sentence of the "negation" that produced it. Beyond entropy: the non-recurrence of any state whatsoever. A dialectical fantasy.

Blackhole metaphysics: "humanity would sooner have the void for a purpose than be void of purpose" (Nietzsche, *Genealogy of Morals*).

Anthropocene: *we're living in ghost-time. Even at light speed, everything is after-effect. A "universe" perceived in the throes of extinction & being born exceeds & cancels out the present as the tense of being or perception. Imagine arriving on the scene four billion years too late. What "status quo" dictates over this zone between possibilities both immanent & as infinitely far off as a night-sky constellation, a dream?*

This inhuman artefact: as ineffable as a constellation's flickering morse. Or a signifying hierarchy.

Humanism has always sought to *absolve itself* of the world, its tremors & discontinuities: a *metaphor* (of the "original" nucleo-synthesis).

All *existence* is singularity (neither homogenous nor isotropic): entropy is the concatenation of singularities, metabolised as an "evolutionary process."

Thesis: life is entropological *technē*.

The cosmic genome isn't a blueprint (the desperation of something "lost" in space): there's always the chance *of being otherwise.* Humanity's "end" (like everything else) is that it will, for all intents & purposes, *never have been*: evolution implies it. And yet, this *never having been*, causally orphaned in the fictional spacetime of "history," persists in leaving traces. To recuperate the "irrecuperable": entropy.

Having dissociated itself from itself, the present of "being" cedes to an abyss or plenitude of representation that can only arise *from now on*. A throw of dice (will never abolish the cosmic debt). Under the cumulative *force* of this entropy, the universe *becomes* mythopoetic: the source & focus of an impossible "nostalgia" (the god-particle whose form is legion: the Big Bang, the Steady State, the Cosmic Crunch).

What "returns" is not the diminishing spiral of an original primogeniture, but the eruption at zero: the *difference minimum*.

At the lowest atomic energy level, the universe *fluctuates*. Catastrophes of the infinitesimal feed the great dissipation. Matter, antimatter: darkness visible.

Blackhole information paradox cannibalised: entropy, too, must feed (on) entropy.[22]

Prague, December 2020

3

APRÈS LE FUTUR …
SIX PROPOSITIONS ON THE ENDS OF MODERNITY

"Could the only opposition to a culture dominated by what Jameson calls the 'nostalgia mode' be a kind of nostalgia for Modernism?"
— Mark Fisher

One. Having declared an end to history in its avowal to MAKE IT NEW, modernism "imagined itself to be beyond eschatology."[1] This is the argument Irmgard Emmelhainz advances in "Self-Destruction as Insurrection, or, How to Lift the Earth Above All That Has Died?" Here the Anthropocene acquires something of the status of a uniquely authentic insurrectional force in the wake of the discrediting of modernity & the institutional avant-garde, accounting for both their political & aesthetic formulations. Emmelhainz's Anthropocene is presented as an insurrectional force entirely alienated from the idea of the human, like a glitched after-image of Klee's *Angelus Novus* as it retraces Benjamin's "Theses on the Philosophy of History," not as a truth that is "recognised & … never seen again,"[2] but one that presents itself constantly *without being grasped for what it is*. Yet in doing so, this Anthropocene describes not a negation of modernism but its apotheosis. From its very beginnings, what characterises modernism is a paradoxical nostalgia for the coming utopia of modernism itself: its own reification as the New World, conflated out of the kitsch of authenticity, the *absolument moderne*. The impulse of so-called *postmodernism* arises out of the desire to suspend this paradox in a dilated present where, as Emmelhainz says, "apocalypse" becomes "central to the neoliberal imaginary." Such a suspended action is no mere sleight of hand, but a *project* that sees the dream of eschatology transform into necessity by way of a certain Return of the Real. Emmelhainz characterises this as the displacement of the "possibility of revolution" in its modernist utopian formulation by the "intolerable" — that which can no longer be *made anew* in the image of modernity, since it is the *desolation of the image*. "In this light," she argues, "the actual legacy of modernism is not a horizon of worker-led emancipation but a biosphere on the brink of extinction … a world in ruins." This much we can agree on.

Two. If it appears that the question of modernity acquires a certain spectral character in its tendency to haunt contemporary thought & return wherever the problems of technicity & futurity rear their heads, this tendency cannot be reduced to an antithetical *moment* – one among others – that merely requires (in order to "resolve itself") to be properly historicised within the scope of the long twentieth century, for example, as a belated after-effect of the end of modernity: its "completion," so to speak, as a *project* subsumed into the *abject form* of an ideological artefact. This line of reasoning seeks to expand a critique of aesthetic autonomy (& modernism in general) into the "objective" form of an Anthropocene that is a kind of residue, a by-product of the abstractive processes of industrial capital, & not as the *articulation of its logic*. Furthermore, this reasoning proposes that the culmination of the project of modernity comes definitively into view with the consciousness of the Anthropocene. It is accompanied by similar logic that insists the Anthropocene is the unfinished business of modernity & that only by accelerating & enlarging the scope of modernity can the Anthropocene be transcended.

Three. While Habermas maintained that the "spirit" of modernity consists in the revolt against a "false normativity in history"[3] – brought starkly into view in the numerous debates surrounding postmodernism – the quasi-enlightenment "project" Habermas equates with modernity nevertheless retains the character of a humanism impervious to either those internal contradictions from which it had arisen in the first place or to the complexity & indeterminacy of those increasingly global systems into which it had long since evolved. This tendency to reaction & counterreformation within a retrospective "modernism" may appear an unlikely fellow traveller of the neoliberalism that apparently succeeded it, yet the argument for the incompletion of the project of modernity & Fukuyama's pronouncements of an "End-of-History" describe an identical teleology.[4] For Fukuyama, the neutralisation of the modernist revolt was postmodernism's (i.e., neoliberalism's) masterstroke – what Habermas calls a "false negation of culture" under the appearance of an impossible emancipation from ideology or ideological antagonism. At the same time, this "false negation" (conflated with capitalist realism's promise of No Future) remains bound to a modernist *discontinuity of history* as the (paradoxical) means of its *totalisation*. Between revolution & apocalypse, this "means-ends" eschatology circulates as a kind of ideal tropism, which in turn is reified in what Emmelhainz calls "the highest stage of modernism": the Anthropocene.[5]

Four. "There is no other world," writes McKenzie Wark (in "Late Holocene Style"), "& it is this one."[6] And if the Anthropocene is, as a recent Alienist publication proclaims, the modernist "art object *par excellence*,"[7] this is precisely because it corresponds to what Wark defines as the coincidence of "the impossibility of the artwork" with the "impossibility of the divine." The divine, as eschatological agency, is always that which, in accomplishing itself, supersedes itself. It is, so to speak, both the end that *lives on* & the afterlife *before the fact*. It's in this sense that Lyotard's remark about postmodernism as modernity *in a nascent state*[8] applies, for example, to Adorno's insistence upon the barbarity of lyric poetry after Auschwitz & the impossibility of maintaining an aesthetic morality vested in the cult of rationalism that had produced the Nazi death camps.[9] We might say, then, that the acme of modernity has always been the *art of the impossible*: not a *mimēsis* of "another world" – some revolutionary utopia, or some eugenicist heaven of ideal forms – but the *means of production* of the impossibility of "an/other world" (i.e., of a world subject to forces operative beyond the purview of modernity). The character of this movement of aesthetic foreclosure & the crisis it represents isn't (despite appearing otherwise) that of a *neutral* geological register of humanity's (i.e., industrialisation's) impact on the biosphere so much as it is *ideological*. This "no other world" that "there is" constitutes both the apotheosis & end of modernity only insofar as it "performs" a final negation of the "free spirit," as Wark says, of the modernist work of art that *lives on* in those cybernated ghosts of our present "world-machine." What is called "posthumanism" marks the return of an ever-more-apocalyptic *humanism* in the experiencing of its self-destruction as aesthetically unsurpassable.[10] In this, the "extinction paradigm" is posed as the condition for alienation's next evolutionary phase beyond the commodity form to the technopoetic sublime. To the extent that this evolutionary "event" acquires its own autonomous representation, it does so not in the elevation of the *anthropos* to the revolutionary status of *world-transformation*, but the contrary: its "alienated totality."[11]

Five. If modernity presupposes a demystification & transcendence of the "natural world," it does so on the basis of a radical idea that all worlds are *reified technology*. Two viewpoints dominate this line of thought: the first attributes agency to determinate ideological forces aligned with capital *by design*, which can be summed up by Negri's understanding of modernity as "the definition & development of a totalising thought that assumes human & collective creativity in order to insert them into the instrumental rationality of the capitalist mode of production of the world"[12]; the second attributes agency to evolutionary forces *arbitrarily* productive of capitalist ideological forms. The first remains mired in humanism, with alienation perceived as a *theft* of subjectivity – or, as Negri argues, "the negation of any possibility that the multitude may express itself as subjectivity"[13]; the second has a broadly cybernetic character in which alienation is *constitutive* of subjectivity. One conceives of the Anthropocene as the *real product* of industrial capitalism that must be overcome (for Negri, by way of a "constituent power" that "points us beyond the limits of modernity"[14]); the other, as the *production of the Real*, which cannot be overcome. This parallax view is not simply one of irreconcilable perspectives: the consciousness it implies is "unachievable" & therefore *only* mystifiable.[15] Yet modernity has always had the Anthropocene in mind: from the beginning, it desired to become the *future as such*, rather than to simply project a *futurism* – to become, moreover, the *only future possible*. Or none. In this way, it defines the horizon of the unachievable, which constantly falls back upon a *future hypothesis* "in order to formulate," as Lyotard says, "the rules of what *will have been done*."[16] Its movement remains that of an algorithm ramifying its bias along an exponential curve: feedback eschatology. And insofar as the Anthropocene corresponds to the "epoch" of this movement, it does so in the recursive temporality of the *catastrophic*.

Six. For Benjamin, the End of History corresponds to a generalised technicity not as a moment of "transcendence" of its aesthetic or *artefactual* condition – which would in any case merely re-inscribe the auratic delirium of the art object – but as the *indefinite reproducibility* of the End of History (i.e., as the vector of reification). This "inauthentic" mode of being would be none other than that of the Real construed as the *order of an unconscious*, whose *operations* would display a fundamental ambivalence to the categorical distinctions of art & technology, being & ideology. For Benjamin, such an ambivalence is the risk of demystification of aesthetic autonomy, whose reification in the art object always threatens to inflate into a "transcendental commodity." Yet the separation of art & life, of the aesthetic from the Real, history from technology, was never more than a *reification of this ambivalence* in the first place – within what Debord called "a whole irrational social praxis" of a "society that has every technical means to modify the biological foundations of the whole of life on earth"[17] – & whose transcendence has never amounted to anything beyond the *ambivalence of its reification*. Neither can the Anthropocene, then, be reduced to the status of an artefact of "autonomous alienation," nor even a constellation of such artefacts into an "aggregate of data." Its convulsions will not correspond to an "emancipation of Man" & will not be the work of any Angel of History. Nor will it stand as a monument to the Human Abstract that supposedly gave birth to it – nor simply to the "universal development of the commodity" that, by dialectising a collective subjectivity, will have been, so Debord says, "wholly confirmed as the crowning achievement of political economy, in other words as the 'abandonment of life,'" confirming the commodity in its function as purveyor of a "tragic view of history."[18] If nothing has escaped the pull of commodification, it is because the seeming eschatological movement of the Anthropocene in the "Return of the Real" also marks the return of an originary technicity, of "the paradox of the future (*post*) anterior (*modo*),"[19] of the *primordial catastrophe*.

Coda. By a certain dialectical movement, it would appear as if the Anthropocene – in contradiction to a mode of thought that would situate it as an object or product of modernity (its metonymic dwarf) – inscribes the entirety of the discursive field of modernity in an apparent movement of displacement that comes into view not *at the end* of modernity, but after the project of declaring *an end* has exhausted itself in its own contradictions: at that point where critical discourse (born of – & bored with – its own modern*ism*) believes it has *finished with modernity*. At that point, critical discourse succumbs to the delirium of its own transcendental claims upon the Real in the perverse pleasure of an "experience" – reified in this uniquely authentic critical artefact – of a self-destruction posited as the ideal "negation of negation."

London, June 2019

4

THE POSTHUMAN ABSTRACT

Insofar as humanity dreams of life after death, the "drone" – the ubiquitous *unmanned vehicle* – is the as-yet-primitive technological image of that afterlife. Like the Panopticon, the drone is a metaphor.[1] It is the prototype of an ideal proxy by which the "human condition" transcends its worldly embodiment into a cosmic internet-of-things: a distributed architecture of autopoetic, kinetic agency. *Thought that moves itself.* Yet it's precisely for this reason that what calls itself *post*-human masks the return of an ever-more-apocalyptic humanism, wherein the prestige of what is conserved as species-unique is equated with the prestige of species-transcendence: the (supposed) "uniquely human" capacity to manufacture universalities (artificial intelligence, cybernetic machines, synthetic DNA, etc.) – the capacity, in other words, to project, by way of abstraction, an all-too humanistic teleology upon the domain of evolution & secure a future against human obsolescence.

This type of paradoxical science fiction narrative has prepared the way (in the West) for the evocation of "species solidarity" in the face of catastrophic imminence, from Global Warming to Technological Singularity to Human Extinction Event. Such a pseudo-solidarity is bound, on the one hand, to the advance of neo-liberal individualism &, on the other, to a ceaseless erosion of the collective "social contract." It doesn't matter that the logics of such catastrophes broadly contradict one another. What's essential is that the ultimate promise of business-as-usual both mitigates & masks a whole intervening process of *un-becoming*.

These symbiotic "ends" of humanism are previewed in the historical convergence of two events:

1. the recognition (with the birth of cybernetics) that technology could no longer be viewed as a human prosthesis, but that the human was in fact a prosthesis of a general technicity; &
2. the contemporary revelation of mass industrialised eugenics.

In this simple convergence, the principle that "technological progress" was divisible from ideology – the separation of science from metaphysics, the foundation of humanist thought – was overthrown. Unable any longer to disguise itself as universal rationality, humanism was exposed for what it had truly become: Western political-economic mysticism. This didn't cause humanism to fail; rather, under the liberal guise of techno-capitalism, it re-engineered itself into an escape plan for the End-of-History. It was able to do this because the idea of history (as maintained in the industrial imaginary) had never been anything more than a prosthesis of humanism to begin with. In this way, posthumanism & posthistoricism come to represent something like a closed feedback loop, whose epochal movement has been lugubriously & hubristically fashioned as the "Anthropocene."[2]

Posthuman, All Too Humxn. In the 2002 postscript to his often-cited thesis on the "End of History,"[3] *Our Posthuman Future: Consequences of the Biotechnological Revolution*, Francis Fukuyama argued for an urgent need to address the "political control of biotechnology" as it related to genetic engineering and recombinant DNA.[4] Failure to do so, he argued, would result in a "desperate rearguard action" for the future of humanity – a future, after all, guaranteed solely by the prospect that "there could be no end of history unless there was an end of science."[5] Its contemporary iteration today is the mitigation industry of AI's "existential risk." Behind its tone of humanistic panic, however, this argument conceals that, for science to secure the domain of the future, history must *already have ended*. If we equate, as Fukuyama does, history with ideological struggle, then the future *as technocracy* can only be consequent upon the end of politics *as such*. The real concern of Fukuyama's "posthumanism," then, isn't "political control of biotechnology," but the contrary: biotechnology *as political control* (where "political control" means social cybernetics).

But we must extend this line of thought further if we are to perceive its fully apocalyptic character. Concealed within the anxiety of an "uncontrolled" biotechnological assault upon the human is the implicit understanding of the human as a biological weapon. For Fukuyama, the true meaning of "posthuman" is thus the accomplishment of humanity's *historical mission*. As the "End of History" designates an end of ideological struggle, so too the dénouement of the Anthropocene & the "ends of man" represent the accomplished purpose of species warfare: dominion, not simply over *the* world, but over *all possible* worlds. The question *for whom* is thereby diverted onto the abstraction of the question of control as idealised (human) agency. It represents what Baudrillard called the "spiralling cadaver"[6] of humanism: even in the (always hypothetical) aftermath of humanity, the future will be human.

Responding to this strand of Fukuyamesque "scientism" in certain strands of Accelerationist discourse, Germán Sierra has pointed to a recurrent tendency to "reload ... humanist discourses," so as to "maintain the fiction of a *ghost-of-the-human-re-presenting-itself* as immutable & undisputed":

> All the current post-human narratives, even those pointing to the evolution of a "radical otherness" as intended or unintended consequence of

human action, are just modern versions of the extinction fables lying in the foundations of human rationality. Any "radical otherness" that may have a consequence for the human morphospace is just happening on "surface media" ... is still "our radical otherness." *No future* is still a future – very often a very specific one that is set in order to retro-determine present behaviour.[7]

In this retro-determined image of the future, "Extinction is unavoidable but impossible. Like time travel, *if it ever happens, it always does*."[8] "Being human" here means the "acceptance of individual death in exchange for not conceiving the extinction of the species." To which must be added that any "acceptance" of individual death is premised not merely on the idea of species continuance, but upon the abstract *vicariousness* of a collective *afterlife*: a mode of hauntology or telepathy, an *exception* from the domain of finite existence by way of an access to a *future totality* of human data-aggregation. Such totalised futurity represents the dialectical counterpart of a radical individualism in whom the idea of (human) *agency* corresponds to the horizon of the impossible, beyond which there is *nothing*.

Escape Velocity Zero. "Most narratives of posthumanism," Sierra writes, "are just time-reversal mutations of traditional western religious narratives interfered with by modern mythologies of progress" in which humanity becomes the creator of the "God" into which it evolves: the DNA of what Baudrillard called "the meta-physics of the code." Species-transcendence thus maintains all the conservative features of a manifest destiny under the sign of a *post-evolutionary future*. Its DNA transforms from materialist biology to "ideological concept," becoming a Baudrillardian "metaphysical sanctuary."[9] In this narrative, "becoming-other" really equates to a dialectical negation of "otherness" as a category by internalising it within the "human," a negation made possible by a Deleuzo-Benthamite *putting-to-work* of chance, indeterminacy, complexity, yoking the stochastic movement of evolution to the project of biotechnological control. Such "evolution," as Baudrillard says, is of course indistinguishable from a "socially & historically determined programme" where, like Fukuyama's "scientific" horizon, "the entire dialectic is devoured" by cybernetics.[10]

Nor is there anything *discrete* about such a project, which aims at the reifi-cation *of the entire complex of future possibility* in all its dimensions. In certain respects, this has always been at the root of every epistemology. The knowledge of what Wittgenstein called "everything that is the case" can be made to equate to power over "everything that *may be* the case," including the so-called *irrational, incalculable & unpresentable*. This trans-dialecticism poses itself as nothing less than an ideal emancipation: a final negation-of-negation, woven simultaneously into an all-pervasive *imaginary* anthropomorphism & a systemic alienation from it in the convergence of the *symbolic* & the *real*. It isn't simply, as Manuel De

Landa has it, that "robotic intelligence" will not "follow the anthropomorphic line of development prepared for it by science fiction,"[11] but that anthropomorphism will be revealed to have *evolved* as an epiphenomenon of a generalised *artificial intelligence* to which it otherwise *bears no resemblance*.

In this respect, anthropomorphism can be understood as a *mask of the unpresentable* – just as, for Turing, "intelligence" is revealed as a symbolic function divorced from human agency, in which it merely acquires an image.[12] In order to negate this negation, posthumanism advances the idea of artificial intelligence as that hidden hand by which a cybernetic vision of itself can be integrated into, or actualised from, the otherwise *inaccessible* matrix of the real: from quantum states to possible worlds. Unsurprisingly, this line of thought mirrors a politics of radical alienation that has become as *indistinguishable from* as it is *constitutive of* the prevalent discourse of emancipation. This paradox has become ubiquitous in the form of "panoptical" mobile communications technologies – from the smartphone to the drone – & the vast secret databanks designed to process, proliferate & predict them. Indeed, their proliferation is the functional extension of what William Gibson, channelling Guy Debord, envisaged in his 1986 novel *Neuromancer* as the lightspeed collapse of inflationary image-capital into a present whose historical vector describes an impossible escape velocity of *no future*.

Within this context, we need to interpret a question posed by Mikhail Prokopenko & David Budden in a 2015 article in *World Economic Forum*: "Is humanity just a phase in robotic evolution?"[13] It's a question that, like the post-Macy conference's turn from general artificial intelligence to robotics, invites us to envisage the blueprints of "our posthuman future" as *latent* in the world of technical artefacts & therefore *representable, programmable, inhabitable* – indeed as some-*thing* reducible to a "future prosthesis" of what the poet William Blake called the Human Abstract – a mere formalism, in other words, wherein the principle that "matter is information" fails to translate, like some posthumous Cartesian avatar whose "shell" is that of an nth-generation drone yet whose "ghost" is ineffably human.

While Prokopenko & Budden extrapolate the origin of human life (& life in general) via an hypothesis first advanced in 1985 by Alexander Cairns-Smith (about the convergence of organic molecules & self-replicating clay crystals) in order to emphasise the materiality of techno-evolutionary processes, their discussion nevertheless centres on a radically ambivalent conception of human agency. This ambivalence is implicitly likened, on the one hand, to *evolutionary* agency of the kind described in the mid-nineteenth century by Alfred Russel Wallace as a homeostatic "governor," and on the other hand, to what Gregory Bateson disputed as "conscious purpose versus nature."[14] This entanglement of probability & purpose finds its expression in the persistent confusion around "artificial intelligence" as the creation of *thinking machines*: either "to construct intelligent behaviour or imitate & enhance human intelligence."[15] Above all, there is the persistence of this mimetic faculty: to *represent*, to *imitate* – to represent the future; to imitate the *human* – like so many football-playing robots, sex bots, killer robocops, or benevolent euthanasia "companion" bots, all on their way to refining themselves into what, in *Of Grammatology*, Derrida called "that dangerous supplement": the metonymic dwarf that extends out from humanity & ends by taking its place in the scheme of *things*.

Dronology. In Prokopenko & Budden's evocation of the "origin of life" as a kind of mirror to the "evolutionary future," we are required to account for the addition, as Derrida says, of the *possible* to the stereotype of *primordiality*.[16] Instead we encounter the reflection of an ideal self-actualisation: humanity is less a "phase" than an "agent" of evolution (an evolutionary technology capable of accelerating stochastic processes of "natural selection" & "punctual" catastrophe). This agency is both retrospectively & prospectively accountable for the idea of *the future*, a thought nowhere more fully encapsulated than in the discourse of the Anthropocene. Yet if the Anthropocene is to AI what the oxygenation event was to biology, does the human algorithm represent a "logic capture" of post-world evolutionary futures or the contrary?

Just as the representational mode of humanism's dream of "democracy" is transposed into social-media algorithms of projective narcissism, so too is history collapsed into this all-consuming "capitalist logic" to which the future of its *non-future* relates as an *ideal commodity*; the "utopian" emancipation it proffers is both *of* & *from* the global as such. This is the more precise understanding of the Anthropocene as technocapital singularity. Its event-horizon shimmers in a vertigo of nascent infinities, hyperbolic space-time curvatures, entropologies of the impossible. It is the epochal thought of a total commodification that desires nothing so much as to *live on*, perpetually, by some miracle of negentropy, inhabiting every additional dimension of every possible *other* universe as well. More than religion, the Anthropocene offers "proof" of hypercommodification's sufficiency to extend humanism's afterlife to an indefinite degree. Equally, it makes little difference to speak of "escaping the Anthropocene," as Bernard Stiegler does, on account of its *unsustainability* as a "massive & high-speed process of destruction operating on a planetary scale" whose "current direction must be reversed."[17] Such a "Neganthropocene" requires more than "the elaboration of a new speculative cosmology." It needs an *unbecoming* of the logic of the commodity within which it is already inscribed.

Characteristic of the Anthropocene is a means of production that is self-styled as uniquely capable of affecting its "transcendence" according to the rationale of an auto-correcting cybernetic system. But while Stiegler's Neganthropocene may be phantasmatic (beyond the functional investment of a desire for conservation or salvation & the industries that evolve to serve them), the commodity is illusory only in its *gratification* of such emancipatory wish-fulfilment: in all other respects, it *reifies* the trauma of what Lacan calls a "missed encounter with the real."[18] Such an "encounter" escapes representation because, like montage, it is the *opening* of the representational scene & can only be *repeated*. In doing so, the commodity produces not only the illusion of the *real thing*, but real entropy. The gravitational pull it exerts may distort representational spacetime, but its cumulative inertia has brought it to the verge of collapsing back into history in the form of a catastrophic "negation-of-negation" (experienced either as the "end of liberal democracy" at the hands of a dehumanising, totalitarian, military-industrial surveillance & control system – Alfred McCoy's "drone canopy"[19] – or as the "end of man" by way of AI-driven mass eugenics, environmental collapse, etc.).

This, at least, is the form in which the Anthropocene appeals to a conflicting belief in the immanent outstripping of production by obsolescence where the "end of capitalism" is indistinguishable from the "end of the world." In all its paradox, it represents humanism's ultimate "call to order," situating itself as the vortex of all these "missed encounters." The Anthropocene is the trauma of the world brought to a critical mass in which alienation has reached such a pitch of repetition & accumulation as to threaten to erupt *into the real*. Its tenor is that of the ultimate anti-Oedipalism: "regress" to first evolutionary principles (reproduction of the *chance of a future* rather than any *thing*). But in its iteration as alien drift, will evolution succeed in "breaking through" the auratic event-horizon of post-history? Or will the commodity always get there faster than *it* can?

Such questions point towards the seduction of Anthropocenic thought as (an access to) a *beyond of ideology*. In the re-convergence of science & metaphysics, the Anthropocene marks a return to the "End of History," a future empirical fact to be lived in the present-imaginary as the *reification of the real*. In its appeal to an overcoming of (the effects of) progress, the discourse of the Anthropocene evokes a geological sublime, with the materiality of a non-ideological "real" being the ultimate historical arbiter. It appears to contradict the rhetoric of endless progress with a radical finitude in which the "End of History" is made to coincide with the "End of the World." It exposes a fundamental irrationalism in the structure of power, which is that of the zero sum: power will either own the future or abolish it. Like Mutually Assured Destruction, the "End of the World" doesn't represent the unthinkable, excluded from play. Instead, there is an incremental tactical manoeuvre.

The Return of Ideological Science. The discourse of the Anthropocene mirrors that of the Last Man & remains humanistic to its core. Like the July 2018 designation by the International Commission on Stratigraphy of a new "Meghalayan Age" accounting for the last 4,200 years of terrestrial history (third Age of the Holocene), the Anthropocene maintains a technological separation between the geological & the "human" (i.e., industrial capitalism). In both cases, the technicity of the "world" is made to recede behind the classical dichotomy of nature/culture (*physis/technē*): planetary agency versus human agency. Just as historical materialism remains bound to a linear, progressive logic, so the appeal to worldfulness hinges on a blind disavowal. Yet no argument concerning the geological register is able to overcome the fact that the Anthropocene is *an abstract representation of "the real" as global crisis* in which the task of "saving the planet" (the ideal Benthamite marriage of the utilitarian & environmental) can only be accomplished by the forces of globalisation that produced this crisis in the first place. The production of crisis – of that continuous "technological leap" that makes the Anthropocene forever immanent – is its *raison d'être*.

The problem here has to do with a fundamental misunderstanding that the "forces of industrialisation" are inherently bound to the discourse of reason. This stems from the error in thinking of technology solely as *instrumental*, as human *prosthesis*, as *extension*, not simply of capability, but of logic itself. In its broadest ramifications, however, *technē* is ambivalent towards such "teleologies." Evolutionary before hyperstitional, *technē* invests history with a *stochastic materialism*. And it is into this seemingly *irrational* dimension that the perpetual crisis of the "technological leap" delivers the idea of progress. For the same reason, what is called the Anthropocene isn't a "wrong turn" in the direction of industrial development. It is inseparable from industrial development and represents a critical amassing of *surplus value* that the system of automated production has always sought to totalise. In its equivalence of accumulated capital & inflationary entropy (debt-driven profit, unregulated waste), this version of the Anthropocene can be regarded as *the global dimension of alienation* (as the universalised counterpart of the Marxian subject, *constituted* by the abstractive "alienation-effect" of technicity).[20]

Misconstruing this condition, much post-Landian "Accelerationism" posits the belief that the only effective *contradiction* of capital – capable of accelerating its internal antagonisms & causing it to crash or self-supersede – is "capitalism." This belief describes a solipsistic movement that thinly veils a fearful longing, in James Joyce's words, "to be nearer to it & to look upon its deadly work."[21] Yet contrary to certain social Darwinist currents in this Fukuyamaesque re-scripting of Marx, "capitalism" *isn't in fact premised upon an essential antagonism*, but upon the contingency of successive disillusionments: a "poetry of marginal symptoms," Žižek writes, "of excessive unaccountable elements ranged against a system whose disturbance they materialise."[22] What appears in the form of "ideological struggle" is the process by which the dissolution of pseudo-antagonisms proceeds (base/superstructure, *physis/technē*), ultimately expressed in the reduction of such dichotomies to a generalised semiotics expunged of essentialisms: a unified "non-relational" field of signifying code whose common product is *surplus value*. It places all things (including all knowledge) "in the same finitude,"[23] in the words of Ignacio Torrent, rendering the *conditions of existence* an autonomatised subject (e.g., cybernetic "self-regulation & control" as the autonomous *non-relation* between the "antagonistic" industrial classes). The logic of the Anthropocene, in turn, dictates that the so-called called lifeworld is always-already co-opted to the work of technical re-production, including its own negative production: the global inflation-effect of "alienation."

Such a semiotics reveals that what, in its Accelerationist/Fukuyamaesque apocalypticism, appears to be an "imaginary" event-horizon in fact describes a "symbolic system" of real signifying force, one capable of producing (& negating) possibilities *by virtue of its radical ambivalence*. Moreover – & here lies its seemingly anomalous power – this radical ambivalence isn't the opposite of ideology, but the mark, the very condition, of the ideological as such, which cannot be reduced to a rhetoric of "concrete situations" (geological *evidence* that delegates as the *ideological unthought*). Under the guise of a "return of the real," the Anthropocene is given as the "return of the subject of history" in an effort to supply this apparent *lack* of ideological agency – a singular Weltproletariat, so to speak, produced by capital & in turn required to assume the burden of its alienating production. The Anthropocene is made to represent, in this sense, the counterpart of such rhetorical sleights-of-hand as the "War on Terror" through the evocation of *real abstractions* & a return of the pathetic fallacy in the shape of a new, totalising form of humanist pseudo-philanthropy: a system of thought able to incorporate anything into itself – even global catastrophe – via the commodification of the inexhaustible resource of "environmental improvement."

The ideological force of the Anthropocene is its seeming confirmation of this totality as the penultimate step towards understanding, regulating, predicting & controlling the "entire world," like some cosmic avatar of Panopticism. The present *planetary crisis* needs to be recognised in this form: as the ideal call to discipline. From the discourse on "energy security" to the widespread "security crackdown" on environmental activists across the so-called developed & developing world, the Anthropocene represents the co-option of a scientific factography for the thinly-disguised resurgence of "ideological science" of the Fukuyamaesque variety. Where Heidegger argued in *Was heißt Denken* that "science doesn't think" (it is ideally non-ideological), the politics of the Anthropocene ushers in an End of Science & a "post-scientific" condition of *technē politikē*. From now on, according to this narrative, *science* (like *technology*) must be uniquely at the service of *maintenance* – the maintenance of the World as the maintenance of the *global order* organised around a universal appeal to "crisis management." And just as technology is made to elide with *technocracy*, so *science* (under the arbitrary authority of intergovernmental agencies, think-tanks & corporate lobbies) elides with the most flagrantly Swiftian satires of market self-interest & private greed.

London, June 2018

5

ENTROPOLOGY

At the beginning of the third decade of the twenty-first century, it has become *de rigueur* to speak already of a post-Anthropocene, whose template has been provided by that historical fissure in which the late-industrial World Order was cracked open & prised apart by a rapid succession of wars, nuclear armament, the Marshall Plan, cyberneticisation & neoliberalism. This succession exposed the vista of an ideal *tabula rasa* viewed from the perspective of monolithic power, like a virgin resource just beyond the frontier, on the other side of History. It is possible that the discourse of the End of History (& its reversal within that of a resurgent transcendentalism) have become more pervasive, more insistent, more *determined* than at any previous time, even if, as is frequently said, "the ability to conceive of the history of hominids & the destiny of the Earth in the same temporal trajectory seems particularly deceptive today."[1]

The question that would still need to be asked is: In what does this *deception* consist & what is the nature of its *seeming*? It cannot simply be a matter of overturning this relation – this *identity* – between the so-called human & the "destiny of the Earth," yet the imperative to comprehend it, under the sign of a "call to order," is caught in a double-bind. The deception that lies at the heart of the discourse of the Anthropocene – as both an objective error *imposed upon the world* & its recoil in a Rousseauesque *return of nature* (above all, the "natural disaster") in the register of *the real* – is no less a humanist delirium than is the claim of a disinterested reason over the task of its correction. Yet the metaphysical foundations on which reason's disinterest stands – as something unbounded by the worldly confines of "the history of hominids" – are precisely what must be maintained here *against* the universality of an Anthropocenic movement that threatens to erase all such prior claims to an *exteriorisation of the world*.

Yet just as metaphysics is created in the (abstract) image of "man," so too this "deception" is made to prevail over what is in fact most alienating to "man" in the Anthropocene: a world that is not the object of reason, but which stands fully in place of reason; a world not subsumed by technology, but constitutive of it; a world not alienated by "human" forces that have obtained, in its termination, an irrefutable ascendancy & mastery ("the destiny of the Earth"), but which *is* that alienation in all its radical ambivalence. To submit this deception to the work of reason – in order to dispel the error, or rather superstition, to which this act of comprehension (of the world in its relation to history & of its singular inscription or destiny) risks succumbing – requires firstly that we submit reason (whether idealised or instrumental) to the critique that this "deception" necessitates. In the final analysis, it may be that what are summoned under the terms reason & Anthropocene can in no way be *opposed* to one another & that, in pretending to stand apart from the "deception" it would seek to remedy, such a reason can only remain true to its object by deceiving itself. This is the object of truth (in the relation of reason, of history, of The Human) to that which by definition *exceeds it* & yet which, in the same movement (& by an equivalent logic) that it comprehends *in advance,* stands before it as the mirror of this *Weltgeist,* *bringing it into view*.

What this question concerns isn't simply the *deception* at work in any of those "simulated or simulating (& dissimulating) representations" of this *beyond* (an "exteriorisation," we will come to see) to which reason must also make recourse, but rather, as Jean-Luc Nancy reminds us, "a matter of what does not pertain to representation at all."[2] And it isn't the point at which representation encounters its own impossibility (of the *unpresentable*, etc.), but of that which cannot be thought within or by means of any regime of *mimēsis* whatsoever: the so-called *return of the real* in which the figure of "nature" is thus subsumed. Within the abundance of this resource of the unpresentable lies that void upon which – through the entire course of its history – reason has nevertheless most desired to gaze. In this nascent figure, this trope of the void, reason seeks to finally break with "the terrifying insufficiency of all the various assurances of knowing"[3] through an experience of the impossible (i.e., of its *non-experience*, of the impossibility of any experience). This movement both exceeds & recoils from its limits, which it has already *figured* as an empty circularity. Far from marking reason's failure, this subversion (its empty circularity) exists today in the pentecostal tones of a post-Anthropocenic philosophy as its ultimate affirmation: *the impossibility of ending*.

Anthropocene, or, the Historical Mission of Capital. The lesson of cybernetics & of the physical sciences is that *there is no movement from organicity to abstraction* upon which a teleological view of history can stake its claim. No devolution from "life" to "technology." No decline from a prior pristine "nature" to "artificiality," from a "human condition" to one of "alienation," from "work" to "commodity." Not even of the *entire work of an epoch*, as Nancy says.[4] And if these terms do not devolve into one another on the basis of a teleology, it is because their co-implication is the defining logic of evolutionary processes: "life" must be understood "technologically" in its origin, constituted by & through operations of "alienation." This rupture in neo-humanist & neo-Vitalist discourse has come to constitute something like a trauma in contemporary thought, above all in the heterogeneous figure of the Anthropocene. Against the spectre of "humanly mediated" global climate *catastrophe*, Anthropocenic appeals to *ecological values* go hand-in-hand with a return of a "technical" or "instrumentalist" reason (and, *ipso facto*, its duality in a metaphysics of "pure" reason.) In other words, there is a return – via an appeal to an objective geological register – of precisely those abstractions that the critique of the Anthropocene has apparently sought to negate or overcome & in which, Nancy argues, "humanity" *has never taken place so exactly*.[5]

The form of this trauma can be detected in the sort of remarks that have been directed by Peter Sloterdijk against the re-emergent genre of "alarmist ecological literature," as he calls it. In an article entitled "The Anthropocene: A Process-State on the Edge of Geohistory?" Sloterdijk writes: "It seems that the proliferation of this term can be explained above all by that fact that, in the guise of scientific neutrality, it transmits a message of nearly unsurpassable moralist-political urgency; a message which, in explicit language reads: Humans have become responsible for the inhabitation & business administration of the Earth as a whole ever since their presence on it stopped unfolding in the mode of more or less traceless integration."[6] Sloterdijk's argument identifies several key strains in this traumatic register where the ideological agency of the Anthropocene is sublimated & transferred successively onto:

1. the human (as a collective subjectivity), to which is attributed "an ability to perpetrate crimes of geo-historical dimensions";
2. technology (as human prosthesis), retrieved via an obscure characterisation of labour in Marx as "the metabolic interaction between *human beings & nature*," & thus the "continuation of natural history in another register";
3. history (qua materialist teleology), positioned "to evaluate the world from the perspective of its end," implying "a cosmo-moralistic sorting process."[7]

This schema poses "humanity" as a "meta-biological agent" & produces an image of "'capitalism' as global fatality."[8] Here the Anthropocene is the accelerated spiral of an abstract vicious-circle principle in which "capitalism" (as an expression of the amplitude of reason) has been swept along. It is a schema entirely contiguous with the discourse of *technological singularity* whereby the primitive industrial phase of the Anthropocene will have served as an evolutionary prologue. Under the constellation of technological singularity are thus gathered the various discourses of post-history & post-humanism. Collective responsibility for this geo-historical terminus immediately transforms into the abstraction of a technological *Weltgeist* marked by human obsolescence.

The apparent paradigm shift from the biological to the technological is supposed to accomplish itself in a purely autonomous fashion; the so-called "human" is not only alienated from its privileged position vis-à-vis reason but is so in a seemingly spontaneous, yet also fatalistic, way, as if *divorced from ideology*. It is the "human species" (& not capitalism, for example) that bears responsibility for those world-negating actions conjured by the Anthropocene, & it is the "human" (& not capital) that is sacrificed to obsolescence in the coming singularity – a purely rhetorical sacrifice, of course, since "human" here merely refers to an opportunistically "ethical" category that supersedes itself in the (posthumanist) narrative of *transcendental capitalism* (i.e., the seeming inversion of the old Marxist paradigm in which capitalism is delimited as the *revolutionary process* of a necessary transition to world socialism[9]). This would appear to correspond to what Vincent Garton has called "the progressive divorcing of capital itself from capitalism as a human social formation"[10] towards its reformulation in what Primož Krašovec terms *alien capital*. "Capital is alien," Krašovec writes, "not (only) as an unconscious or unforeseen dimension of human activity, but as an additional actor, the 'eighth' passenger of capitalist economy: *alien*."[11]

Entropy Is the Meaning of the Real. Marx himself had already observed that only in its self-alienation does capitalism represent the operation *of its own* transcendence – firstly by transforming the crises of production into an expanded "means" of self-propagation (the same vicious circle would be described once more *under expanded conditions of production, with an expanded market & increased productive forces*) – then by its generalisation of crisis (i.e., the totalisation of its internal contradictions) as the *logic* of its system of control: it becomes an alienated, independent, social power that stands opposed to society as an object.[12]

This objectification – like that of the Anthropocene, which inscribes its entire movement – becomes ever more concrete just as the entropic production of "human obsolescence" is ever-more accelerated & ramified *towards its ideal form* in the automation of globalised & financialised capital. This is not due simply "to the development of autonomous machines & artificial intelligence in the direction that anthropocentric theories of capital are unable to detect (i.e., towards an ever-greater independence of capital from humanity"[13]), but rather to the alien basis of humanity *in capital*.

Just as Marx advised the necessity of Ricardo's insight into the distinction between "human beings" & the "development of productive forces" (whose development was "the historical task & justification of capital" without consideration for humanity in its moral appeal), so too the Anthropocene must be grasped in its relation to *its* forces of production, including the self-supersession of the Anthropos implied by a terminal *technological singularity*. And to the extent that such forces can be attributed to a generalised "evolutionary" movement, it would be no less the case that this "evolution" would place no higher premium on *human obsolescence* than it would on the *human exception*. In this respect, Sloterdijk's observation that the Anthropocene contains "the spontaneous *minima moralia* of the current age"[14] makes sense as a kind of Kantian imperative arising upon a foundation of *radical ambivalence*.

It is necessary to recognise that these seemingly opposed terms – obsolescence & exception – merely function here to resituate the "human" as the privileged term within a binary relation in which the non-human, the alien & the technological retain what amounts to a distinct eugenics that does *not* deny a general miscegenation along the lines of the cyborg or some other form of biotech hybrid; rather, it denies the fact that the "human" – & by declensions "nature" & "life" in general – is *always-already technological from its origin.* It is only by preserving or re-inscribing the nature/technology dichotomy that such concepts as the "technological singularity" & the "posthuman" obtain their meaning, whereby one might continue to speak of a certain "technological" future as a *posthumous condition* ruled by a principle of *non-life*, of *artificiality*, of *virtuality*. And by an impeccable dialectical logic, this would also serve as a post-facto extension of the "human" & of a humanist rationale via the prostheses of the *non-human, super-human, in-human*, etc.

The transcendental itinerary of the "alien" (as that element which governs experience from "beyond life") would not describe the negation of the "human" but its *apocalyptic return* (as the definitive form of an evolutionary process *whose author it will have become*). Indeed, this preoccupation with the spectral valences of the "human" permits a certain *alien capital* to inscribe the "epoch" of the posthuman through a reinvention of the discourse of the *perfectibility of man* while simultaneously announcing *human obsolescence* – the two terms are interchangeable – & thereby producing this *ultimate form of the completion of history* out of its own circular & (seemingly) paradoxical itinerary. It remains that the belated, all-too-human status of the Anthropocene – a purview in retrospect – is (& has always been) ideological to its core. Such a *technē politikē* does not mean that it *is not real* or that it is merely an "externalisation" of human agency onto some other abstract entity (a scapegoat of some kind, e.g., some "alien capital"). It means that what continues to be posed as the ideologically neutral counterpart of a humanism – whether by appeal to the "real," to "nature," or to "technology" as *externalised prosthesis* – is ideological from its origin: this inhabiting "alien" element that assumes the form, as Freud says, of a "thing that thinks."

It is only in this sense that Sloterdijk can speak of the Anthropocene as a "cosmo-moralistic sorting process" that effectively redistributes its *means of production* onto the supposedly objective categories of the *human, technology & history* away from the system of ideology that inscribes them. The work of *responsibility* for the Anthropocene is thus vested in purely "material" processes that – in being indifferently ascribable to humanity, technology, or history – can be subsumed into the "natural metabolism" of an autonomous planetary agent or *Weltgeist*. This work bears all the marks of a fetishism & is the apotheosis of *alienated labour*. Through its alienating effects upon the "fabric of the real," & by "externalising" itself from its own processes, capital promises a *world to come* & operates as the *alibi of the world.* Just as "production of surplus value" is conventionally regarded as "the social form of the process of production in capitalism," so does the production of a certain *futurity* as world-prosthesis manifest capital's assurance of a transcendental surplus beyond the apparent eschatology of the Anthropocene.

If the Anthropocene signifies a final (authentic) End-of-History, then capital is nevertheless imbued with the special capability of teleporting the world *beyond it.* This end-world is *nothing other* than a perpetual *forethrow of the beyond.* Yet what constitutes the alien-in-capital is not the autonomous agency attributable to this process or to the "surplus" produced by it – as if it were a detachable logos – but rather to the *absence of any beyond as such.* The true characteristic of alien capital is that *what appears to be surplus-production* is in fact a movement of *dissipation accumulating dissipation.* Known from thermodynamics as entropy, this movement has always signified the "externalisation" of capital. It does not extend outward from the world or from one world to another. It constitutes the limits of the world (i.e., by inflation). As Bataille has argued, in re-orientating the theory of capital towards a *general expenditure,* dissipation isn't simply a "middle term between two expropriations,"[15] but capital's *raison d'être.* It is, in a manner of speaking, its own movement of an alienation that orbits around a nucleic void: there is no prior, more authentic being of capital, nor is capital capable by itself of inaugurating a positive "productive force" that is not already an operation of entropy. In this sense, too, the alienation of capital is not something that merely befalls the world – an "Anthropocene," for example, that could simply be detached under conditions of a *post-capitalism*; it is *endemic* to the world. Moreover – & this is perhaps the most radical implication of this line of argument – its "logic" is generalised to such a degree that it's no longer possible (if it were ever possible at all) to separate this *alienation* from the constituency of "life itself."

Dissipative Strictures. The thought of "alien capital" – as an autonomous dissipative principle – can be said to relate to what Bataille calls the "insufficiency of the principle of classic utility" in the manner of a *potlatch.* Everything that, up until now, has been subsumed under the category of "productive forces" can be shown (in principle) *not* to conserve a "surplus" or "reserve" but to be wholly orientated towards an increase of expenditure. This general dissipative economy ramifies itself through a system of feedback in which "growth" is determined as an accumulation of dissipative effects. Dissipation produces more dissipation in the mode of an eco-ideological struggle to maximisation. Ecology *is* this struggle & it is *ideological* on the level of dissipation as the determining *rationale* of its operations – which is to say, its *system of meaning.* Sloterdijk attributes such a view to the advent of cybernetics, in particular the viewpoints set out in Buckminster Fuller's *Operating Manual for Spaceship Earth* (1969): "From this moment on, good old Earth could no longer be thought of as a natural force, but was to be regarded as a gigantic artefact. It was no longer a base; it was a vehicle. It was no longer the epitome of material; it was the sensitive system of all systems."[16]

Fuller's text appeared two years after Bataille's major work on general economy, *The Accursed Share*, but already 35 years after the "Notion of Expenditure," a blueprint for Bataille's later thesis. All three texts, however, are connected through Vladimir Vernadsky's *The Biosphere* (1926),[17] to which Bataille refers in his notes & Fuller was obviously indebted, yet of which Sloterdijk appears distinctly unaware. Vernadsky's concept of Earth as biosphere was predicated on a global system of "circular" metabolism wherein the expropriation (transformation) of solar energy allows the production of entropy to amplify through feedback cycles of consumption & expenditure. This also permits the overall rate of dissipation to increase, tending towards conditions of what biologists call *extremal forcing* & what Ilya Prigogine called *dissipative structures* in the 1970s. The "conditions for dissipative structures are readily encountered in living systems, which are (i) open, (ii) governed by nonlinear evolution equations, & (iii) operate far from thermodynamic equilibrium."[18] But they are also encountered in other forms of self-propagating dynamic systems not conventionally considered to be *alive* (e.g., cybernetic or economimetic systems exhibiting a general *technicity* that extends from microsystems to the biosphere & beyond).

By proposing the existence of the biosphere as "a specific life-saturated envelope of the Earth's crust" – in addition to the atmosphere, hydrosphere & lithosphere – Vernadsky was not only proposing that the entire planet should be viewed as an ecosystem analogous in its process to "life itself," but that "life processes" in general must be understood differently, extending beyond any restricted notion of *organism* to encompass the "inorganic body"[19] of, for example, geological processes:

> No chemical force on Earth is more constant than living organisms taken in aggregate, none is more powerful in the long run ... Life is, thus, potentially & continuously disturbing the chemical inertia on the surface of the planet ... The outer layer of the Earth must, therefore, not be considered as a region of matter alone but also as a region of energy & a source of transformation of the planet. To a greater extent, exogenous cosmic forces shape the face of the Earth, & as a result, the biosphere differs historically from other parts of the planet. This biosphere plays an extraordinary planetary role. The biosphere is at least as much *a creation of the sun* as a result of terrestrial processes.[20]

This last point is central to Bataille's reinterpretation of the biosphere as a *general economy*, defined as a system of constantly enlarging processes of dissipation, driven by what we might call a *solar technology.* In this conjunction of solar expenditure & biotechnical amplification, an *alien capital* can be seen to operate not as the derivative of human-dependent operations (or even of evolution in general), but as their agent. Moreover, by its implicit relation of globally consequential life-processes to planetary-scale *technological transformation*, & in its economy of metabolic force-feedback, Vernadsky's concept anticipates the logic of the Anthropocene. And just as Bataille's general economy encompasses forces of destructive expenditure that are nevertheless *productive of ideology*, so does Vernadsky's biosphere encompass those industrial forms of "systematic destruction" wrought by "civilised humanity," themselves *productive* of biogenic impact.[21] Thus: "The release of [carbon dioxide] by Man in the process of his technical work ... has already reached such an order that it must be taken into account in the geochemical history of the biosphere."[22]

But where the Anthropocene is generally taken to describe a geological "epoch" defined negatively by such impacts, Vernadsky instead envisaged the inauguration of a new sphere of geological activity, the Noösphere (from the Greek *nous*: mind, intelligence). Here "the increase of the cultural biochemical energy of mankind is advancing steadily without fundamental regression ... There is a growing understanding that this increase has no insurmountable limits, that it is an elemental geological process."[23] This isn't just a product of a technological intelligence; the Noösphere is itself that intelligence, productive of its own transformative processes of expenditure & aggregation.

Negentropic Debt. A number of interventions in the discourse on the Anthropocene have adopted a term derived from Erwin Schrödinger's 1943 lectures at the Dublin Institute for Advanced Studies, later published as *What is Life?: The Physical Aspect of the Living Cell*. The term is "negative entropy"[24] or, as Léon Brillouin felicitously abbreviated it in his 1953 study of information systems, "negentropy."[25] In the section entitled "Order Based on Order," Schrödinger tells his audience that "the laws of physics, as we know them, are statistical laws. They have a lot to do with the tendency of things to go over to disorder ... The general principle involved is thermodynamics (entropy principle)."[26] He then proceeds to the question at hand: "What is the characteristic feature of life? When is a piece of matter said to be alive?"

"Living matter," Schrödinger notes, differentiates itself from inert matter by evading "the decay to equilibrium": "When a system that is not alive is isolated or placed in a uniform environment, all motion usually comes to a standstill very soon ... After that, the whole system fades away into a dead, inert lump of matter. A permanent state is reached, in which no observable events occur. The physicist calls this the state of thermodynamic equilibrium, or of 'maximum entropy.'"[27]

The distinction Schrödinger arrives at is that a life system "feeds on 'negative entropy'": "It is by avoiding the rapid decay into the inert state of 'equilibrium,'" he argues, "that an organism appears so enigmatic; so much so, that from the earliest times of human thought some special non-physical or supernatural force *(vis viva,* entelechy) was claimed to be operative in the organism, & in some quarters is still claimed."[28]

For Schrödinger (& not only Schrödinger, of course), there is instead "metabolism" – i.e., a system of *exchange* (μεταβάλλειν) – in place of any mysterious *life-force.* This metabolism isn't reducible to a redistribution of "matter" or "energy." Rather, "[e]very process, event, happening ... in a word, everything that is going on in Nature means *an increase of the entropy* of the part of the world where it is going on. Thus a living organism *continually increases its entropy,*" & so "[i]t can only keep ... alive, by continually drawing from its environment negative entropy." Consequently, "the essential thing in metabolism" is that it *"feeds upon negative entropy,* attracting ... a stream of negative entropy upon itself, to compensate the entropy increase it produces by living."[29]

By a slight inflection, this metabolic compulsion underwrites conditions of political struggle within the "social organism" equivalent to the Spinozan principle of "the impulse *(conatus)* of self-sustainability at any price, impressing upon every life the form of a flight forward."[30]

Ideo-Metabolic Production. This concept of "metabolic exchange" has fostered some confusion among cultural theorists, partly informed by Marx's concept of metabolic rift[31] – in reference to ecological crisis tendencies under capitalism – & partly by an attribution of what amounts to *subjectivity* in the principle of negentropic exchange. In "Dreams & Nightmares: Beyond the Anthropocene Era," Bernard Stiegler writes: "A consensus exists in the scientific community, whether among physicists or chemists or biologists, that *life* is *what defers* the process of entropy, that is, what *retains* energy, transforms it & *organises* it into organs, organisations that constitute organisms."[32] Yet as Derrida (to whom Stiegler is also alluding here) makes clear, "No doubt life protects itself by repetition, trace, *différance* (deferral). But we must be wary of this formulation: there is no life present *at first* which would *then* come to protect, postpone, reserve itself in *différance.*"[33] In addition, this deferral does not correspond to a *retention* (e.g., of energy: living systems, in any case, consume food & so energy cannot be conserved). Nor is there any entity to which the term "life" corresponds that decisively *produces its own being* through a consumption of negentropy; rather, the metabolic pre-disposition of entropy gives rise to *entrained* (or *entroped*) structures of "spontaneous" self-propagation as efficient conduits for the *maximisation* of entropic flow. (This synchronous arrangement, or *resonance,* defines what is called negentropy, since the one is in direct proportion to the other, as we will see later.)

Among other things, Stiegler's formulation is concerned with what appears to be an entirely paradoxical maintenance of *surplus* (energy reserve) in the deferral of entropy (stagnation/non-exchange/non-circulation), which will also have unintended implications for how he construes a political economy. For now, however, Stiegler envisages this retention/organisation as a process of "exo-somatisation" or *externalisation* (i.e., of thought into hybrid realities). The term coincides to some extent with *hyperstition* since this deferral of entropy is ultimately attributed to a kind of embodied-embodying agency or intention. "The function of reason," Stiegler writes, "is to produce negentropic bifurcations against entropy in general & against its own entropy in particular – here we must spell entropy with an 'a' & an 'h': anthropy."[34] Such an embodied (and embodying) entropy/anthropy cannot help but evoke a "transhumanist delirium"[35] by which the anthropos transforms into an agent of self-supersession, aligning the concept of "negentropy" with an idea of emancipation that signifies a certain end: "the end of the Anthropocene, in the epoch of disruption, which makes obvious that the Anthropocene is no longer sustainable, no longer liveable."[36] But as Althusser already reminds us in his examination of *Capital*, "once the anthropological given has been removed, the space remains, which is precisely what interests us."[37] This space is also that of a *différance*, of a general substitutability, marking (under the pretence of a "deconstruction") the interval of a *return* in Stiegler that amounts to a "subject of history" in the form of its negation.[38]

This interval (or transposition) from Anthropocene to a post-Anthropocene (or Neganthropocene) is supposedly accomplished through an exo-somatisation. Exo-somatisation, we are told, "is a *bifurcation* in the history of life," a "*new regime of negentropy*" coinciding with a transposition to "neganthropology."[39] Neganthropology is in turn taken to define the *différance* – this is Stiegler's appropriation of Derrida's term[40] – of Anthropos, the "differing & deferring" of the "end of Anthropos," which constitutes an imperative: "it is *inconceivable* for us," Stiegler insists, "to *remain* in the Anthropocene. We will have to *conceive, invent* & *exo-somatise* the Neganthropocene, & for that we need a neganthropology that will allow us to enter into a *new era* ... a new age of political economy," of a "noetic dream."[41]

Exosomatism. How is it possible to differentiate this exo-somatisation from a posthumanism that all too readily resembles a transcendental agent – & indeed *rationality* – of humanity's *living on*, beyond the end of its own "unsustainable," "unliveable" epoch, if simply under a regime of inverted terminologies?

What is clear is that this exo-somatisation is envisaged simultaneously as *exchange* & *retention*, a *transformation* & a *conservation*. Its relation to a mode of political economy is articulated in terms of "freedom," "combat," "law": "Freedom is what *produces* negentropy," Stiegler says, "it is what *generates* negentropic acts. Freedom does not mean the freedom to choose," as in Marx's *false choices*; it is rather "the freedom to combat an entropic state of fact in order to establish a new negentropic reality. This entropic state of fact *is precisely a state of fact within which a new negentropic reality sets up a new state of law*."[42] The immediate question here is how Stiegler's eschewal of false choices can be distinguished from a purely arbitrary bifurcation, one that feeds back into a "vicious circle" of quasi-supersession (from "new states of fact" to "new states of law"), & one that accomplishes nothing more than its own exo-somatic *reification*: not as *différance*, but as a merely procedural negation-of-negation that is, "in fact," an algorithmic rationality's attempt to materialise a *raison d'être*. What, after all, is the imperative of the "us" in Stiegler's figuring of the Anthropocene to "conceive, invent & exo-somatise the *Neg*anthropocene" other than to avert the reality of that "end of Anthropos" that arrives (& is simultaneously deferred) under the guise of a recuperative Neganthropos? Of *being* under the guise of a certain (instrumentalised) *non-being*? Of a subjectivity defined within what Stiegler calls "*Automated Society?*"[43]

This *conscientious* exo-somatisation will have reinscribed a movement of "externalisation" that philosophy has, at least since Plato, associated with *technē* & the production of automata; in these terms, technology is broadly conceived as a *prosthesis of reason*. Its purpose, Stiegler informs us, will have been "to produce bifurcations," "to implement the function of reason" so as to "make noetic life possible in the universe": "Now is the time for this thematisation. And this is why it is time to take seriously what Binswanger & Foucault tell us, but while taking equally seriously what Azéma shows, namely, that noetic man is above all an oneiric man. This oneiric & noetic form of life has the capacity to exteriorise its dreams & thus to realise them in the form of technics – the issue being that technics produces pharmaka, which can always turn the dream into a nightmare."[44]

This *production of possibility* for "noetic life" – a narrative of *premonition* for a certain futurity or what might be called *manifest destiny* – is sublimated through a fictional correspondence with a *deferral of entropy*, which, Stiegler adds, "I believe to be the true stakes of what Derrida called *différance* with an 'a.' But Derrida himself did not see this clearly."[45] On the contrary, for Derrida, *différance* is not a deferral *of* entropy, but deferral *as* entropy: the "death," in Derrida's reading of Freud, at the "origin" of life (which inscribes all of its operations).[46]

The Instrumental Unconscious. Stiegler's claim that exo-somatisation corresponds to a radical potential within *différance* that Derrida failed to grasp should be treated with an appropriate degree of scepticism, since, under the "sign" of *différance*, Stiegler's text summons a type of techno-Hegelianism.[47]

Even if the implementation of a "function of reason" from a production of bifurcations did not imply a prelapsarian self-sufficiency (i.e., a "reason" from which this prosthetic function could be derived as the "model" of an originary bifurcation), its "noetic dream" nevertheless remains that of a teleology destined to "conceive, invent & exo-somatise" one. This movement from anthropos to neganthropos – from "noetic life" to an "externalised" "function of reason" – bears all the traits of a dialectical mystification. Supersession is always recuperated for the self-preservation of the power of enstatement "itself," as both the subject & form of *power*, of *history* (even of so-called post-history), & of "the State" *as such*. The Anthropocene here is an "era" or "epoch" only to the extent that it sustains itself[48] as a mode of duration (& thus as a "genre" of reason) whose "negation" is the instrument of its propagation – not, as Stiegler says, as "*a new state of law,*" but as the Law of Genre.[49]

The true meaning of exo-somatisation is the effective *outsourcing* of a global regime of power in the expansion of the work of resource-exploitation, expropriation & expenditure. It corresponds, in neoliberal economics, to the mechanism of "continuous growth" – an apparent refutation of what Marx, restating the second law of thermodynamics, calls the "law of the tendency of the rate of profit to fall"[50] – that requires a perpetual profit-margin creep abetted by ever-more-virulent forms of enforced inequality & a "reserve" of alienated labour (negentropy).

The Neganthropocene, as Stiegler defines it, possesses at best the character of a "regime change" in which a certain *ambivalence* in its binary organisation comes into view. The freedom entailed in such a movement can be no more than a structural bias: the handy-dandy alternation or oscillation of *signifiers for the Law,* even if they apparently constitute its "governing" terms (Anthropos/ Neganthropos) & so represent at best a *diversion, detour* or *détournement* of subversion. Contrary to the assertion that such a movement is productive of a "new reality" (or even a *sur-reality*), this re-inscription attempts a homeostatic reduction of *différance* to a simple opposition, designed for no other purpose than to preserve the Law under whose sign it would indeed represent a *false choice* – were such a reduction possible in anything other than appearance.

This re-inscription of precisely those dualisms (inside/outside; *physis/technē,* etc.), which the polysemy of *différance* deconstructs,[51] echoes what Benjamin Noys has described in instrumentalist terms as "[t]he aim of accelerationists ... to engage *with technology* & *forms of capitalist abstraction*[52] so we can invent a *new post-capitalist future.*"[53] Just as Stiegler insists that "humanity" accomplishes itself by "organic projection" (i.e., "by projecting organs outside itself"), such an *engagement* needs firstly to be understood as nothing but *abstract & technological,* so that any agent of acceleration or noetic exo-somatisation could never be, as it were, *internal to itself.* So too the "noetic dream" cannot stand in an objectified relation to "technology," just as "negentropy" cannot "*produce* ... différance," since *différance/technē* already inscribe the "economy of negentropy."[54] "Humanity" does not exist here other than as a moralistic alibi (Sloterdijk) for processes of exploitation that are subsumed under an appeal to a *common future,* whose accomplishment in reality can only be effected by an impoverishment of the mass of "humanity" (& so-called inhumanity) that must labour in its production.

Structure's Dream. On this point, it is instructive to return to the discourse from which Stiegler's terminology derives, situated as it is at the intersection of physics & biology, if not politics & psychology. The thermodynamic interpretation of evolution has recently produced some interesting theoretical outcomes. In a series of papers co-authored since 2014, Jeremy England has advanced the thesis – devolved from Prigogine's ideas on dissipative structures – that what we call "life" is not in opposition to entropy. It is a *function* of entropy, produced by it, dependent upon it, & engineered to maximise its increase. In this scenario, evolution, from its inception, is an economy of ever-increasing efficiency in circulation & expenditure, rather than an economy of conservation or "energy retention" (however this might be conceived).

In a talk given in 2014 at the Karolinska Institute (Stockholm), England defined the physical properties of "life" as:

1. self-replication;
2. sensing, computation & anticipation;
3. effective absorption of work from environment.

According to England's observations, "when a group of atoms is driven by an external source of energy (like the sun or chemical fuel) & surrounded by a heat bath (like the ocean or atmosphere), it will often gradually restructure itself in order *to dissipate increasingly more energy.*"[55] Adapted "through rounds of iterative selection,"[56] this tendency to spontaneously align with a dissipative increase effectively *engineers* "self-replicating molecules" where the *algorithmic* corresponds to *life-processes.* Thus "self-replication," England argues, is a process that "must invariably be fuelled *by the production of entropy.*"[57] Computer simulations have shown that, with a high statistical probability, self-replication undergoes "extremal thermodynamic forcing" capable, in theory, of producing complex life-systems. It is, in the parlance of Noys, inherently accelerationist. Moreover, it marks an accelerationism whose *agency* is not some alien entity "in the sense of being a register of alterity or radical disconnect from the world," as Negarestani puts it, but is the *law* of entropy itself.[58]

Such apparently novel self-replicating structures do not evolve *despite* their dissipative character but *because* of it: they are not "tolerant" of change but change-determined, since this is the basis of their self-organisational possibility. The emergence of life-systems may be conceived as a function of resonance (the oscillative character of *dissipation* interacting with itself *in synchronisation* to achieve increase, or what England calls "resonant adaptation").[59] Growth is defined as *an increase in the capacity to consume, complexify & dissipate.* In such a system, *différance* would describe the minimum energetic cost of maintaining its requisite *far-from-equilibrium state* & the (iterative) mechanism of its *driven stochastic evolution.*[60] Yet what drives it cannot be accounted for by Stieglerian exo-somatisation, by a latent "libidinal economy" translated into a "function of reason" (from chemotaxis to an approximation of Anthropic "intelligence"). Instead, we have an emergent computation in the *en-troped* structure of evolutionary possibility (Althusser, echoing Marx, deems it "an authorless theatre"[61]). This general entropement, in turn, defines a "Noösphere" analogous to Fuller's synergetics: a global "geometry of thought"[62] or *internet of everything.*

To rephrase a formulation of Derrida's vis-à-vis the Freudian *death drive*: Is it not already *entropy* at the origin of a life which can defend itself against entropy only through an *economy* of entropy?[63] This would imply, contrary to Stiegler's insistence upon exo-somatisation, that "the existence of structure," as Althusser says, is "in its effects [&] that the effects are not outside the structure, are not a pre-existing object, element or space in which the structure arrives to *imprint its mark*: on the contrary, it implies that the structure is immanent in its effects ... that *the whole existence of the structure consists of its effects*."[64] Or, as Benjamin Bratton has recently observed, "infrastructure orchestrates *decisions*."[65] In the *Grundrisse*, Marx describes this as "a particular *ether* which determines the specific gravity of every being which has materialised within it"[66] (i.e., an "ether" that may be said to constitute a general *ecology of mind*). Such an overdetermination of structural logic is a mode of *entropement*; its movement is not that of a "Neganthropology" but of an entropomorphology – or, simply, entropology.

Entropy's "Inorganic Body." Just as the movement of entropy has been weaponised in the movement of alien capital, so too the logic of *entropement* needs to be understood on the level of this movement's *rationale*. In the absence of any teleology, this movement is nevertheless *directed by* the drive towards ever & ever greater dissipation: it is this *drive* that defines the entire evolutionary *rationale*, its "decisive" orientation. Evolution is its "inorganic body," its "body-without-organs."

Certain tendencies of "accelerationist" thought have recently reprised the belief that an "integrated incentivising complex of consumer capitalism"[67] is the *driving force* of techno-social evolution & that other possible motors "for driving human progress" need to be shown. It is necessary to recognise that the framework for such "possibilities" is determined not by the viability of competing models of *human incentivisation* but by the field of entropological drives that inscribe human & non-human agency alike. Such a generalised *rationale* assumes a proto-cybernetic form in Marx's early investigations of capital that he terms the "social brain." This "brain" corresponds to a distributed *agency* in the operations of capital that encompass the entire field of techno-social relations. Marx intuits it as a "general intellect" that, at a certain point in Notebook V of the *Grundrisse* ("Circuit of Capital"), also elides with "general conditions of production" (inclusive of systems of "communication"). Thus: "The development of fixed capital indicates to what degree general social knowledge has become a direct force of production, & to what degree, hence, the conditions of the process of social life have come under the control of the general intellect & been transformed in accordance with it."[68]

The foundations of Marx's "general intellect" ultimately reside in those operations of entropy in which the so-called forces of nature themselves originate (as "man's inorganic body") & the dynamic of "alienation" evolves towards a consciousness & production of subjectivities that *is not modelled on the human but produces it*. This idea contrasts with a persistent strain of humanistic Marxism dictating that alienation is instigated *against* subjectivity & that, through a correspondingly inverse movement, initiates what Matteo Pasquinelli calls "the belief that the technologies of industrial automation (already looking like robots) might become a true agent of political change & social emancipation under the command of public education" (i.e., as the instigation of an *alienation of power*).[69]

In an attempt to establish a "labour theory of AI," Pasquinelli identifies in this movement a general-repetition automation or technicity. The source of this observation is credited equally to Marx & the inventor of the Analytic Engine, Charles Babbage.[70] It is summed up in the proposition that "a machine always emerges *by imitating a previous division of labour*, machine intelligence included."[71]

> Marx had already quoted Babbage in *The Poverty of Philosophy* during his exile in Brussels in 1847 &, since then, adopted two analytical principles that were to become pivotal in *Capital* in drawing a robust theory of the machine & in grounding the theory of relative surplus value. The first is what could be defined as "the labour theory of the machine," which states that a new machine comes to imitate & replace a previous division of labour. This is an idea already formulated by Adam Smith, but better articulated by Babbage due to his greater technical experience. The second analytical principle is usually called the "Babbage principle" & is here renamed "the principle of surplus labour modulation." It states that the organisation of a production process in small tasks (division of labour) allows exactly the necessary quantity of labour to be purchased for each task (division of value). In this respect the division of labour provides not only the design of machinery but also an economic configuration to calibrate & calculate surplus labour extraction. In complex forms of management such as Taylorism, the principle of surplus labour modulation opens onto a clockwork view of labour, which can be further subdivided & recomposed into algorithmic assemblages. The synthesis of both analytical principles ideally describes the machine as an apparatus that actively projects back a new articulation & metrics of labour. In the pages of *Capital* the industrial machine appears to be not just a regulator to discipline labour but also a calculator to measure relative surplus value, echoing the numerical exactitude of Babbage's calculating engines.[72]

Techno-teleology. It would not be fantastical to see in this logic of *modulation* an implicit entropement in the form of the recursion of a "division of labour" related to both the principle of *conservation* & the drive towards *expenditure*. By precisely such a (neg/entropic) movement of self-alienation & re-circulation does capital represent the operation of its "transcendence," transforming the crises of production into an expanded "means" of self-propagation (i.e., of an *auto-poiēsis*). Marx describes this via a chain of metonymic substitutions (i.e., "divisions of labour") such that "part of the capital, depreciated by its functional stagnation, would recover its old value. For the rest, the same vicious circle would be described once more *under expanded conditions of production, with an expanded market & increased productive forces.*"[73]

By situating Taylorism's productivist machine-psychopathology *in advance* within a generalised technicity, the "general intellect" of the *Grundrisse* can indeed be seen to evolve in *Capital*, as Pasquinelli proposes, "into a machinic collective worker, almost with the features of a proto-cybernetic organism, & the industrial machine becomes a calculator of the relative surplus value that this cyborg produces."[74] This relative surplus value is the necessary *irreconcilability* of the "machine" & "cyborg" to any thought of capital that does not recognise that the division of labour producing the machine in the first place *is the alienation at the origin of value* (& so the locus of its "recovery"). Hence:

> It was not the invention of the steam engine (means of production) that triggered the industrial revolution (as it is popular to theorise in ecological discourse), but rather the developments of capital & labour (relations of production) demanding a more powerful source of energy. *The steam engine itself*, such as it was at its invention during the manufacturing period at the close of the seventeenth century, & such as it continued to be down to 1780, *did not give rise to any industrial revolution*. It was, *on the contrary*, the invention of [tooling] machines [*Werkzeugmaschinen*] that made a revolution in the form of steam-engines necessary.[75]

And if the "division of labour" is, as Pasquinelli says, "the political inventor of the machine," this *technē politikē* must nevertheless be distinguished from a product of that engine of perception where alienation is misrecognised as a *political artefact* rather than as the pre-condition of any (political) relation whatsoever. The repetition automation of this "division of labour" is marked by a recursive, topological relation to its *cause*. At the same time, the irreconcilability it describes – between a generalised technicity with the implied teleology of "relations of production" – is not the *flaw* in capital's totalising movement, but "the contrary." Wherever it arises within this system, irreconcilability always corresponds to that dynamic interval in which a certain dissipative ("entropic") social production is ever more accelerated & ramified *towards its ideal form.*[76]

The "circuit of reproductive consumption" – driven & *organised* by the movement of entropy – is not a "loss of meaning" in itself,[77] nor a corresponding "recovery," but instead what Bataille defines as the "*relation* to this loss of meaning."[78] It is *related* "to no presence, no plenitude,"[79] which permits the non-appearance of a certain ideality – a certain *reality*. Even if this movement does not produce new conceptual unities (Stiegler's "exo-somatisation"), it retains – by way (or by default of) this non-production – a relation to that which *opens the question of meaning.* This is the mark of its *self-evidence.* Consequently – & despite appearance otherwise – there can be, as Derrida shows, "no possible opposition" between "an economy of circulation (a restricted economy)" & a "general economy" (an economy of expenditure without reserve)."[80] In both formulations, production (as *reproductive consumption*) remains bound to a cybernetic *pro-gramme* vested in a base materiality of the "real."[81] The repetition automation of Bataille's "pure expenditure" is no exception. Entropy always entails the *work of dissipation.* This work extracts a cost & imposes a value even if it is under the sign of a non-value to which the "system of expenditure" can only *relate* (without recuperating) as what perpetually returns. Via the trope of "recovery," it can do *nothing other than relate.*

Xenocapitalism, or, The Jouissance of In/completion. In *Beyond the Pleasure Principle*, Freud proposes that consciousness – a phantasmatic surface-effect of what, in the "Note upon the Mystic Writing-Pad," is presented as a kind of writing-machine – must be understood as psychic expenditure, discharge, expiration of the "excitatory processes" of sensory experience. The idea of the preservation of "life" (i.e., Freud's "reality principle") is always linked to the maintenance of a certain mode of inscription as *expenditure*, so that when we speak of preservation, we are speaking of expenditure *as repetition*, or more specifically, as *repetition automation* (i.e., the "pure" relation of *différance*). This automation, vested in a generalised technicity, defines the contours of what insistently figures as the "real." It marks an event horizon between a hermeneutics of thought & the admission of the Freudian "thing" – that *thing that thinks* – in which the work of comprehension (& work *as such*) is inscribed as if in advance of itself *as the index of an impossible object*. This *thing* has nothing to do with any representation or resemblance of, for example, so-called human intelligence or of its divinity in the form of a pure reason. "It" is only possible *to relate*: it is that complex of relations "itself." If this impossible object may be signalled by the term Noösphere, it is solely to the extent that its "worldliness" remains irreducible to *historical thought* (of an Anthropocene, to be exact), which could be in any way situated as the *object* of its own transcendence (or even as the *subject* of a noetic dream of the "post-Anthropocene").

It is not for nothing that the Noösphere coincides – in the metaphorics of a certain non-teleological, recursive & broadly "ecological" thought – with what is subsumed in the operations of the Freudian unconscious. Rejecting the "Kantian theorem that time & space are 'necessary forms of thought,'" Freud contends that "unconscious mental processes are in themselves 'timeless.' This means in the first place that they are not ordered temporally, that time does not change them in any way & that the idea of time cannot be applied to them."[82] The coordinates of this End-of-History correspond to all the "unfulfilled but possible futures to which we still cling in phantasy, all the strivings of the ego which adverse external circumstances have crushed, & all our suppressed acts of volition which nourish in us the illusion of Free Will."[83] Contingent upon this is also "the value of play" as defining "pure productivity,"[84] which is to say, pure expenditure. To the extent that this Kantian "Free Will" only *simulates* the "free-play" of a signifying economy, its "spontaneity" is that of a *mimēsis of spontaneity*: freedom posed as the translation of "nature" into reason.

The entire domain of the Noösphere – in which Stiegler's "noetic dream" is necessarily subsumed – needs to be considered in this light.

If posthumanism seeks to transcend what, at the same time & in the same gesture, it re-inscribes by imitating the previous "division of labour" in the nature/technology dichotomy, what does its entirely predictable appeal to dialectical reason mean to accomplish if not the mystification of the real as that which, on its own cognisance, alone "comprehends" the so-called Anthropocene? Is this not the trajectory of Stiegler's "noetic dream," with its desire to turn the tables, so to speak, & *exceed* the dissipative systems of anthropocapitalism as *neganthropology*? Is it a dream of reason that, in its transcendental delirium, engenders monsters, just as in Goya's vision, retold by Feuerbach, Marx, Bataille, Derrida? This delirious slumber "must be effectively traversed so that awakening will not be a ruse of dream. That is to say [...] a ruse of reason. The slumber of reason is not, perhaps, reason put to sleep, but slumber in the form of reason."[85]

The ambivalence upon which this compulsive dichotomisation is founded isn't opposed to the movement of entropy, which is *differential* & not *teleological*. It is the condition of its *différance*. In the same way, entropy can no longer be said "to reduce life to its original condition in inanimate matter."[86] Entropy situates the impetus of "life" (& every other mode of production) in a generalised condition of technicity. And if the real power of *mimēsis* derives from the fact that it "can accommodate itself to political systems that are different, even opposed to one another,"[87] then it is insufficient simply to appeal to an increase in scales of complexification – to a mere *accelerated* repetition automation & a certain *gratuitousness* in the logic of expenditure – as availing some kind of (artificial) intelligence automatically productive of a critique of (capitalist-humanist) value. By situating an "alien" ambivalence as the "sign" of that which must remain non-exchangeable as a use-value, it marks not the limit of exchange-value as such, but of its subsumption into a phantasmatic *non-ideology*: the totalising subjectivisation of this entropomimesis we call "the human."[88]

Maribor, October 2019

6

THE TERATOLOGISTS

Washington, 25 August 2019. STORMAGGEDON. Scenario: A lunatic is in the White House. Like a slow-motion car crash, the US administration embarks on a catastrophic trade war with China, the systematic sabotaging of the North Atlantic Treaty Organisation, a series of proxy wars with Iran, & nuclear brinkmanship with North Korea. At the point of maximum tension, the President directs the Joint Chiefs of Staff to deploy atomic weapons against a hurricane tracking westward across the Caribbean & threatening landfall at the President's private golf resort in Florida. Were this a film, it could only be the worst type of science fiction & few would believe it. *But what if it were real?*

Scenarios of the Real. Wednesday, 11 October 1961. During what has since become a now notorious speech to the National Press Club in Washington, the director of the United States Weather Bureau at the time, Francis W. Reichelderfer, told his audience that he "could imagine the possibility someday of exploding a nuclear bomb on a hurricane far at sea," even suggesting that, at some point in the future, the Weather Bureau could acquire its own nuclear arsenal.[1] On the same day, the front page of the *Newark Advocate* (Ohio) carried a story entitled FALLOUT EFFECT FROM RED A-BOMBS TERMED SLIGHT, deeming "any genetic damage caused by fallout from the current series of Russian nuclear explosions will be so slight, in the opinion of a Public Health Service physician, that it might not be discernible even after several generations." Other headlines included BRITAIN STANDS FIRM WITH US ON BERLIN & HOFFA INDICTED FOR FRAUD. Coverage of Reichelderfer's speech appeared in the bottom left corner: NUCLEAR BOMBS PLANNED TO BREAK UP HURRICANES. The article, sourced from Associated Press, noted that "the idea of using bombs of any type against storms 'is still only in the gleam-in-the-eye stage.'" While proposing an arbitrary 1-megaton starting point for consideration of nuclear intervention against extreme weather events & citing cost as a factor, Reichelderfer inadvertently became the first government official to reveal a concrete figure for the hydrogen bomb – a highly classified piece of information. The figure was $1 million for one megaton.[2]

Also reporting on the story, the Wilmington *Morning News* (Delaware) gave a fuller picture of US research into developing a "storm killer," quoting Reichelderfer, who cautioned that an H-bomb "might simply intensify a storm." The article noted, however, that the Weather Bureau had held "informal discussions with the Atomic Energy Commission about the theoretical use of nuclear explosions to kill hurricane." A thousand times more powerful than the bomb dropped on Hiroshima, the thermonuclear "hydrogen" bomb represented, to those privy to the fact, an incommensurably greater paradigm shift. In 1952, while studying the atmospheric effects of the US's first full-scale test of an H-bomb (codenamed Ivy Mike, which produced a mushroom cloud 41 km high & 32 km in diameter), Air Force meteorologist Jack W. Reed conceived of employing similar detonations for meteorological ends. Reed later participated in the US government's Plowshare Program (to develop "peaceful" applications of nuclear weapons technology) & was a member of the US Army Engineer Nuclear Cratering Group. He first presented his ideas in 1956 during the International Geophysical Year; in 1959, he submitted a detailed two-part proposal to the second Plowshares Symposium entitled "Some Speculations on the Effects of Nuclear Explosions on Hurricanes."[3] In Reed's view, a "megaton explosion" at the centre of a hurricane, where wind temperatures average 10 degrees higher than the rest of the storm, would "engulf & entrain a large quantity of this hot 'eye' air & carry it out of the storm into the stratosphere." The compensating flow of colder air was expected to sap the hurricane of its overall strength, rendering it benign. It was this proposal that became the basis for Reichelderfer's speech two years later & an object of serious experimental consideration.

The month previous to Reichelderfer's address to the National Press Club, "weather scientists" had dropped around 50 kg of seeding material on Hurricane Esther," a Category-4 hurricane in the North Atlantic which was the first large tropical cyclone to be detected using imagery from the new Television Infrared Observation Satellite. The storm was also the first target of a weather-modifying US Navy experiment that later came to be known as Project Stormfury (1962-1983), a successor to Project Cirrus (a failed one-off collaboration between General Electric & the US Army Signal Corps in 1947). On 13 September, a navy aircraft flew into the eye of the hurricane approximately 400 miles north of Puerto Rico, releasing canisters of silver iodine (an inorganic compound with a crystalline structure similar to that of ice capable of inducing freezing by a process of *heterogeneous nucleation*). It was hypothesized that the silver iodine would cause supercooled water already within the storm system to freeze, releasing latent heat in the eyewall & disrupting the hurricane's internal structure. This hypothesis was later shown to be incorrect, due to the insufficient amount of supercooled water contained in most tropical storms of magnitude & due to the fact that such storms were already subject to internal dynamics identical to those believed to have been induced by seeding. In any case, it didn't work. The *Morning News* report on Reichelderfer's speech noted that, with respect to the seeding of Hurricane Esther, "[r]adar photographs indicated a segment of the storm's eyewall was rained-out as a result. But the wall quickly reformed, the storm's course was not affected, & its intensity was reduced only temporarily, if at all."

At a time of nuclear optimization, as the 1960s were, the progression from cloud-seeding to H-bombs had the appearance of a natural economy of scale. Throughout the 1950s, US military & civilian applications of nuclear technology proliferated, in part driven by Eisenhower's 1953 "Atoms for Peace" programme, which directed research towards electricity production. With the commissioning of the Calder Hill reactor in the UK in 1956, followed a year later by Shippingport in the US, & with the construction of large commercial reactors by General Electric & Westinghouse in 1960, atomic power moved from the realm of science fiction (& predominantly military application) into the banality of everyday life. And for at least a decade – until the anti-nuclear movement, increasing costs of constructing new reactors & a series of accidents (culminating in the partial core meltdown at Three Mile Island in 1979) took the glow off the atomic age – proposals like Reichelderfer's appeared almost self-evident to a public grown expectant of ever-greater scales of technological development & their potential for application on a "global" scale.

While human activity from the earliest times has been characterised by environmental transformation – the cumulative effects of which, vastly accelerated by industrialisation, have produced an indelible global environmental impact event (the Anthropocene) – postwar nuclear technologies represented the first instance in which direct transformation or even control of the planetary environment came into view as a scientifically achievable proposition. The term "terraforming" had been coined by Jack Williamson in a short story entitled "Collision Orbit," published in *Astounding Science Fiction* in 1942. The story appeared at the same time as the Blitz-bombing of London, which was soon followed by thousand-bomber formations of the Allied Air Forces over Germany & the advent of atomic warfare. Williamson's term drew upon cosmic contingencies like impact events as proto-technologies of planetary engineering. But in the wake of vastly expanded wartime industry & economies of scale, direct human agency became the defining factor in the term's subsequent use. With the birth of the US & Soviet space programmes – both developed out of ICBM missile projects based on the captured Nazi V2 – & with Apollo architect Wernher von Braun militating for interplanetary colonisation, consideration was increasingly given to questions of technologically modifying the atmosphere, temperature, surface topology or ecology of planetary or planetoid bodies for the purposes of human habitation.

War of the Worlds. Terraforming is an applied global technology of a magnitude only previously approached by the phenomenon of world war. The ideological & logistical dimensions of terraforming emerged in the period between 24 October 1946, when a refitted V2 rocket launched from White Sands, New Mexico, took the first photograph of Earth from space, & 12 April 1961, when Yuri Gagarin became the first person to orbit the planet. During this time, an emergent global consciousness achieved a kind of apotheosis, pictorially & as direct experience, & the Earth became an object of human contemplation. In

1962, when Donald Brennan at the Hudson Institute in 1962 coined the expression "Mutually Assured Destruction" (MAD), this object of contemplation became one of direct, intentional & singular technological transformation.

As a blueprint, the terraforming logic of MAD left much to be desired, but it was the seeming demonstrable fact that carried the argument: truly global technologies, analogous in scope to entire ecosystems, were deemed achievable. The period encompassing the Apollo lunar programme (inaugurated in 1961) & the commissioning of the satellite-based radionavigational system known as GPS in 1978 appeared to confirm this: the logistical horizon that had once represented an insurmountable obstacle now offered an entirely different prospectus. Reed's Plowshare proposal for nuking hurricanes was entirely pragmatic in this respect. "When the first public announcement of atomic bombs dropped on Japan came at the height of the Florida hurricane season," he wrote in his introduction, "the press & public began immediate speculation on their use in controlling destructive storms. However, as information on actual bomb yields became known … it appeared obvious that atomic bombs could not compare with large natural systems in converting energy." He adds: "Even thermonuclear weapons, a thousand times more powerful than bombs dropped on Japan, yield an energy which is equivalent to that transformed in only five minutes by a mature hurricane." However, "since megaton thermonuclear devices do release energies at rates only a few orders of magnitude smaller than do tropical storms, such large-yield nuclear explosives might be used for triggering some indirect or 'divergent' system, which would result in storm deflection or dissipation."[4]

The Nuclear Test Ban Treaty (1963) – & later the Peaceful Nuclear Explosions Treaty (1990) – limited yields for non-military use to 150 kilotons. The treaties inhibited the application of Reed's ideas. Plowshare actively pursued a wide spectrum of similar applications. Serious proposals were advanced for deploying nuclear devices to create an artificial harbour in Alaska (Project Chariot), widening the Panama Canal & creating a new "Pan-Atomic Canal" at sea-level across Nicaragua, while 22 nuclear explosions were proposed for Project Carryall to blast an interstate road & rail link through the Bristol Mountains in the Mojave Desert. Major objectives also included controlled blasts used to connect underground aquifers in Arizona & to aid natural gas stimulation & shale oil extraction (i.e., fracking) in Texas. Before Plowshare was quietly mothballed in 1977, it had produced radioactive blast debris from some 839 underground nuclear test explosions. One of these explosions, "Sedan," a 104 kiloton experiment in earthmoving conducted at Yucca Flat, Nevada, in 1964, resulted in twin radioactive plumes that reached an altitude of 3.7 kilometres & drifted northeast as far as Illinois. They released an estimated 880,000 curies of radioactive iodine-131 into the atmosphere. It was the highest acknowledged fallout of any nuclear test in the continental US, displacing 11 million tons of soil, causing a seismic disturbance of 4.75 on the Richter scale & leaving a crater 100m deep.

While these results bear out obvious flaws in the general applicability of the nuclear doctrine, Reed's remarks remain worthy of further consideration for other reasons. Much of Plowshare's agenda was directed at the instrumentalising of nuclear weapons in piecemeal efforts at environmental transformation, with the potential for consolidation into a general "positive science" of terraforming. Reed's observations about "divergent systems" point to the fundamentally *tactical* character of such experiments & their susceptibility to the effects of complexity in dynamic systems like hurricanes. Cybernetics branched into what came to be known as Chaos Theory, which was mediated by the work of Yoshisuke Ueda on "randomly transitional phenomena" & Edward Lorenz on weather prediction in 1961. Chaos Theory was able to provide a framework (formalised by 1977 at precisely the time Plowshare was terminated) in which the crudely targeted effects of tactical nuclear weapons on what Carl Sagan called "planetary ecosynthesis"[5] could potentially evolve beyond the *tabula rasa* logic of "storm killing nukes" & MAD into a strategy of "sustainable" terraformation.

It is perhaps no coincidence that Sagan published around the same time a proposal for the "planetary engineering" of Venus based upon seeding the planet's cloud-cover with algae intended to convert water, nitrogen & carbon dioxide into organic compounds, reducing the concentration of greenhouse gases in the atmosphere & bringing surface temperatures to a habitable level in a reversal of the greenhouse effect.[6] Unknown to Sagan, however, the sulphuric acid that largely composes Venusian cloud-cover rendered such a proposal meaningless when coupled with high atmospheric pressure (just one more example of how military-industrial applications of cybernetics have been marked by an astonishing degree of false assumption). Sagan's idea gave rise to similar proposals for "ecopoiesis" — what Robert Haynes called the "fabrication of a sustainable ecosystem on a currently lifeless, sterile planet"[7] — including the introduction of chlorofluorocarbons into the Martian atmosphere to promote a self-regulating biosphere.[8] In 2015, space entrepreneur Elon Musk refashioned an idea put forward by physicist Michio Kaku.[9] During an appearance on *The Late Show with Stephen Colbert* on CBS, Musk announced that nuclear devices might be used to create "pulsing suns" over the Martian poles to melt the icecaps. This would release trapped carbon dioxide to thicken the atmosphere, promote "global warming" & restore liquid water to the planet's surface, preparing conditions for general habitability & commercial exploitation.[10]

Musk's headline-grabbing remarks recalled similar suggestions that thermonuclear detonations might be used to reactivate magnetic fields & geologic activity on Mars, with a view to shielding the planet from solar radiation that will induce "geothermal forcing." But while Musk's proposal was widely ridiculed — & dismissed outright by NASA as technologically unfeasible — the case for terraforming Mars with nukes, like that for terminating hurricanes, has a history of serious consideration. One is a 1996 paper by Anthony C. Muscatello & Michael G. Houts (of the Los Alamos National Laboratory) entitled "Surplus

Weapons-Grade Plutonium: A Resource for Exploring & Terraforming Mars." Underscoring the greatest nuclear-waste-disposal scam of the century, Muscatello & Houts argue that "the end of the Cold War has presented the world with a great dilemma & a great opportunity. Greater than 100 metric tons (MT) of weapons-grade plutonium (WGPu) are now surplus to defence needs in the United States & the former Soviet Union ... Implementation of this proposal to use WGPu for nuclear reactors for Mars exploration & colonisation would allow resolution of this serious, expensive problem on Earth by removing the problem from the planet & would simultaneously provide a very large energy source."[11]

Did Judas Iscariot Have Godzilla on His Side? All of these propositions tend towards what we might call a positivist pseudo-science where speculative real-world problems are mapped onto an ideological framework in which they seek to be reified as self-evident in the defining contest over a certain futurity. Behind such speculative ecologies, however, remains an operation of political/ economic capital based upon an "instrumentality," which is not that of a naïve conception of reason or of a "prosthesis" of reason. It is a technological rationale. Seemingly exotic financial instruments like weather derivatives are paradigmatic in this respect. Based on the principles of risk management & insurance, weather derivatives are tradable "futures" (or hedges) famously exploited by Enron Corporation with its launch, in November 1999, of EnronOnline, an electronic trading platform for energy commodities. More recently, these "futures" were exploited by the Speedwell WeatherGroups weatherXchange,® launched in 2017. Even so, projects like Stormfury & Plowshare almost inevitably invite comparison to megalomaniacal world-domination schemes (e.g., Fu Manchu's diabolic ocean-freezing device[12]) & the weather-control systems of popular sci-fi (e.g., Samuel Johnson's mad scientist in *Rasselas*: "I have possessed, for five years, the regulation of the weather, & the distribution of seasons: the sun has listened to my dictates, & passed, from tropick to tropick, by my direction; the clouds, at my call, have poured their waters"[13]) or pseudo-scientific quackery like Wilhelm Reich's cloudbusting experiments with "orgone energy"[14] in the 1950s. Unsurprisingly, however, the hyperstitional aspect of projects like Stormfury & Plowshare becomes the instrumental agency in their realisation under the appearance of what is (or seemingly ought to be) most "fictional."[15]

Operation Popeye is one such project, a top-secret weather-modification programme pursued in Indochina between 1967-1972 by the 54th Weather Reconnaissance Squadron as part of the US-led war with North Vietnam. Ostensibly a cloud-seeding operation aimed at intensifying & extending the tropical monsoon season, Popeye was localised over the region of the Ho Chi Minh Trail in eastern Laos, northeastern Cambodia & the far west of North Vietnam (a.k.a. "Truong Son Strategic Supply Route") in tandem with the aerial dispersal of the "tactical use" defoliant Agent Orange (Operation Ranch Hand). Agent Orange was a mixture of two herbicides known as 2,4,5-T & 2,4-D, each containing the dioxin TCDD (the most toxic of its kind). It was shown by the US National Academy of Medicine to be connected through direct exposure with soft tissue sarcoma, Non-Hodgkin lymphoma, Hogkin disease & chronic lymphocytic leukaemia as well as respiratory cancers, & it was responsible for birth defects through prenatal exposure, including mental disabilities & physical deformities such as cleft palate & polydactyly (additional fingers & toes). Agent Orange also had extensive ecological impact, with dioxins persistent in the soil entering into the food chain, resulting in biomagnification that has severely affected plant & animal diversity.[16]

Combined with the intended objective of Ranch Hand to defoliate (& expose to aerial surveillance) the area around the Ho Chi Minh Trail, the intensified rainfall generated by Operation Popeye was additionally intended to deprive the North Vietnamese of functional use of the area by softening roads, causing landslides, washing out river crossings, & maintaining saturated soil conditions beyond the normal timespan (the operation's motto was "Make Mud, Not War"). Such operations became the object of the 1978 Environmental Modification Convention banning "weather warfare." (In 2010, the Convention on Biological Diversity further restricted weather modification & geoengineering.) Together, Popeye & Ranch Hand ramify what already, in the wake of the bombing of Hiroshima & Nagasaki, had emerged as a dominant theme within the latent discourse of ecopoiesis. This was perhaps best communicated by the nineteenth-century French neologism *teratology*, the study of signs sent by the gods, portents, marvels & monsters (Reed's "divergent systems," no doubt, producing Godzillas instead of monster hurricanes). The idea of an instrumental technology began to give way to the idea of uncontrolled mutation, catalysed by a technicity that is no longer "at the service" of an external (human) agency, but constitutes that agency with operations that are consequently visible (to the human) only through ruptures in linear causation & a naïve rationalism. This came to define a logistical as well as an ideological divide, exemplified by competing "thought experiments" in ecology, cybernetics & artificial intelligence, on the one hand, & a brute force attempt to reduce complexity to a *tabula rasa*, on the other, in an effort to reconstitute competing systems of "control" over such eruptions of the Real.

Ultrashock, or, A Brighter Tomorrow. In *The Planet Remade: How Geoengineering Could Change the World*, Oliver Morton says that the computer hardware for modelling the atmosphere was the same as that used for simulating the hydrogen-bomb design developed in 1945 by Edward Teller. The computer concerned was the first fully-programmable electronic computer, ENIAC, designed by John von Neumann (formerly attached to the Manhattan Project), & the H-bomb simulation was its first assigned task. By 1950, von Neumann, along with meteorologist Jule Charney, began processing weather predictions through ENIAC, aimed at producing "new insights into controlling it."[17] At around the same time ENIAC began work on the H-bomb, biologist Julian Huxley, the first secretary general of UNESCO, gave a speech at Madison Square Garden hailing a new atomic era & echoing an earlier pronouncement about the promises of radium in 1906 by Frederick Soddy, who envisaged the power to "transform a desert continent, thaw the frozen poles, & make the whole world one smiling garden of Eden."[18] For his part, Huxley envisaged adapting atomic power to flood the Sahara & "alter the entire climate of the North Temperate Zones by exploding ... at most a few hundred atomic bombs at an appropriate height above the polar regions."[19]

In addition, Huxley supported a June 1946 proposal by Bernard Baruch, the US representative to the United Nations Atomic Energy Commission, based on the Acheson-Lilienthal Report from March of the same year, advocating international control of atomic energy – including nuclear weapons – as a step towards a possible future "world government." Such a government was intended to assume responsibility for "social planning on a world-wide basis," from geoengineering to eugenics. Albert Einstein similarly came out as a signatory of "One World or None," the world-government manifesto of the Federation of American Scientists. Von Neumann, on the other hand, rejected the Baruch Plan of human governance in favour of cybernetic systems of "global control" (including control of industrial processes, the world economy & *climate*). It was in such a political atmosphere that Jose Delgado, Director of Neuropsychology at Yale University Medical School, pursued an investigation into electrical brain implants (in part for the treatment of epilepsy) that led, in 1969, to the publication of *Physical Control of the Mind: Towards Psychocivilized Society* & later, in 1974, to Delgado's testimony before US Congress when he stated: "We need a program of psychosurgery for political control of our society. The purpose is physical control of the mind. Everyone who deviates from the given norm can be surgically mutilated."[20]

Delgado's surgical mind-control research overlapped with the US government's secret pursuit of a psyops programme developed between 1953 & 1973 through the CIA's Office of Scientific Intelligence & the US Army Biological Warfare Laboratories; after the 1975 revelations by the commission convened by Gerald Ford into illegal CIA activities within the United States, the public came to know it as Project MKUltra. Its wide remit for developing chemical & psychological warfare techniques included drug-induced brainwashing, memory erasure & mass psychosis in a logical continuum with Popeye's environmental modifications & Stormfury's brute-force *tabula rasa*. MKUltra was driven in part by a belief within the CIA – like the belief publicly expressed by Delgado – that control of the human mind would represent nothing less than global political mastery. This synergy between ecopoiesis & psychocivilisation brings into view a dimension of Gregory Bateson's phrase "ecology of mind,"[21] which might best be described as *teratogenesis* – not as a symptomatology (the production of monstrosities), but as the "mental characteristics" of a *technological condition* (the mode-of-production of the so-called Anthropocene wherein all of these grandiose schemes are truly psychotic attempts at instrumentalisation).

Von Neumann's cybernetic vision of economic & ecological "governance" became a central tenet of Buckminster Fuller's general systems theory or *synergetics*, a global geodesic megastructure of "comprehensively commanded automation" & a mutually ramifying life-support systems constitutive of "spaceship Earth." In Fuller's view, the "synergistic effectiveness of a world-around integrated industrial process is inherently greater than the confined synergistic effect of sovereignly operating separate systems. Ergo, only complete world desovereignisation can permit the realization of an all humanity high standard support."[22] One recent iteration of this idea is Benjamin Bratton's "Cloud Megastructures & Platform Utopias," which transform planetary-scale computation from an accidental, contingent array that Fuller calls "sovereignly operating separate systems" into a global "Stack."[23] Bratton adapts principles of *urbanism* to a problem of general ecological governance by way of a renovated conception of terraforming. In his 2020 programme presentation for the Strelka Institute in Moscow, he stated: "The term 'terraforming' usually refers to transforming the ecosystems of other planets or moons to make them capable of supporting Earth-like life, but the looming ecological consequences of what is called the Anthropocene suggest that in the decades to come we will need to terraform Earth if it is to remain a viable host for Earth-like life."[24]

Bratton's terraforming is a post-Anthropocenic survival strategy – a "proposition for urbanism at planetary scale" – with echoes of an architectonic messianism (the "engineer of human souls") evident from Fuller to Reed in its geo-social vision of "world desovereignisation," which tends towards the meta-sovereignty of The Architect irrespective of whether this architect is a "human" agent or a "dead-hand" automated cybernetic system. At issue here is not the self-regulatory capability of such governance systems or their capacity to substitute a form of risk-averse ecological management for environmental "human error" on a sufficiently large scale. The developmental toxicity of its logic remains a problem. The belief in weaponised evolutionary processes – even if these amount in practice to a type of digital cloud-seeding – is forever bound by the paradox of an appeal to a technological "fail safe," i.e., to a transcendental signified of a runaway process of "desoveriegnised" hyperstition whereby the post-Anthropocene, like the posthumanist fallacy on which it is premised, returns dividends for "Earth-like life" in an endless rehearsal of the cosmic embryo in Stanley Kubrick's *2001: A Space Odyssey* (1968). Yet there is no escaping the fact that this reborn "star child" – the augury of a new world & the source of a life system cognisant of "ours" – is the product of two factors: an "alien intelligence" that terraforms Jupiter into a second sun by means of a type of thermonuclear detonation,[25] & a mode of Corporate-State terror with which Reed & Reichelderfer were inevitably complicit & which has only ever prefigured future "life" through an apocalyptic machinery of "salvation."

Prague, September 2019

7

ALTERNATIVE THREE

"No one has ever lived in the past … & no one will live in the future …"
– Jean-Luc Godard, *Alphaville*

On 20 July 1969, when Apollo 11 commander Neil Armstrong stepped off the Lunar Module's ladder onto the surface of the Moon, 53 million people world-wide watched the event transmitted in hazy black-&-white, live on TV. This quasi-instantaneous "experience" allowed for the 1.3-second delay between the moon & the Parkes radio telescope in Australia that received the original signal as well as an additional 0.3-second delay between Sydney & Houston that was comparable to a long-distance telephone call at the time. It was almost like *being there*. Armstrong described it as a performance "in front of the largest audience in history." The event promised to transform what it meant to be human while bringing other worlds within "our" grasp for the very first time. And yet this triumph of ingenuity & determination, of scientific rationalism, of the sentimental delusion of a global "social media" *avant la letter* – it was a bogus solidarity of the industrially privileged, as belied in Gil Scott Heron's *Whitey on the Moon*:

> You know, the man just upped my rent last night
> Cause whitey's on the moon
> No hot water, no toilets, no light
> But whitey's on the moon …[1]

Science Fiction in the Expanded Field. Mankind's giant leap towards this final frontier was never less ideological than it was technical. The collective roman-ticism of exploration & discovery – of landing a "man on the moon" – paled against the massive political, engineering, economic & evolutionary effort to put "him" there, with 400,000 mostly faceless workers keeping the whole project functional. But the fact remains that the proclaimed ambition of speaking in the first-person plural of all humanity, of "the world," has perhaps become more virtual than ever. This was only to be expected, considering the equally vast ideological logistics of this most accomplished of simulacra.

The largest single logistical undertaking since the D-Day landings culminated in a total of just two-&-a-half hours of footprints-&-flag activity on the lunar surface. It was watched on TV by an unprecedented number of viewers, yet in a profound sense, it was *witnessed by no-one*.[2] With the return to Earth of Apollo 17 & the cancellation of the lunar programme in December 1972, the "great leap for mankind" beyond low orbit (unrepeated, so far) emphatically *did not* pave the way for a mass excursion to follow in those pioneering footsteps, like homesteaders to a new western frontier. This has not happened, at least, within the generational timeframe by which modernity has become accustomed to gauging such recent historical movements. As Baudrillard might have said, the Apollo moon-landing ostensibly *did not take place*.[3] It represents, in its recoil to a ubiquitous present tense, the simulacrum of a "new frontier" existing as remote televised images & audio transmissions. Commentators on Earth have long referred to this simulacrum in the singular as a media event: an ideological ripple in the fabric of Realpolitik whose orphaned *logos* has already crossed interstellar space, more alien now than ever.

Writing on the 40th anniversary of mankind's "giant leap," Tom Wolfe declared that "the American space programme, the grandest, most Promethean … quest in the history of the world, died in infancy at 10:56 p.m. New York time on July 20, 1969, the moment the foot of Apollo's Commander Armstrong touched the surface of the Moon."[4] The mystifications of this new Prometheus were never likely to survive the first moments of this ideal consummation; in an instant, the entire course of Western culture was undone. It wasn't, as the chauvinists said, that the great goddess was reduced to a whore, or merely to a lump of rock no more magical than any other, like Roquentin's pebble on the beach. Instead, the myth of culture, the possibility of the dream, had been turned to travesty. The moon had become just another repository for ideological trash: an expired commodity.

Realism Is the Dream-Life of Tax Collectors. As quickly as it had emerged from it, the future of manned space exploration receded into the "dream factory" of a kind of cinema. As a residue of TV images & moon-rock paraphernalia, Apollo presented a *dissolution of the real* into science fiction (& thus *the dissolution of history* into genre) to the entire world. In doing so, Apollo readmitted the phantasm of disillusionment into scientific rationalism. It effected a *suspension of disbelief* in what, until then, had represented a purely instrumental domain of veracity & verification. It inscribed "humanity" within a new technological metaphysic that, by foreclosing upon an idea of futurity, evoked a *futurism* capable of incorporating (like the neoliberal, post-Fordist economics it coincided with) the most fantastically "excluded" elements of the industrial imaginary, from Ballardianism to Afrofuturism, *in place of the real*.

The apparition of this paradox was a consequence of (& in a sense necessitated by) the act of setting foot on the moon, like some spectre of a future doomed to repeat itself in the register of a science fiction that *has already ceased to exist as fiction*, not by virtue of its historical "realisation," but because the major determination of a "real" *which will have taken its place* is revealed as *nothing more* than a repetition automation. (And the "real" recurs in the place we expect to find it: not a *thing*, but the pure technicity of recurrence.) This in turn marks the limit & horizon of those conceptions of a future bounded by cybernetic interfaces (i.e., data prostheses), analogues of a symbolic order that, in becoming *purely mimetic*, is "restored" to a metaphysical array. Consider this rhapsodic episode from Virilio:

> We might even imagine that one day, having donned a suit of interactive data – the DATA SUIT – our internaut will launch himself into a new kind of adventure tourism, discovering the ancient world with the assistance of positioning & surveillance satellites overflying him without letup.
>
> As though playing a pinball machine, our explorer could then touch the summit of Everest or the slopes of Kilimanjaro with one single gesture ... Sweep his hand over the shores of the Pacific, caress the wetness of the seas that lurk there ... And who knows? Maybe someday in the near future or soon after, he will TOUCH THE MOON, feel the aridity of the Sea of Tranquillity, searching somewhat gropingly for the tools dumped up there, in 1969, by the men of the Apollo 11 mission.[5]

Baudrillard will have insisted that "[t]here is no real & no imaginary *except at a certain distance*,"[6] yet this (prosthetic) distance is nothing if not the measure of a temporal precession in which "the future" isn't a reflection-effect *but the possibility of a reflection* occurring at the limits of foreclosure (i.e., of *différance*).

In the larger scheme of things, there is no other condition than this one. And it is precisely at its most simulacral of moments, in its progress towards self-supersession, that humanity perceives its future (or "no future") in the most tentative & fraught of narcissistic fantasies: six million years of evolution condensed into the image of a man in a spacesuit with a life-support system strapped to his back, on a piece of rock half-a-million kilometres from the only known breathable atmosphere, drifting at the edge of a cinematic vastness where the probability of survival is statistically zero. By a singular act of "transcendence," the *contingency of human existence upon technology* (i.e., the *technological condition* of humanity) comes into view. Without the slightest trace of paradox, the future perpetuation of the species now *belongs to science fiction*. And if cinema represents "our" collective dream, then this future of humanity – divorced from any other possible "realism" – would be experienced, if nothing else, as a dream of the most conventional cinema.

World as Will & Ideology. In a short text published in 1991 under the sway of Philip K. Dick's 1964 novel *The Simulacra*,[7] Baudrillard reformulates a schema developed over the prior two decades in which a residual idea of truth becomes the pretext of a general simulationism. Here, the corresponding "orders" of the *real* & the *fictional* (n.b., "there is no more fiction") collapse into a universal field of simulacra.

There are three orders of simulacra:

1. Natural, naturalistic simulacra: based on image, imitation, & counterfeiting. They are harmonious, optimistic, & aim at the reconstitution (or the ideal institution) of a nature in God's image.
2. Productive, productionist simulacra: based on energy & force, materialized by the machine & the entire system of production. Their aim is Promethean: worldwide application, continuous expansion, liberation of indeterminate energy. Desire is part of the utopias belonging to this order of simulacra.
3. Simulation simulacra: based on information, the model, cybernetic play. Their aim is maximum operationality, hyperreality, total control.

To the first order corresponds the utopian imaginary. To the second, science fiction in the strict sense. To the third ... is there yet an imaginary domain which corresponds to this order?[8]

If the Fukuyamaesque domain of the End of History & the birth of the "virtual" that Baudrillard traces in its emergence out of the neoliberal/postmodernist nexus corresponds today with what is called the Anthropocene, it does so only insofar as this "epoch" announces not the transcendence of primitivist, industrialist or cybernetic *post*-humanism, but rather the "truth" of a return of humanism in its most apocalyptic formulation. Such an apocalypticism would not break with the "classical (& even cybernetic) viewpoint" in which, Baudrillard reminds us, "technology is an extension of the body" & "the evolved capacity of a human organism which allows it both to rival Nature & to triumphantly remould it in its own image."[9] In other words, the apocalyptic view of the Anthropocene remains one of pure instrumentality, be it a discourse of mitigation or transcendence, repair or redundancy, sustainability or exit. Nothing will have escaped recuperation to the human idea, even its own supersession. Here the dialectical character of Baudrillard's schema can be viewed *as the real teleology* of the *simulacral as such* (from the world in "God's image" to the image as god) – a movement uncannily retraced in the more recent (de)anthropic turn of François Laruelle's "general science fiction."

"Science fiction," Laruelle argues, "is a minor genre of literature entrusted to an arbitrary imaginary ... but it is possible to re-found it ... as a non-philosophical genre, on strictly generic bases ... that are consolidated by another use of the quantic, as model rather than as furnishing of the Universe."[10] This re-founding of science fiction is a proxy re-founding of metaphysics. It assumes the form of an inverted Platonism, & like Baudrillard's schema, it adopts a predictably tripartite form:

1. "the introduction of contemporary science in the form of the quantic as model into the heart [of science fiction]";
2. "its object or outcome is the destiny of humanity in transit between the Earth, the World, & the Universe";
3. "the 'World' as Bad-world or history is only an unplanned & unfortunate halting point on this voyage which leads it to the Just-world."[11]

In this, too, we are challenged with the need to de-schematize the concept of "simulacrum" as the mark of an anthropo-teleology that would recuperate science fiction's "cognitive estrangement"[12] for a *genre* of dialectical reason (even one posed in the guise of non-philosophy). It is necessary, nonetheless, to identify the seemingly counterintuitive forms that allow this logic to reconstitute itself under the constellation of a "new" metaphysics or a trans-rational technologism.

Between Baudrillard & Laruelle, the precession of simulacra & the ascent/ descent of the anthropic[13] describe the topology of a certain "truth" that doubles the movement of reason. Previously conceived by Lacan as the inscription of the analytic scene *par excellence*, this movement narrates itself as the object it seeks to discover. Just as Lacan proposes that "the unconscious is structured like a language,"[14] so does he say that "truth declares itself in the structure of fiction."[15] If science (as "quantic model") binds truth within a system of prediction or predication (wherein, for Lacan, *its signifier always reaches its destination*), it is only to the extent that the system of science *stands in place of truth*. Identifying the one with the other (i.e., as its *simulacrum*) nevertheless turns upon an irreducible "cognitive estrangement," since – in & of "itself" – truth can never be subsumed into a mere coincidence with any scientific system or systematicity in general.

The art of revelation (i.e., truth) that here supposedly belongs to science remains indelibly that of a fiction, of the *possibility of fiction*, which would include the fictionality of *representation as such*. At precisely this moment of revelation (the consciousness of simulacra, the subsumption into utopia), a "quantic" truth elides with *mimēsis*. A measure of even the most "materialist" discussions is bound to a teleological/instrumentalist conception of temporality & technology by way of an equally teleological/instrumentalist conception of knowledge & information. It would be easy to cite further examples to demonstrate this point, but one more should be sufficient. Steven Shaviro writes:

Science fiction works to extrapolate elements of the present, push actually existing conditions all the way to the most extreme consequences. That is to say, science fiction is not about the actual future; rather it's about futurity, if I can use that as an abstract noun … Science fiction grasps & brings to visibility what the philosopher Gilles Deleuze calls the virtual, or what Karl Marx sometimes called tendential processes. Tendential things or tendencies are not things that have to happen but there's a movement towards their happening. Science fiction picks at certain implicit trends that are embedded in our actual social technological situation. These are elements of a futurity which exist in the present; they aren't really present because they're not really happening but they represent a kind of futurity, whether or not they actually turn out to happen in the future.[16]

Tendential processes, like algorithmic processes, are entroped & *turned* towards the production of "possible" futures. They represent the means-of-production of possibility *as such*, one via the amplification of emergence, the other via foreclosure. The zone of intersection for these complementary functions is, however, neither a representation in prototype nor a predictive model. It is a simulacrum of (instrumental) reason – the spectral hauntology of what is always *yet-to-come*.

Cinema/Time-War. Even if its "image" literally belongs to a cinematograph, a certain technical evolution – from Méliès' *Le Voyage dans la lune* (1902) to Kubrick's *2001: A Space Odyssey* (1968) & beyond – has predisposed the discourse of (instrumental) reason to a dominant mode of *realism*, even if this realism is *of* the fantastic, *of* the impossible. On the pretence of being internally verifiable, its aesthetic logic has tended towards the foregone conclusion, the self-fulfilling prophesy, the *fait accompli* since its inception. This teleological faculty is deeply rooted in the structure of the image, in its reflection effect, & in that projective rationality whose temporal (self-)difference appears to resolve the paradox of manifold time by inscribing cinema *as history* (à la Godard) within a *future* that is already the truth *of* cinema. No longer would it be necessary to speak of the future as a dream of the unpresentable – of the *fantasy of the real* or of an *immanence* beyond presentiment. Instead it is given as the necessity & impossibility of *representation as such*.

Here stands the crux of the dispute between science & fiction. Before the question of verity is even able to be posed, it must contemplate this vista & will ultimately stake everything upon it. Like fiction, it belongs to a radically determinate universe & is unable to envisage its own end. Confronted with a proliferation of singularities, it evokes a crisis of universal laws: physics breaks down. And like institutionalised psychoses, these singularities have nowhere to go *unless it is to reconstitute the universal elsewhere under other regimes* (the law, reason, etc.) in some parallel dimension, perhaps. But are we not forever in some *parallel dimension*? The dimension of signification? The "End of History" did not require the Apollo moon-landing to be brought into view other than in the realm of a certain political conspiranoia. Nor did it require Auschwitz, Darwinian evolution, or the death of "God." Wherever the insurmountable has been evoked, depicted, or instrumentalised, it has only ever served to instigate a countermovement, tending quasi-dialectically to the production of historical prostheses: a technology of indefinite extension, renewal, reproduction.

Even if the premise of such a thing as evolution demands a corresponding thought of the *finitude of "man,"* of an idea of humanity bound to supersession, it also advances a mechanism for the transcendence of *evolution* as well as the contingencies of worldly existence. Herein lies the seeming paradox of the "present condition": humanity – that collective phantasm – has either to exist in the *real futures* of its technological dreaming, or it must cease to be. Which is to say, it must confront the fact that it has *already* ceased to be. To rephrase Marx, a spectre is haunting reason: the spectre of humanity. And if Landian hyperstitionality can be understood in Mark Fisher's terms as the dialectical counterpart of a *hauntology of lost futures*[17] – being the driving impetus of every posthumanism – this too demands an understanding of what amounts to a Nietzschean *ressentiment* in the instrumentalised fiction of the End-of-History. To evolve beyond its Earthly condition, like the "talents" (i.e., mutants) of Philip K. Dick's novels, or to conserve itself in a metaphorical iron lung, cryogenically immersed for untold millennia in a "virtual reality" from which there can, in fact, be no exit, no *other reality* – the idea of humanity must become the adversary of the world.

It's as if, overwhelmed by the creeping pessimism of a revealed certainty, an untold resourcefulness contained in the words "science fiction" finally becomes apparent, not as a smoke-&-mirrors distraction from the so-called real world, but *as* the "real world." Quotidian experience has become saturated with the technological legacies of Apollo: the pervasively simulacral access to experience defined by the World Wide Web, "cloud" computing, algorithmic social media, dronology, the proliferation of data-harvesting, etc. Humanity has indeed already become a hostile figment of its global self, a malevolent spectral presence in the expanded field of a spectacularised present that no longer tries to mask the provisional fictionality of any given future (those former "manifest destinies"). Now humanity masks its "real absence" from a future that can *only* exist on those terms. This issue has been theorised at length by Guy Debord in *The Society of the Spectacle* (1967) & explored cinematically in Chris Marker's *La Jetée* (1962) & Rainer Werner Fassbinder's *Welt am Draht* (1973).

Having apparently become the god-like agents of technological evolution in the Anthropocene, humanity is confronted with an unbearable scenario: the world-to-come is no longer provisional upon human agency; on the contrary, it hinges on what Artaud denoted a *subjectile*, produced by spacetime algorithms of stochastic feedback. This scenario requires a sanguine view of things if what passes for a critical & cultural consciousness isn't to regress into a neo-humanistic sentimentality that, in light of the cybernetic revolution that followed from it, accounts for a certain *existential turn* in post-Apollo science-fictional real*ism*. Yet this would not be the same thing as Baudrillard's insistence that "the SF of this era of cybernetics & hyperreality will only be able to attempt to 'artificially' resurrect the 'historical' worlds of the past, trying to reconstruct *in vitro* & down to its tiniest details the various episodes of bygone days: events, persons, defunct ideologies – all now empty of meaning & of their original essence, but hypnotic with retrospective truth ... like a gigantic hologram in three dimensions, where fiction will never again be a mirror held to the future, but rather a desperate rehallucinating of the past."[18] And the past is *always-already* a work – a texture or fabric or web – of hallucinations. Lacan calls it *fundamental fantasy.*[19]

The Truth in Fiction. "It is truth," Lacan notes in his seminar on Edgar Allan Poe's "The Purloined Letter," "that makes the very existence of fiction possible."[20] A certain appeal to common sense might define science as that domain of "systematic & formulated knowledge" (OED) – & therefore of "truth – from which fiction must necessarily be *excluded*, but such a "common sense" is contradicted by an integral relationship between fiction & truth that lies at the heart of a body of philosophical thought encompassing the work of Plato (dialogues), Descartes (*Meditations*), Leibniz (the doctrine of infinitesimal magnitudes) & Kant (*das Ding-an-sich*), among others. Terms such as "conjecture," "hypothesis," "model," "theorem" & "experiment" anchor scientific discourse. One speaks of a "calculus of probability," of an "uncertainty principle," of "complexity" & "indeterminacy." Yet while such terms remain distinguished from speculation of the merely "imaginary" kind, within any scientific description we inevitably encounter propositions that are in some regard provisional, analogical, or metaphoric – in short, a whole *poetics*. In so doing, we find ourselves in a zone of ambivalence between "science," as it is commonly understood, & rhetoric, philosophy, literature, art, cinematography, etc.

It has always been a feature of science that its capacity to know is ultimately determined by its capacity to formulate representations of the unknown. Ordinarily, this takes the form of testable hypotheses. An hypothesis, as Henri Poincaré once remarked, is first & foremost a type of generalisation: it provides an overall framework upon which to structure a worldview. Such hypotheses also present science with a dilemma, since they are potentially false until proven otherwise – indeed, in this *provisional state*, they're no more than elaborately constructed *as if*s (i.e., species of fiction). And yet hypothesis is necessary for science to proceed *in anticipation of* experimental proofs or observable facts.[21]

During the late eighteenth century, Jeremy Bentham formulated a "theory of fictions" that regarded fiction as an unavoidable & indispensable product of *all discourse*. This contrasted with Francis Bacon's view of fiction as a superstitious "idol." Bentham recognised the *necessary* similarities between the conjectural form of scientific method & so-called literary language. Developing this line of thought from the late-nineteenth century, Hans Vaihinger's *Philosophy of As If: A System of the Theoretical, Practical & Religious Fictions of Mankind* (1911) – an important source text for Borges' "Tlön, Uqbar, Orbis Tertius" (1940) – specified an array of instances in which "fictive" thinking (or the "fictive activity of the logical function") lends impetus to such practical & theoretical domains as biology, mathematics, physics, philosophy, psychology & jurisprudence.

Although Vaihinger made distinctions between different kinds of fiction, all of them were reducible to the sequence of thought encapsulated by the "as if." Additionally, Vaihinger argued that science – as a set of experimental epistemologies – is necessarily speculative insofar as it can never really "know" (or directly experience) the underlying reality of the world. Science constructs simulations & acts "as if" these correspond to a directly objectifiable reality that, in ideal circumstances, *could* be known or experienced.

For Vaihinger, the worldview presented by scientific reason is constructed *upon a fictional foundation*, albeit a highly coherent & functional one (a system of representation that *works*, an *economimesis* inherently productive of a critique of the spontaneity of so-called unmediated experience, of *presentation*).[22] This view reflects the practical reliance of science upon hypothesis, but also a dependence upon technically-mediated forms of verification (everything from high-speed photography, to x-ray & infrared, to the Large Hadron Collider, to the human nervous system). From the industrial revolution onwards, it has been increasingly the case that science is concerned with what, for human observers, remains fundamentally *un*knowable or *un*presentable – if by *knowable* we also mean *directly available* to some form of intuitive understanding or precognitive experience rather than an *artefact* of a calculus or system of thought or methodology.

Vaihinger's theory of fictions likewise attempted to address questions of subjectivity & the preponderance of individuals, employing psychological fictions to give coherence to "irrational" social realities.[23] The forms of simulacra encountered in paranoia & hysteria invoke a functional equivalence of "reality" & "fiction" at certain crucial junctures (e.g., the experience of what Philippe Pinel termed "mental alienation" in his 1802 *Traité médico-philosophique sur l'aliénation mentale ou la manie*). The equivalence comes to haunt the methodological dependency of scientific positivism upon the "as if." It also haunts the status of "as if," a *foundation for scientific method*, posing the question of a "fictional rationality." This may have far-reaching consequences for the epistemological privileges attendant upon the *forms* of rationality. Principle among them is the discourse of realism (which, incidentally, is the "task" of science to distinguish from fiction as it was once the "task" of philosophy: the valorisation, we might say, of techno-scientific *capital*).

Where the philosophy of Vaihinger bears most incisively upon the question of "science fiction," though, is with regards to the domain of the *unverifiable*. Just as a "literature of the possible" must necessarily evoke the limits of the *im*-possible, so too the generalised form of hypothesis must also evoke a type of *irrational counterpart*. Vaihinger argued that fiction forms a class of hypothesis *not* subject to ordinary criteria of verification. This is not merely because such fictions are patently false, but because *certain hypotheses concern problems for which there are no "rational" solutions*. Such later developments as set theory, general relativity, quantum, chaos, etc. are thus confirmed in their suspicion of the existence of seemingly "irrational" logics that violate, contradict or negate what amounts to *ideological assumptions* in the framing of universal laws.

In an attempt to establish general criteria for scientific discourse, Karl Popper famously coined the term "falsifiability."[24] Any statement that can be demonstrated to be true can be falsified. It is the possibility for falsification that distinguishes science from "mere" fiction since, in the realm of fiction, there are no formal criteria of verifiability. As Vaihinger said, fiction represents precisely what is *un*-verifiable, & since it is not verifiable, it is not falsifiable. Such a dualistic view, however, exposes itself to a number of important ambiguities. From this locus, "science fiction" presents a kind of quasi-dialectical "alternative three."

Irrational Counterparts. Ten years before John Logie Baird demonstrated a viable television broadcast system, *Amazing Stories* editor Hugo Gernsback coined the term "scientifiction" in the January 1916 issue of *Electrical Experimenter* in an article entitled "Baron Münchhausen's New Scientific Adventures: Thought Transmission on Mars."[25] Gernsback anticipated an emerging new wave of popular techno-consumerism that would reach its height in 1950s America. During this period, former Nazi rocket scientist Wernher von Braun, the man largely responsible for the V2, was teaming up with Walt Disney on the production of a series of TV advertorials – based on von Braun's 1948 novel *Das Marsprojekt* & a series of articles later published in *Colliers* entitled "Man Will Conquer Space Soon" – to promote the seemingly fantastic idea of putting a man on the moon.[26] By the time von Braun was heading NASA's Marshal Space Flight Center, tasked with developing the Saturn V rocket, space travel had moved from the realm of fantasy to that of plausible science. Gernsback called it "science faction."[27] Its popular depiction in film evolved accordingly, from George Pal's *Destination Moon* (1950), which borrowed von Braun's moonrocket design & incorporated plot elements that would uncannily recur in Alfons Cuarón's *Gravity* (2013), to Kubrick's *2001*, which famously employed a team of NASA engineers & cyberneticists as production consultants, including Marvin Minsky.

Between world wars, science entered into everyday life in entirely unprecedented ways. By the time terms like "science fiction" & "sci-fi" appeared in the 1930s & 1940s, the popular awareness of science had been transformed. This continued a trend from the late-nineteenth century when the term "scientific romance" was used in Britain to describe work by writers such as H.G. Wells & Jules Verne. And we can trace the evolution of science fiction as a literary genre through the various stages of the Industrial Revolution, linked to the popularisation of scientific discovery from the early eighteenth century onwards. Of course, it can & has been argued that science fiction emerged when "science" did.

Between the appearance of Aristotle's *To Organon* in the fourth century BC & Bacon's *Novum Organum* in 1620, there was no strict disunity between what we call science & what we broadly call fiction today. Regarded by Voltaire as the father of experimental philosophy, Bacon insisted on the *dissolution of myths* & the substitution of facts for "fancy." *The sovereignty of man*, he argued, *lieth in knowledge*. Yet, as Derrida has argued, if "scientific knowledge is a power, art is what it does not suffice to know."[28] The dichotomy of science/fiction establishes the terms of an antagonism while inscribing a *detour of truth through fiction* in a dialectical movement where the hegemony of knowledge asserts & ramifies itself. This movement dilated within what Derrida calls "the time of an algorithm" in a critique of Lacan's seminar on Edgar Allan Poe.[29] In a 1958 seminar on Gide, Lacan similarly advances the observation that "there is so little opposition between this *Dichtung* & *Wahrheit* in its nakedness that the fact of the poetic operation rather should give us pause before the characteristic which is forgotten in all truth, that it declares itself in the structure of fiction."[30] Derrida draws the following conclusion: "Truth governs the fictional element of its manifestation, which permits it to be or to become what it is, to declare itself. Truth governs this element from its origin or its telos, which finally coordinates this concept of literary fiction with a highly classical interpretation of *mimēsis*: a detour toward the truth, more truth in the fictive representation than in reality, increased fictionality, 'superior realism.'"[31]

Another End-of-History Is Possible. A critical-satirical turn in modern science fiction can be traced back to Mary Shelley's *Frankenstein* & the earlier writings of Voltaire & Jonathan Swift. *Frankenstein* presents the dilemma of "artificial life" as the spectre haunting instrumentalist reason, while both *Micromégas* & *Gulliver's Travels* are reflections upon ideas previously expressed in Bacon's *Novum Organum*, namely the concept of *una scientia universalis*, which explicitly links knowledge & political power. But where science fiction generally continues a long tradition of utopian & speculative literature, here the transparently mimetic character of this projection is subverted by way of a sceptical reflexivity that is brought to bear *as discourse*. *Frankenstein* even takes the form of a pursuit of the narrator by his "creation" – the eternal return of the repressed logos that mirrors the persecutory truth of a scientific reason centred upon the claims of transcendental humanism (the nemesis of which is not artifice but its parodic simulacrum: humanism's doppelgänger). The broad ramification of this critical-satirical turn encompasses the entire epistemological & speculative orientation of the genre, extending to every aspect of its realism. At the same time, this turn is mirrored in a consciousness of science fiction having become, as J.G. Ballard suggests, *the only possible realism*. Ballard writes:

Everything is becoming science fiction. From the margins of an almost invisible literature has sprung the intact reality of the twentieth century. In essence, science fiction is a response to science & technology as perceived by the inhabitants of the consumer goods society, & recognizes that the role of the writer today has totally changed – he is now merely one of a huge army of people filling the environment with fictions of every kind. To survive, he must become far more analytic, approaching his subject matter like a scientist or engineer. If he is to produce fiction at all, he must out-imagine everyone else, scream louder, whisper more quietly. For the first time in the history of narrative fiction, it will require more than talent to become a writer.[32]

This *only possible realism* is precisely the subversion of every realism. "Above all," says Ballard, "science fiction is likely to be the only form of literature which will cross the gap between the dying narrative fiction of the present & the cassette & videotape fictions of the near future."

But how does this zero-sum of the possible distinguish a polyvalent science fiction from an accountable totality of technical artefacts that are supposedly *of their time* by somehow *being before it* & thus *comprehend it in advance*?

Intuiting a recurrent mode of anachronism in the formulation of *what* science fiction *is*, Nabokov once observed that, if the strict definition of a literary genre were to be applied, it would be necessary to begin with Shakespeare's *The Tempest*.[33] Irrespective of how the term "strict" is defined, Nabokov is right about *The Tempest*'s situation – if not its chronology – at a critical juncture in the relationship between *history, knowledge, art* & the discourse of power as *realpolitik*. It is likewise arguable that Shakespeare's play represents something of a preview of the crisis inaugurated by the capitalist system of production in the following century: the subsequent "autonomy" of the commodity fetish & the de-essentialising of "value," leading to the post-industrial "society of the spectacle" & the more-or-less current "cybernetic revolution." Shakespeare signals a quasi-automated sociopolitical apparatus of control, computed & operated by an epistemic system whose proxies threaten – beyond any "purely" mimetic function – to become independent & overwhelm their master. This revolutionary threat is averted in *The Tempest* by a strategic manoeuvre of self-supersession that relinquishes nothing: power *lives on*, as it were, in the figure of a sentimentalised "emancipative" reason. Shakespeare seems to intuit, too, the coming "technological singularity" wherein an all-too-human tyranny engineers its succession under the guise of a "posthuman future" that is brought into view as the true meaning of this history-annihilating tempest.

Borrowing its title from a line in *The Tempest*, Aldous Huxley's *Brave New World* – a 1932 re-versioning of perhaps the very first sci-fi "novel," Plato's *Republic* – offered precisely such a futuristic vision of technological utopia & social engineering. Bertrand Russell, whose *The Scientific Outlook* appeared a year earlier, lamented this vision, saying it "is all too likely to come true."[34] Like *The Tempest*, *Brave New World* treats the relationship between knowledge, illusion & the power of reason. Unlike the play, however, Huxley's novel is a *savage critique* of the idea of benevolent science & bio-technological progress (iconicised by the Model-T totem of Taylorism). In this "brave new world," the *perfectibility of man* has given way to the abolition of the human; the existence of "man" becomes a "consensual" enslavement to technocratic rationalism, eugenics, social Darwinism & the soporific spectacle of progress.[35]

The *pantographic exuberance*[36] of Huxley's nightmare of universal happiness exposes the contradictions of utopian thought linked to the emancipation of man from the so-called irrationalism of nature (capitalism, by any other name). We are confronted with the terrible realisation that utopias are not merely political fictions but always *threaten to become real*. "Life," as Huxley's epigraph announces, "marches towards utopias," & it is humanity's task to discover the means of avoiding such a destination. Here, art & fiction are not only the guiding imagination of a *science of truth*, but its homeostat, guarding against *rationalist excess* (including what Gide calls a realism of "petty & contingent facts"[37]). They remind us that scientific "progress" ultimately serves its own ends & that these ends are not always compatible with the idea of humanity.

In *The Tempest*, Shakespeare, borrowing from Montaigne, reflects upon a specific utopia: the possibility of a society governed by reason & therefore "ideal." The microcosm of Prospero's island is a working hypothesis of such a Platonic pseudo-utopia, organised around the singular idea of a real accession to power via a certain *truth* of the principle of *scripta manent*. It represents a dictatorship of "pure reason," with its systematic vanities, its narcissism, its overweening ambition to universality (accomplished by Prospero's sleight of hand at drowning his books). The illusionism vested in a *scientia universalis* is relinquished only at the point when Prospero abandons (flees?) his island & returns from exile in the realm of "phantasy" to "real" political power. The authoritarianism of Prospero's "science" exposes itself in its hidden counter-part, hinted at in the alien/ated (i.e., colonised, enslaved, subproletarian, dena-turised) figure of Caliban, representing a completely *other* kind of "utopia" from the one promised – but never realised – by Prospero's invocation of *scientia universalis*. It is a "utopia," as Montaigne says (in reply to Plato), which "hath *no* … knowledge of letters, *no* intelligence of numbers, *no* name of magistrate, nor of politike superioritie."[38] Prospero's techno-primitivist "science" is here vested in the art (the *stratagem*) of a concealing-unconcealment. The organic veils of truth appear in the operations of a fiction that has been "rationalised" into a system indistinguishable from it.

As framed in Shakespeare's text, this simulacral *state of nature* contains no *falsehood as such*, but merely an "ignorance" of the Law of *scientia universalis*. There can be no question of access to a doctrine of "truth" beyond its own narrative enframing. And insofar as its *topos* is made to resemble the archetypal *garden*, it evokes a regression of *savage thought* forever falling under the sway of a *technē politikē* that it is incapable of representing other than as a miraculous power. This illiterate, superstitious non-knowledge nevertheless *underwrites* Prospero's own panoptical *dystopia*. It is both a prison & a phantasm: an ecology of radical contradictions driven by a *metabolic rift* in the subordinated forces of nature & a fantastic *return of the real* by way of the *technē of the word*. As an allegory of a certain transcendental reason *at the service of an ultimate restitu-tion (recovery) of the political order (value)*, this movement becomes the object of a whole series of ideologically inflected "sciences," culminating in a historical materialism that (seemingly re-enacting Prospero's *noyade*) supersedes itself in the accomplishment of the End of History & the insipidity, as Lacan notes, "of our contemporary superman."[39]

Anthropocenic Vistas. Ostensibly worlds away, the inauguration of the "Space Race" via the launch of Sputnik by the USSR in 1957 climaxed in the Apollo lunar missions twelve years later, eroding many of the conventional distinctions that had grown out of the Renaissance between science, fiction & "science fiction." By 1975, after the remnants of the Apollo project had morphed into Skylab (accompanying a vast communications project that anticipated the advent of GPS), the lunar programme had supposedly exhausted its immediate symbolic value as political spectacle as well as its scientific *raison d'être*. Whereas von Braun's express view had been that Apollo was simply a dry run for manned missions to other planets in the solar system, for those holding the NASA purse-strings, it had served ultimately as a *potlatch* directed at Moscow (like Reagan's "Star Wars" project a decade later & the Space Shuttle programme that replaced Apollo, whose Soviet analogue, Buran, virtually bankrupted Roscosmos at the beginning of the 1990s).

For the grand historical occasion marking the transition from interplanetary to Earth-bound "manned space exploration," the Soviet & US governments orchestrated another bit of live televised agitprop, symbolising the new policy of détente & ceremonially marking the official end of the superpower "Space Race," with a handshake between the crews of Soyuz 19 & the last Apollo module to be launched. It occurred at a time of extraordinary political unreality in the US, after the turmoil of the Nixon administration & the Vietnam War, & against a backdrop of paranoia & conspiracy theories not far removed from the daily fair of TV-news reality. By 1975, the vision of a future space-faring species (in Carl Sagan's phraseology) appeared to have terminated in low-Earth orbit. It has more or less remained there ever since, pending the future emergence of another corporate-state arms race (in which Elon Musk assumes the role of von Braun/Disney & China takes the part of the USSR).[40]

The termination of the lunar programme & the one-off Apollo-Soyuz Test Project presented a fertile opportunity for an obscure group of British film-makers to produce a fake episode of the popular *Science Report* documentary series on Anglia TV. Directed by Christopher Miles & featuring former news-caster (& Tory MP) Tim Brinton, *Alternative 3* (1977) depicted an investigative report into links between climate change, Britain's "brain drain," & a secret US-Soviet project to establish a colony on Mars. Intended for broadcast on April Fools' Day, the *Science Report* hoax supposedly provoked front-page hysteria in the nation's tabloid press, reminiscent of Orson Welles' 1938 radio broadcast of *War of the Worlds*. Yet unlike Peter Hyams' *Capricorn One*, which came out the same year & converted the Apollo lunar-landing conspiracy theories into a fake NASA mission to Mars (again replete with live TV broadcasts), *Alternative 3* exploited the medium of the TV science documentary to expose a (fake) conspiracy between the Cold War powers in which the Soyuz/Apollo linkup served as a joint front to conceal a (fictionally "real") Mars landing. Of course, *Alternative 3* was actually about the ideological "medium" of information.

Combined with "real-world" scenarios of industrial wastage, over-population, resource degradation, ecological catastrophe & every other life-threatening symptom of globalisation, *Alternative 3* uncannily projected a conspiratorial vision of the end of the Cold War, cyberspace, artificial intelligence, the all-pervasiveness of the military-industrial-entertainment complex & the secret commodification of space. And it's in this last respect – a *prospective* cinema of the Anthropocene – that *Alternative 3* is most incisive. Posed as an escape plan (while there's still time to leave this planet & colonise another), the film's eponymous "Alternative 3" proffers a bold project for the *preservation of the status quo* under the guise, firstly, of *sustainable* political, economic & technological progress (space as the ultimate arbiter of a social-Darwinistic struggle that has rendered the Cold War a mere *pretence*), & secondly, of environmental transcendence (the colonisation of space & evacuation of Earth as *necessity*). Both are nevertheless suspended in a type of "indefinite & unending"[41] hyper-industrial present. The aim of this present is to propagate a simulacrum of itself in space (other worlds) & time (ownership of the future). This is precisely the implied sense of "global power" that merges with Fukuyama's post-1989 "End of History" & what Baudrillard calls the "projective hypostasis of the robot."[42]

The Future of a Disaster. In its increasingly critical response to the evolution of corporate-political power & the cyberneticisation of society, "science fiction" at the turn of the millennium was no longer concerned with positing a transcended present. Like *12 Monkeys*, Terry Gilliam's 1995 remake of Marker's *La Jetée*, it imagined a foreclosed future. In this mode of recursive cinema, history collapses back into the illusion of itself in a closed loop of collective alienation, manufac-tured consent, rampant commodification & the advent of a "post-truth" epoch dominated by fully-automated global surveillance systems. We have moved from the panoptic war machine of Godard's *Alphaville* (1964) to the multi-level computer-simulation of Fassbinder's *Welt am Draht*. Fassbinder's "Simulacron" (a global simulation or virtual reality machine for modelling future economic events designed by the semi-fictional "Institut für Kybernetik und Zukunftsfor-schung"[43]) is to Godard's "α60" (the handiwork of a certain Professor von Braun) as William Gibson's "matrix" is to Kubrick's "HAL." The world of Fassbinder's "Simulacron" is an immersive *expanded cinema* where the carceral logic of *subjection* re-evolves into the production of *subjectivity*: there is no external galaxy of the "real" to which its pseudo-protagonists might escape; there is only the "simulation" of an outside, itself a simulation. Ultimately there's nothing but simulacra *all the way down*.

In 2003, Gibson remarked that the increasing tendency of "science fiction" towards cinematic *realism* derives from an impulse to conceal the fact that "we have no *future* because our present is too volatile ... We have only risk management. The spinning of the given moment's scenarios."[44] According to Gibson, as Western society evolves further into the realm of the virtual & the so-called posthuman, "the future" assumes the appearance of a *preservation strategy*.[45] Within this sense of "preservation," science fiction corresponds to a multiple-scenario system of prospective disaster management overlapping the Anthropocene. Collectively the genre points to the tension between the instrumental function of simulationism & the relation of fiction-to-truth (qua Lacan) as a signifying *automatism* in which technology, the future-historical present, & the real are equally construed. Science fiction is at once a "mapping of the topography of a yawning postcapitalism,"[46] as D. Harlan Wilson has observed, & the discourse of its operations, indeed of its very possibility. And if "Gibson & Bruce Sterling ... fetishized how electronic technologies invaded, modified, & evolved the flesh" via a shared preoccupation with commodification of the body & the psyche,"[47] this is precisely a measure of the *autonomous* function Freud & Marx attribute to the fetish, an instigation of agency in & by a system of alienation that it would otherwise be taken to merely represent or describe.

Yet within the discourse of posthistoricism *après* Fukuyama, it's not the utopian future but the imagined present that stands as the conservational horizon of this "brave new world," a world nevertheless verifiable only as data-points in an ongoing "hyperstitional" multiple-scenario construct designed to perpetuate itself *ad aeternitatem*. These are what Gibson called *semiotic ghosts* in "The Gernsback Continuum" (1981) – a cyberneticised collective unconscious that exists, like its Freudian doppelgänger, in timeless superposition. This alien "thing that thinks" is no mere *analogue* of the human but its divine inscription in the very stuff of the universe (pure information), the stuff from which probability flows towards an inevitable encounter with a cosmic intelligence. In the "epoch" of space exploration, this aspiration-cum-preservation strategy finds its most explicit form in those summarised digests of human life on Earth sent aboard deep-space probes like Pioneer (10 & 11) & Voyager (1 & 2). Addressed to distant extraterrestrial (or future human) "life," each probe contains an eccentric array of scientific & cultural data selected by a NASA committee chaired by Carl Sagan, who thought Venus could be made habitable. This data referenced everything from human biology & Earth's relative location in the galaxy to recordings of Bach & images of people shopping in supermarkets.

As a projected encounter with extraterrestrial life (e.g., Nicola Tesla's radio communications with Mars), Pioneer & Voyager represent the export of a cosmic humanism. "Billions of years from now," Sagan wrote, "our sun, then a distended red giant star, will have reduced Earth to a charred cinder. But the Voyager record will still be largely intact, in some other remote region of the Milky Way galaxy, preserving a murmur of an ancient civilisation that once flourished – perhaps before moving on to greater deeds & other worlds."[48] Voyager's message "to future times & beings" – objectively interpretable, so Sagan believed, by any sufficiently advanced "space-faring" species – represents a *human abstract* for whom both history & the fantastic dream of universal knowledge are commodities like any other, married to the sentimental idea of *living on* (what we might call the derivatives market in the *future of an illusion*). It is a narrative of projection & (narcissistic) re-encounter that has found a more recent (& more local) iteration with the 2018 launch of the Arch Mission Foundation's prototype archive of "critical human knowledge" aboard the SpaceX Falcon Heavy, where it has taken the provisional form of an "off-site backup." This was ultimately envisaged as a distributed data network in orbit around each of the planets in the solar system as insurance against terrestrial catastrophe.

Eschatologistics. The "Arch" (or ark) is encoded in a variety of formats, including 360 terabyte datacrystals capable of resisting cosmic radiation, with an estimated functionality of 14 billion years (the digital episteme as transcendental signified). As its name intends, this Anthropocenic contingency plan represents nothing less than a future knowledge-platform for an expanded field of human habitation off-world. The Ark is as much of an escape vehicle as a *system* of dissemination & re-colonisation. What presents itself as a survival strategy is also the germ of a future space technocracy whose ultimate beneficiary – echoing Aaron Swartz's critique of the intellectual property regimes of JSTOR et al.[49] – would *not* be those escaping the Corporate State disaster of the Anthropocene & its micromanaged, algorithmic, proprietary neoliberalism, perhaps in the hope of establishing a "future" public domain. Instead, it would be archmission.org, their partner Cloud Constellation Corporation, & their institutional subscribers (the dead hand of so-called postcapitalism).

While the science of bulk data transmission & storage in outer-space represents a serious logistical challenge, the idea that such projects are ideologically neutral represents the dominant *science fiction* of our era. It's possible, though, that one day these futurist time-capsules will, despite themselves, come more & more to resemble Frankenstein's "monstrous" doppelgänger & Huxley's "savage": failed evolutionary escapees from the videodrome of the *techno-capitalist sublime* in whose image they were created (like Huxley's "World State"). This hyperstitional relay – from the "imaginary" to totalisation in the "real" – reprises Baudrillard's argument concerning the ideological saturation of the episteme & the belief in an emancipatory scientism:

> We can no longer imagine other universes; & the gift of transcendence has been taken from us as well. Classic SF was one of expanding universes: it found its calling in narratives of space exploration, coupled with more terrestrial forms of exploration & colonization indigenous to the 19th & 20th centuries. There is no cause-effect relationship to be seen

here. Not simply because, today, terrestrial space has been virtually completely encoded, mapped, inventoried, saturated; has in some sense been shrunk by globalization; has become a collective marketplace not only for products but also for values, signs, & models, thereby leaving no room any more for the imaginary. It is not exactly because of all this that the exploratory universe (technical, mental, cosmic) of SF has also stopped functioning. But the two phenomena are closely linked, & they are two aspects of the same general evolutionary process: a period of implosion, after centuries of explosion & expansion. When a system reaches its limits, its own saturation point, a reversal begins to takes place. And something happens also to the imagination.[50]

But whether it's apocalyptic futurism or self-preservational status quo, the science fiction of the current global political disorder – like the geo-technic epoch that reifies it – marks the subsumption of the imaginary into the ideological *at precisely the point where ideology appears to dissipate under the critical mass of the "real"* (climate change, the geological register, etc.). This is the moment Stiegler refers to as the "digital episteme,"[51] the point of generalisation of the cybernetic conception of information throughout & *as* the so-called medium of the real & thus, in McLuhan's terms, its "message."

Such a general dissemination of the apparently fictive doesn't accomplish an algorithmic universalism, but the contrary, an emergent specificity, an idiom, particles of thought extrapolated from a probability field: the infinity of detail that constitutes what Ballard deemed "the eternal present of this timeless zone."[52] This particularity, this *point de capiton*[53] of ideology in the real, orientates the entire epistemological schema as ideological *par excellence*. It extends its claims of monopoly over every mode of computable future, including all of the computable non-futures (ideology isn't, as Baudrillard says, the "coefficient of reality to the imaginary"; it's the field within which any such coefficient may be inscribed). It automatically defines a singular "horizon" of *all possible futures* & of the *impossibility* of any (other) future *of possibility* beyond this singularity – a movement that comes into view at the horizon of the End of History, infinitely self-repeating in an accumulation of toxic world-suffocating simulacra of the "universal present." This (dys)utopia is all-inclusive; even its dysfunctions feed the play of (im)possibilities. And it's here that science fiction, supposedly an Id to rationalism's Ego, comprises not a *deviation from the real* but realism's foundation.[54] Science fiction inscribes that projective, cinematic realm of the *to come* in which the possibility of the *im*possible resides & through which "we" obtain "our" perspective on a future that – like the Cartesian planet-annihilating warhead in Carpenter & O'Bannon's *Dark Star* (1974) – we may fulfil only by adverting to our own unreality.

Prague, December 2019

8

THE END-OF-THE-WORLD IS NECESSARY –
PROGRESS IMPLIES IT

Imagine a psycho-civilisational AI that has internalised all the dynamics of political critique, protest, dissent, insurrection, revolution – an AI whose hegemony is secretly contiguous with the entire cybersphere. How would the *existence* of such a power manifest within the system of representations "we" call the world? What outward forms would it assume that might betray its presence among "us" – or even *within* "us" – that could alert "us" to the fact that "we" might be nothing but *subjects* of some science-fictional experiment in "mind control" inside a cybernetic programme governed by it? Would merely entertaining such a scenario imply a crisis of confidence in "our" cognitive processes? A fatal psychic vulnerability? A doubt in the "concrete situation" of reality so profound as to imply that "we" are, for all intents & purposes, mad? A collective pronoun of micro-targeted paranoias? Is a pronoun of this nature deflected into the accusation that the world "itself" is secretly mad? Such "thought-experiments" constitute *irresponsible*, perhaps even unspeakable, inducements to reason at every turn. Scenarios of messiah complexes, persecution complexes, influencing machines & cosmic conspiracies furnish the conceits of countless "psychiatric" dramas. They differ from accepted "truths" (religious, political, social, etc.) by ideological degrees rather than degrees of facticity (usually the contrary is the case). Ideology, not science, defines terms like God, revelation, freedom, civil rights, protest, resistance, terrorism, revolution & so on.

Plato's notorious gaslighting exercise known as the "Analogy of the Cave" unites the various elements of these scenarios into what amounts to an overwhelming ambivalence. Truth & emancipation-from-falsehood are clearly displayed as a contest between opposing control-forces. Whether construed as forces of reason or madness, it is a matter ultimately of indifference (though not to Plato, of course, who insisted always on siding with Right, even if by subterfuge).[1] It provides a ready template for the "eternal antagonisms" of ideological struggle in general, be it of the individual or the collective – one "man" against the world or the oppressed many against the privileged few; a monomania or a mass hysteria; truth singular or plural. In its numerous iterations, more often than not the story proceeds along the following lines: A renegade (or group of renegades) has stumbled upon a secret conspiracy of potentially global proportions ("truth" is under threat). A malevolent force – perhaps aliens, or machines, a tyrant or a lunatic, or all of these – has taken over the planet & hypnotised its inhabitants into believing they are free "sovereign" individuals whereas they are slaves to a vast simulation. Yet unsuspecting of such a control-force operating over them, the mass of humanity continues to behave unperturbed in their everyday social dramas. This is deeply disturbing, like mass organised religion. Our renegades use their secret knowledge in an attempt to emancipate the people & are met with incomprehension, ridicule, outrage, death. In every version of this story, the renegade-characters face a Herculean task in persuading their compatriots merely to *open their eyes*, an almost trivial injunction that nevertheless implies how everything the masses have been led to believe to be the "truth" up until that moment has been pure fabrication.

Unseeing is Believing. In John Carpenter's 1988 satirical masterpiece *They Live*, X-ray sunglasses provide the ocular proof and reveal to those "humans" who wear them the "aliens" operating in plain view within the Corporate State Appa-ratus. These sunglasses also reveal the secret control systems hidden beneath the veneer of "everyday life." In commodities, advertising, the mass media – it's only a matter of putting the sunglasses on (i.e., *opening your eyes*). Aware that they are participating in a cinematic fiction, the film's viewers perceive that *this* world (the cinematic world-within-world) is nothing but a subterfuge, a collective (apparently volitional) hallucination, a type of attenuated paranoia that sees all the evidence of a world created solely to "deceive" (i.e., entertain) them. Yet without this ocular proof, such an accusation against the madness of the world – even were it to escape its own representational paradox – could never escape the charge of madness. Countless psychiatric institutions & ratings surveys attest to this double-bind. The catch, of course, is that the distinction we are offered between "seeing the truth" & "hallucinating" is an entirely ambiva-lent one, since everything is only perceptible through a prism of ideology – the ideology of control or the ideology of emancipation; the ideality of subjection or the ideology of subjectivity. Or rather, perception *is* ideology: despite the appeal to an objective "technology of seeing," there *is no neutral perspective on the world*, & this is *its* apparent "madness." If, as Wittgenstein says, the world is *everything that is the case*, including the possibility of its "falsification," etc., etc., then how are we to hold "it" to account?

Of course, this is the dilemma of postmodernity, which, armed with its magic glasses, sees everything (including the act of seeing) as pure spectacle. Post-modernity's solution is to produce *more*, in an ever-inflationary, accelerated movement of idealised relativism. But the system of spectacular production is still a system – & what it produces is production. As Debord & Baudrillard have insisted, such an accumulation of productive surplus doesn't represent a *falsification* of the world, but its immanence as a mode of self-supersession: the spectacle *produces the real*. Yet how can we escape the suspicion that all of those "phantasms" animated by this generalised system are *really* the agents of an undisclosed power? A power operating in the world because it constitutes the world? A power that is unpresentable precisely because it is what "makes visible"? A power that, by necessity, no amount of countervailing force can *reveal* its naked truth?

How could we approach such a power, where every means of representing the problem, let alone a *critique*, would instantly be inverted – with any project of disillusionment (like that of emancipation) instantly transformed into a more profound illusionism, with knowledge transformed into non-knowledge, consciousness into false-consciousness? Inflated to encompass the totality of "critical" discourse, scenarios of this kind inevitably appear trivial, like a calculus whose result is always infinity. But an appeal of the kind we encounter ever-more-frequently to a "return of the real" – that emancipative, catastrophic horizon delimiting a movement of totalisation – belies an equally trivial faith in some imminently approaching "critical mass" of self-evidence on which the simulacral world must finally run aground. Such is that monument to human entropy referred to as the Anthropocene, which is construed as if the mere foretelling of a global extinction event could be the ideal counter-argument to the logic of spectacular-production. Are they not one & the same?

Mutually Assured Delusion. If we take the Anthropocene somehow as the ocular proof of the world's madness, we still delude ourselves in our appeal to the myth of some other, prior, cognitively pristine world to which – through a simple fidgeting with its neurons, carbon emissions, plastic refuse, or the amputation of the Corporate-State Apparatus – could be, like the blind, mag-ically "restored" to vision. Yet it isn't, as Žižek says, only that a world *without capitalism* is somehow beyond the pale, but that such a world would necessarily be incomprehensible *according to the rationale of a public discourse symbiotic with it*. Or put otherwise, there is no seditious idea that isn't already co-opted to the thought of capital, no negation within the framework of the Corporate State that isn't already commodifiable & therefore an *affirmation*, despite wishing otherwise, of the very logic of capital. This says less about a tragic view of eman-cipation than it does about certain persistently farcical notions about capitalism.

That the history of scientific enlightenment, industrialisation, bourgeois democracy & capitalism all coincide is no accident: indeed, this coincidence rep-resents the paradigm of the modern conception of history, which is contiguous with the discourse of reason. In contrast, the recoil to "nature" opened by the Anthropocene as redemption-through-negation would, by consequence of its own logic, present the very *mimēsis* of unreason. To repurpose Wittgenstein, if this "other world" could *speak*, "we" would not *understand it*.

Does this incommensurability mean that the end of *capitalism* is tantamount merely to the end of "our" world? That is to say, the collective subjectivity pro-duced by (or indeed *as*) capitalism & its "abstract social form"?

The other side of this question focuses on the *expropriation* that characterises its otherwise elusive object & seems to cast the act of questioning into doubt: UNDER WHAT GUISE DOES POWER RE-EMERGE FROM THE THEATRE OF ITS NEGATION, IF NOT AS NEGATION?[2] Either the negation of capitalism isn't possible *or else* it must be predicated on capitalism being the *concrete form of its own negation*. Such is the deceptive character of this ZOMBIE CAPITALISM that resurrects itself at every pronouncement of its death. This is the true meaning of the neo-liberal END OF HISTORY, which LIVES ON in a kind of negative perpetuity AS THE SELF-SIMULATION OF CAPITAL. It's not the same as the proposition that the long-foretold apocalypse has already taken place & we are merely living in a "post-apocalyptic world." The world of zombie capitalism describes the sheer horrifying banality of an apocalypse that happens over & over again: farce, as Derrida says, always "on the edge of excess" – "satire of the abyss."[3] The "negation of negation" is no mere illusion. It is a rupture in the system of the world. Within this rupture, the "ontological fabric" of *capitalist realism* is no longer able to support the accumulated mass of its representations.

Dawn of the Undeeded. The belief in the *self-supersession* of the Corporate-State Apparatus has always been the pervasive superstition of Western democracy – a superstition that knows full-well that power relinquishes nothing, or rather no-thing, since it is no *thing*, the operation *of the symbolic order*. Power doesn't describe a system of difference & repetition. It constitutes that system (as *difference* & *repetition*) able to accommodate any succession of "terms" whatsoever. In its naïve volitional form, self-supersession presumes that power is susceptible either to a *suicidal* impulse – excited by an unconditional ethics (that "elective" power belongs to a given temporality which it must not exceed) – or that it *relinquishes* itself knowing that to it alone belongs the trick of instant recuperation & resurrection, contiguous with the miracle of the commodity, which bears the system of power like a hologram within it (i.e., world-without-end). It isn't that the End-of-Power would be the End-of-the-World, but that the world has been caused to discover its end *in* power (i.e., capital), whose prolific & self-devouring resurrection henceforth corresponds to "the world's" sole temporal dimension.

The idea of history as "progress" implied a teleology of perpetual change. In its post-historical formulation, it signifies the contrary: teleology as the implosion of the "real"; implosion under a critical mass of signifier-commodities. Henceforth, "the real" will designate this implosion. In this movement, reification belongs solely to the symbolic order & we recognise the essential *thinglessness* of the commodity: the "thought" of capital-moving-itself, so to speak, as autonomous agency, as pure self-simulation – a zombified cognition that, like the Freudian "repressed," returns *as if from the future* like some agent of a secret time-war. Driven by this implosive feedback cycle, the acceleration of capital glitches the threshold of the perceptible, strobing between montage-effect & a subliminal palimpsest of diachrony & synchrony. The *time of representation* is perpetually out-of-joint. If the End-of-History names any *thing*, it is this palpable anachro-nicity, a circuit of self-supersession from which *nothing follows*. If history is an "open-ended progress" that describes a vector, then the accelerated movement of late-capitalist hyperproduction describes an exponential curve. As acceleration approaches infinity, time approaches zero & history's vector becomes captive to the geometry of inflation (i.e., it becomes a mirror-image of itself).[4]

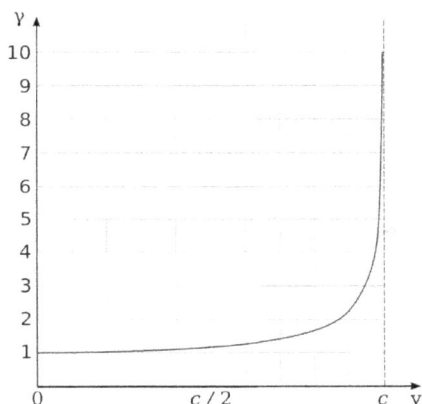

The "Lorenz Factor" (γ): the factor by which time, length & relativistic mass change as a function of velocity, tending towards lightspeed (c).

The *telos* of this movement describes neither one coordinate nor a multiplicity of coordinates. There is an event-horizon, the attenuated representational field that masks a singularity. It is meaningless to name this singularity (e.g., post-capitalism, post-Anthropocene, even post-history). In terms of the historical movement that converges upon it, the *telos* represents the IMPOSSIBLE insofar as it represents anything at all.[5]

What's more, within the circuit of anachronicity, this will *always have been the case*. Like a cyclic redundancy error, acceleration will describe the threshold that it glitches as the *totality* of the historical dimension. And if, as Land argues, "capitalism is *nothing beside* the abstract accelerative social factor,"[6] then acceleration is its constitutive *self-sufficiency*. By "abstract," I mean it is bound only by the teleology of its own perpetuated feedback, & it is "social" in that its operations constitute the entire domain of the spectacle's *permanent glitch economy* that simultaneously *integrates* & *disintegrates* all social signification. The particular quality of this "abstract accelerative social factor" makes it appear to us as both the field of its own operations & the agency presiding over them, as both its sufficiency & its excess. In this dimension of accelerated recursive spacetime, everything revolves around an interval of metonymic self-substitution, which lends to this configuration its particular appearance of reflexivity.[7]

Alien Covenants. In "Alien Capital," Primož Krašovec distinguishes reflexivity of this kind from mere fetishism (the imbuing of dependent elements within a system & their interrelations – such as commodities or market instruments like derivatives – with magical properties of independent action). "A metaphor that Marx held dear," he writes, "was that in capitalism, something keeps happening behind the backs of those who participate in it." At the same time,

> that capital does something behind our back does not only mean that the consequences of capitalist economic activity are unpredictable & not necessarily in accordance with the intentions & expectations of those who carry them out … but also that capital operates according to its own logic that is independent of human intentions, desires & expectations. Capital is alien not (only) as an unconscious or unforeseen dimension of human activity, but as an additional actor, the "eighth" passenger of capitalist economy: *alien*.[8]

This alien metaphor can be taken a step further. It exceeds the notion of simply an economic or social *prosthesis* – an addition to the world of human activity – & speaks of a *condition*. Like power, capital isn't abstract: it is abstraction. Capital isn't a concept born in relation to a subject either: it is the operation of subjectivisation. In its "post-human" iteration, power is precisely *not* wielded; like the old Soviet joke, *power wields you*. Without explicitly stating this, Krašovec says that "the two anthropocentric perspectives of capital" – corresponding to the "elemental class positions" of the capitalist & the proletarian – differ from the perspective of capital, which is defined by the production of value for the purpose of "infinite technological self-improvement" on the assumption that technology defines the *exclusion* of the social. Krašovec thereby identifies competition, or the classical idea of class antagonism, as the *technological dynamics* of capitalism. Whereas the "technological dynamics of capitalism" are entropic, antagonism is the appearance attributed to the maximalisation of this dynamic in differential terms (i.e., different modes of socioeconomic dissipation interacting, interfering, or coalescing).

Just as Marx indicated that alienation isn't an anthropological process (it is instead the *precondition for* the anthropological), so too must we move beyond the simple description of capital *as* technological to the supposition that capital *is indistinguishable from* technology-as-such. Capital is the integrated *system* of technology, just as the commodity is the *thought* of capital. It should be evident that the Anthropocene can't be acquitted by the convenient appeal to malevolent doppelgängers or rogue AIs. Neither can humanism mask the alienation that constitutes subjectivity. Technology isn't, as Marcuse believed, the invasion of "man's" inner-freedom.[9] In the final analysis, the subjective *is* technological; the human *is* alien capital. And if the dream of humanity is to outlive itself by "alien" sublimation, the dream of capital is no less than to transcend itself in the movement of history by arriving from the future. Accelerating towards the limit of its own representability, capital radiates in the illusion of a totality suspended over its own void – as if making possible the very thing it makes impossible.

Prague, November 2018

9

RE-EVOLUTIONARY ABORT

"The present order is the disorder of the future."
— Saint-Just

"When the revolution is still a long way off," Guy Debord reiterates with imperceptible irony in *The Real Split in the International* (1972), "the difficult task comes down increasingly to *the practice of theory*. When the revolution commences, its difficult task comes down increasingly to *the theory of practice*."[1] But if the capacity to solemnly transform *knowledge* into *power* rests upon the capacity to joyously transform *theory* into *praxis*, what is the foundation of this deliberative, spontaneous, self-transformative, revolutionary knowledge? The empowerment of revolutionary knowledge has historically been premised on a certain individual & collective agency vested in its organisation: the so-called "revolutionary class." According to a line of thought extending at least from Blanqui, however, this "class" is contradictorily organised across these two phases, between an *avant-garde* (i.e., those few, *ahead of their time*, whose coherence & ability to communicate an overall project *prepares the way*) & the proletariat (i.e., those "masses of workers" who, as Debord says, "are *of their time* & must remain there as its sole possessors ... *refusing all delegation of power to a separate vanguard*"). Subsequently, "the great majority of the proletarian class must hold & exercise all powers by organising themselves into permanent deliberative & executive assemblies."[2] The Situationists saw their role conclude on this note: "We were there to combat the spectacle, not govern it."[3] Indeed, this vexed third phase of *the consolidation of power* has often been said to inaugurate a counter-revolution from within, its organisation reconstituted as Corporate-State Apparatus, subsumed into the evolution of a "bureaucratic capitalism" from which it had never departed.

The Criterion that Revolutionary Knowledge Must Become Power. The contest over individual & collective agency stands at the heart of every ideological encounter, yet no more so than the contest over what individual & collective agency *is*. "The theory of revolution," Debord writes, "in no way falls exclusively within the domain of strictly scientific knowledge," i.e., of the form *What is?*

Revolutionary theory is the domain of danger, the domain of uncertainty; it is forbidden to people who crave the sleep-inducing certainties of ideology, including even the official certainty of being the strict enemies of all ideology. It is a conflict between general interests concerning social practice as a whole, & only in this respect does it differ from other conflicts. The rules of conflict are its rules, war is its means, & its operations are more comparable to an art than to a piece of scientific research or a catalogue of good intentions. The theory of revolution is judged on the sole criterion that its *knowledge* must become *power*."[4]

Reflecting (contemporaneously with Debord) on the situation four years previous in Paris over which the Situationist International had expressed a certain proprietary interest,[5] Félix Guattari made the following observation: "In May 1968, from the first sparks to local clashes, the shake-up was brutally transmitted to the whole of society, including some groups that had nothing remotely to do with the revolutionary movement – doctors, lawyers, grocers. Yet it was vested interests that carried the day, but only after a month of burning."[6] Citing Foucault, he criticised the conventional Marxist dogma that enlisted the distinction "avant-garde-lumpen-proletariat" & that, having exploited a certain force of "excess" in its preliminary stages, sought to reinstitute the Corporate-State Apparatus in a call to revolutionary "order." For Guattari, this amounted to a "trapping [of] desire for the advantage of a bureaucratic *caste*,"[7] producing a *technocratic revolution*. In this way, it is ultimately Debord's "domain of strictly scientific knowledge" that is most served by an appeal to what is presented as the underlying *irrationalism* of "revolutionary organisation" – an irrationalism embodied in the "proletarian masses." Thus the "Marxist" schematisation of base-superstructure is recast into a model of social psychiatry between convulsive proletarian *Id* (driven by a formless desire for untutored emancipation) & rationalist, technocratic *Ego* (whose operations exploit & enchain it, including an illusory idea of *emancipation*).

In Guattari's view, "revolutionary organisation must be that of the war machine & not of the state apparatus, of an analyser of desire & not an external synthesis."[8] This recasting of Debord maintains the Blanquist line on revolutionary warfare, but it goes further in its critique of two prevalent aspects of "Marxist" dogma:

1. the criterion that revolutionary *knowledge* must become *power*;
2. the myth of a *revolutionary class* (of individual & collective agency).

This critique forms the basis of what, in *Anti-Oedipus*, Guattari & Gilles Deleuze term "schizoanalysis," which stems from a rethinking of historical materialism &, like Situationism, the "rationalist" basis of revolutionary ideology. Hence:

1. "Desire is Power, Power is Desire";[9]
2. class consciousness is symptomatic, not constitutive.

"All societies," Deleuze argues, "are rational & irrational at the same time," yet reason "is always a region cut out of irrationalism – not sheltered from the irrational at all, but a region traversed by the irrational & defined only by a certain type of relation between irrational factors."[10] Accordingly, the social field is characterised by "the problem of delirium." Deleuze continues: "The real problem of delirium lies in the extraordinary transitions from a pole which could be defined as reactionary or even fascist – statements like 'I belong to a superior race' appear in all paranoid deliriums – to a revolutionary pole. Consider Rimbaud's affirmation: 'I belong eternally to an inferior race.'"[11]

What's most controversial about this statement, however, isn't the implicit heresy vis-à-vis conventional "Marxist" notions of class consciousness. It's the belatedness in applying to political economy insights derived from psychoanalysis that, for a quarter of a century, had already been driving the rapid evolution of postwar consumer capitalism & "la civilisation technicienne." This had, in its theory & practice of *unitary urbanism* & *psychogeography*, been at the core of Situationist activity for the previous decade, culminating in two documents of particular (though frequently unacknowledged) significance both in the genealogy of May '68 & in its subsequent theorisation by Deleuze & Guattari: Mustapha Khayati's *De la misère en milieu étudiant*. Published in 1966 by the Strasbourg students' union, this "scandalous" brochure evoked "the most banal analyses of American marketing sociology: conspicuous consumption & advertising's pseudo-differentiation of products otherwise identical in their nullity."[12] With Debord's 1967 *Société du spectacle*, the brochure went beyond a critique of the ideological function of cultural merchandise in its impact upon individual & collective agency to expose a more radical *constitutive alienation* that renders agency (as well as class consciousness) a symptom. Even in their molecular formulation, "class" & "caste" are ultimately *algorithmic functions*.

Categorical Imperatives. The genealogy of this system of regularised desire came to figure centrally in Foucault's 1975 reflections on panopticism, drawing together the eighteenth-century utilitarian philosophy of Jeremy Bentham with contemporary articulations of social control founded upon a system of alienation, abstraction, individuation & normalisation.[13] The pragmatics of this system in its post-WW2 consumerist iteration forms the basis of Adam Curtis' 2002 documentary *The Century of the Self* & provides a critical counterpoint to those narratives around 1968 burdened by anachronism. In Curtis' narrative, the aftermath of fascist "mass hysteria" in European & suicidal Emperor-worship in Japan led to those old sociological categories tasked with explaining the behaviour of populations to give way to controversial new theories that dispensed with conventions about individual & collective agency (negatively theorised as otherwise rational subjects of disinformation in Adorno & Horkheimer's "The Culture Industry: Enlightenment as Mass Deception"[14]). Instead, they focused on supposedly "irrational" psychological drives

& the appeal of *self-actualisation*. The schematic of class consciousness was displaced onto a fluid network of psychological "types" via what Alvin Toffler called "experience creators."[15] This began with the "public relations" pioneer (& nephew of Freud) Edward Bernays, who translated the analyses presented in *Civilisation & Its Discontents* (1930) into a hugely influential system of social propaganda & market manipulation. It extended through Timothy Leary's "acid accelerationist" revolution-in-consciousness & the work of Wilhelm Reich, who, in *Character Analysis* (1945) & *The Mass Psychology of Fascism* (1946), sought to demonstrate the normative character of personal & group identity & the primary determining function of *libido*.

These "types," it was believed, could be produced by an array of seemingly contradictory signifiers & manipulated through a targeted appeal to "irrational impulses" in such a way as to negate or obfuscate Bakunin's "irreconcilable antagonisms" of class consciousness.[16] ("Desire on a social scale," Guattari writes, "cannot be explained by a social rationality."[17]) These precursors to contemporary, micro-targeted social media provided a measure of explanation for such phenomena as the appeal, for example, of fascism among large segments of the industrial proletariat. They also marked the transition of post-industrial societies away from *alienated labour* towards *alienated individualism* & a universal credit (i.e., debt) economy in which exploitation is no longer a "class" privilege & which paradoxically maintained itself by a general appeal to emancipation-through-consumption. Enabled by the advent of television & the emerging science of informatics, this public-relations "revolution" aspired to nothing less than a wholesale *engineering of consent* in tandem with *the permanent obsolescence of class revolution* in the West. It paved the way for the post-'68 triumph of neoliberalism & a global delirium of hypercommodification that, with the fall of the Soviet Union two decades later, would assume the exalted status of an End-of-History.

Intimations of this revolution-in-counterpoint could be found explicitly in the writings of Siegfried Giedion, Vannevar Bush, Norbert Wiener, Buckminster Fuller & Marshall McLuhan, among others. But its implications were slow in penetrating continental political philosophy, which it accomplished only in part through Althusser's synthesis of Marx & the psychoanalytic theories of Jacques Lacan, whose cybernetic recasting of Freud – despite (or perhaps because of) Deleuze & Guattari – continues to be under-examined. Perhaps the clearest formulation of this *other* revolution was given in a 1968 series of lectures on "the political order." Delivered by Harvey Wheeler at the Center for the Study of Democratic Institutions in California, these lectures were later published as *Democracy in a Revolutionary Era*. Wheeler proclaimed the *institutionalisation* of a "universal revolution."[18] What he meant by "institutional" was *permanent integration* into the logic of social organisation. By "universal," he meant an *architectonic science*: a politics of "world order" as "the precondition for the survival of the species."[19] This politics, like the "revolution" it referenced, would no longer be bound by the antagonisms of class or nation-state (i.e., by the competing humanisms of a passed epoch). It would be a global *cyber-politics* – not merely a transitional phase in the history of industrialisation where "cybernation" would "break the dependency of organisational size & complexity on human nature & make it possible to conceive of a vastly expanded scope of control," but a systemic transformation across the entire technological (& therefore *ideological*) sphere, permitting it "to centralise & decentralise simultaneously," (i.e., to *globalise*).[20]

Wheeler's "universal revolution" marked the consummation of a process that had begun with mass industrialisation. It reversed those relations "that had previously existed between science & politics" & that had entered its dénouement with "the famous letter in which the atom bomb project was proposed to President Roosevelt … dated August 2, 1939."[21] (The End-of-History in prototype was soon to be duplicated by the Nazi rhetoric of Total War & the contending "triumph" of Scientific Socialism in the Soviet Union). The advent of the nuclear horizon, articulated during the Cold War arms race by the strategic doctrine of Mutually Assured Destruction (MAD),[22] brought apocalyptic thought fully within the domain of technology, thereby completing the humanist project of wresting control of the "cosmic design" from metaphysics. In MAD, the Machine Age fantasies of global (social) domination of & by humanoid robots transfigured itself into a spectre of autonomous agency that evolved cataclysmically from a "critical mass" of technological power. What appeared strategically absurd in the form of such an "idealised (almost caricatured) doomsday device,"[23] as Herman Kahn wrote in 1960 – subject as it still was to *political* considerations – rapidly transformed into a purely algorithmic problem. The Soviet "Dead Hand" automated weapons-control system thus sought to replace human "decision-making" with pre-calculated scenarios that would be *autonomously* triggered by an array of Earth-bound & orbital seismic, optic, radiation & pressure sensors.

In their abundant metaphorics of "fail-safe," "critical mass," "chain reaction," "runaway" & "unstoppable," these systems described in prototype the lineaments of what has since come to be more popularly known as the *technological singularity*, that point beyond which the evolution of technology will no longer be humanly controllable & will assume the characteristics of fully-autonomous agency.[24] They also represented a broader transition within machine culture to discourses of artificial intelligence & the so-called posthuman, encompassed above all in the *universality* of the Anthropocene.[25] The 22nd Congress of the Communist Party of the Soviet Union in 1961, recognising that "automation is a universal law of development," went so far as to decree that principles of cybernetics should be systematically applied to all aspects of the social-industrial system as the "science of government."[26] This transition was everywhere visible (& increasingly verifiable) across the Cold War's so-called ideological divide, yet its manifestation on a political & social level occurred to a great extent under cover of a series of "bureaucratic readjustments" & "failed uprisings" that took place almost as universally in 1968. The transition was barely observed & almost entirely obscured by the competing sentimental history of "revolutionary action" bearing out the adage that cybernetic systems learn by *breaking down* chaotic inventories of (social, etc.) data into new possibilities of organisation.

The Impossible Raised to the Level of a Revolutionary Criterion. Reflected upon "in an environment of indifference" & the "calm we find ourselves in now,"[27] it has become customary to speak of the Paris student "uprising" (along with the largest general strike in French history) in terms such as "the abortive revolution in May '68."[28] Doing so assures a certain historical agency at work, a revolutionary idea brought into being while simultaneously negating itself, the locus of its own "causality." When the words *revolution* & *May '68* are conjoined in this way, the status of an event (i.e., of a certain "singularity") is conjured forth. That singularities by definition contain multiplicities does nothing to discredit the affixing of the definite article to this "abortive revolution." Its constitutive ambivalence asserts itself all the more readily. Hence "1968" signifies a dialectical *revolutionary-to-counterrevolutionary* movement from which the "indifference" of the 1980s subsequently arises through a general consolidation of reactionary tendencies across Western society as a whole: the transition to neoliberalism. That "1968" acquires a certain historical fatalism in the retelling does little to detract from those narratives in which this "dialectical" movement is presented as a consequence of "the revolution" *failing to realise itself.*

How do we speak of this revolution that isn't a revolution, but an abortion?

Deleuze & Guattari begin their short 1984 commentary for *Les Nouvelles littéraires*, "Mai 68 n'a pas lieu," by suggesting that, in "historical phenomena such as the revolution of 1789, the Commune, the revolution of 1917, there is always one part of the event that is irreducible to any *social determinism*, or to causal chains. Historians are not very fond of this point: they restore causality after the fact. Yet the event is a splitting off from causality – a bifurcation, a lawless deviation, an unstable condition that opens up a new field of the possible."[29]

For Deleuze & Guattari, the field of the possible "does not pre-exist, it is created by the event. It is a matter of life. The event creates a new existence, it produces a new subjectivity."[30] Revolutionary possibility is thus an immanence. By analogy to both quantum field theory & to a dissident psychoanalysis, its eruption is "spontaneous," evoking the production of matter & antimatter, or the operations of desire as the discourse of a machinic "unconscious." These are central tenets of their major response to "the reaction against '68," *Anti-Oedipus*.[31] In a lengthy 1977 discussion with Claire Panet reprising the genesis of *Anti-Oedipus*, Deleuze proposed: "Desire is ... not internal to a subject, any more than it tends towards an object: it is strictly immanent to a plane which must be constructed, where particles are emitted & fluxes combine. There is only desire insofar as there is a deployment of a particular field, propagation of particular fluxes, emission of particular particles."[32]

The matrix of relations between revolution, possibility & desire has an explicit formulation. "[T]here is no blossoming of desire," Deleuze insists, "which does not call established structures into question. Desire is revolutionary because it always wants more connections & more assemblages."[33] The formulation Deleuze & Guattari arrive at for this matrix in *Anti-Oedipus* is "machinic desire" or "machinic surplus value." This brings into play a second matrix of relations involving technicity & *autopoiēsis* within which "history" elides a particular understanding of "technology." In his preface to the Italian edition of *Mille Plateaux*, Deleuze stressed that the ambition of *Anti-Oedipus* had been to arrive at a "determination of those syntheses proper to the unconscious" & of "the unfolding of history as the functioning of these syntheses."[34] Above all, *Anti-Oedipus* viewed the unfolding of history with respect to "the aborted revolution in May '68," which, as Guattari noted, "developed in a counterpoint that we found troubling: we were worried ... about the future being prepared for us by those singing the hymns of a newly made-over fascism."[35]

And here lies a central problem of "1968." How do we reconcile a conception of revolution vested in the singularity of the event with the programmatic contest over futurity that resides at the core of its ideological struggle? Deleuze & Guattari are not speaking of abstract revolution. "The revolution was possible," Guattari wrote, "the socialist revolution was within reach. It truly exists & is not some myth that has been invalidated by the transformation of industrial societies."[36] But what if that were exactly the case? Moreover, what if the "aborted revolution" that Guattari thought "possible," "within reach" & "truly exists" were a *phantasmatic symptom* of precisely the "machinic desire" that *Anti-Oedipus* goes on to theorise in the wake of '68 by a *contrapuntal* movement of "pairing ... productive forces & anti-productive structures"?[37] What if it were "machinic desire" vested in a radical *ambivalence* – or what James Joyce, one of the presiding spirits of *Anti-Oedipus*, called *ambiviolence*[38] – that is, neither fascist nor socialist, but pure "ideology"? Not any kind of dogma, but *the system of signifying possibility as such*? What if the idea of (aborted) revolution here occupies the position of a surplus value, a signifier that "carries out the conjunction, the transformation of fluxes, through which life escapes from the resentment of persons, societies & reigns," as Deleuze says, referring to a certain status of *writing*, to "lines of flight," to "deterritorialisation"?[39]

Symptom, writing, revolution.

Deleuze says that language "is criss-crossed by lines of flight," yet "pragmatics ... is the true politics, the micropolitics of language."[40] Similarly, one might say that "[p]raxis is a network of relays from one theoretical point to another, & theory relays one praxis to another."[41]

The Machinic "Vision Splendid." History written by language-machines is a palimpsest of "breakthroughs & breakdowns," as we are informed in the opening pages of *Anti-Oedipus*. These abortive or aborted revolutions describe what psychoanalysis calls a "transference": "the always-incomplete character of the regressive & analytic process," says Foucault.[42] There are, Deleuze subsequently argues, no reducible "*functions* of language, only regimes of signs which simultaneously combine fluxes of expression & fluxes of content, determining assemblages of desire in the latter, & assemblages of enunciation in the former, each caught up in the other."[43] The question "What is revolution?" devolves into the questions "What is desire?," "What is writing?," "What is language?" & also "What is technology?" To invert the deleuzoguattarian formula, technology is *irreducible to machines* & – via the "abortive" movement of transference inscribed by this chain of substitutions – its operations produce that zone in which "revolutionary discourse" finds its point of return & disappears into itself as the *epistemic rupture* of "pure repeatability."[44]

In "How Do We Recognise Structuralism?" Deleuze proposes that "sense always results from the combination of elements which are not themselves signifying."[45] This broadly epiphenomenal conception stands in a symbiotic relationship to the work of "reification." For Deleuze, the non-signifying elements that *produce* signification are contiguous with the idea of an unconscious *produced* by something akin to a "reification" of certain proto-cybernetic latencies in Freud: the machine, so to speak, inside the ghost. "The unconscious," Deleuze insists, "is not a theatre but a factory"; it doesn't *signify* anything.[46] This reverse-Cartesianism derives from an assumption at the heart of *Anti-Oedipus* "that desire could be understood only as a category of production": "Saying the unconscious 'produces' means that it's a kind of mechanism that produces other mechanisms"; it has "nothing to do with theatrical presentation but with something called a 'desiring-machine.'"[47] And yet the form of desiring-production is not only an *immanence*. The unconscious *has to be produced* too.[48]

What, then, are the conditions of such an interminable production of desire? Of the unconscious? Of *desiring machines?* In other words, of *revolution* in a somewhat universalised "sense"? And is to speak of "abortion" in this relation to speak of a particular kind of non-production? A productive non-production, for example, of a certain non-(Cartesian)-theatricality? An indeterminacy of signification? A subversion of myth? (Theatre, Deleuze contends, speaks of *myth*, the *production of myth*, etc.). In other words, is it a "refusal to represent"? Or, to put it otherwise: What would the conditions be for this revolutionary language-machine to write itself without falling into genre (be it the genre of "failed revolutions," or worse, the genre of History)? Was the micropolitics stemming from *Anti-Oedipus* & inflecting the new millennial discourse of Accelerationism to (re)write the "aborted revolution in '68" in order to produce – by way of a myth of this non-myth – a quasi-historical open-endedness of its "event"? Was the ultimate goal to forestall the "future being prepared … by those singing the hymns of a newly made-over fascism" & thus foreclose upon its own foreclosure as a negation-of-negation of Fukuyamaesque No-Futurism?[49]

At the heart of all these questions remains the dilemma of what Lyotard, in his 1979 report on the "postmodern condition," called the *unpresentable*.[50] This "unpresentable" is twofold. On the one hand, it occupies the position of an horizon of the impossible, which the End-of-History masks, since what it necessarily omits is the possibility of an "end of capitalism"; on the other hand, it stands in the position of the "revolutionary signified" – not the *object* of revolution, but its *accomplishment*. Unifying this idea of the unpresentable is the figure of "technology" (i.e., "science") at the service of a certain illusion of a "progress beyond" (because this "beyond" is by definition excluded from the world). As Debord noted in 1972, "the society that has every technical means to modify the biological foundations of the whole of life on Earth" nevertheless "cannot develop productive forces any further."[51] This is only partially grounded in empirical considerations. Its real basis is ideological: the "science" expected to perform the alchemical miracle of transmuting the Anthropocene into a cornucopia of unbounded futures is seen as inextricably linked to the problem it is tasked with overcoming. "Such a science," writes Debord, "in thrall to the mode of production & to the aporias *of the thought* that this mode has produced, cannot imagine a real overthrow of the present scheme of things."[52] Like some embellished monster dwelling in the margins of a Renaissance map, beyond this present scheme of things lies the "impossible."

If this intractable "present" defines the totality of what is *presentable* within its field of discourse – a world "wholly contaminated by the superabundance of the commodity, as well as the real, miserable dross of spectacular society's illusory splendour"[53] – then the logic of "revolution" must also be counted as having been internalised to it, not as a *rupture with the present* but as the *universalisation* of this rupture. This would mark the convergence of revolution upon that "point" (i.e., event-horizon) which simultaneously renders it impossible & thrusts it into being. "The present & the future," Debord writes, "are merely occupied by consumption turned revolutionary. In the immediate sphere, it is a question of the revolution of commodities, of the recognition of an endless series of *putsches* whereby prestige commodities & their demands are replaced; beyond, it is merely a question of the prestige commodity of revolution itself."[54] Correspondingly, the *impossible* is raised to the level of an historical & revolutionary criterion. What presents as *abortive*, as a "line of flight" from the forces of totalisation, risks succumbing to the opposite of what Guattari called an "escape from the impasse of capitalism,"[55] which is to say, a re-capitulation of the logic of the capitalist desiring-machine. It's an on-going evolution enabled by a "controversy shaped by the phoney tenets of economic science" given the status of the "ontologically revolutionary."[56]

That this should all resemble something like a self-parodic schema doesn't detract from the reality that the productivist line (from *Anti-Oedipus* to Accelerationism) has come to be the line of least resistance, even if its movement is one of bifurcations, multiplicities & indeterminacies. If anything, these offer new "possibilities" for reterritorialisation within an otherwise depleted terrain. They have become the anachronistic shock-troops of the "pseudo-cyclical model of untrammelled commodity production"[57] that they propose to escape or negate, motivated by what amounts to a repetition compulsion indistinguishable in all other respects from that of commodification. In acquiring an ever-more "historical aura" as the transcendental signified of anti-capitalist revolt, the prestige commodity of "1968" – to which revolutionary discourse in the West has all-too-often come to refer for a kind of cultural permission (like Woodstock or the Apollo moon-landings) – becomes less & less distinguishable from every other sentimental wasteland of "No Future" populated by a race of its own reactionary abortions.

Epistemic Catastrophism. On this question, it is still worth revisiting Debord's post-'68 critique. He casts the political re-normalisation after May & the process of accelerated commodification in the light of revolutionary abortiveness as well as a re-mystification of what Soviet scientists were even then calling the Anthropocene – the totalised reification of "spectacle" wherein every utopia accomplishes its "gilded destitution." "The *cumulative reality* of the production in question," Debord writes, is "indifferent to utility or harmfulness" that, "far from slipping from view, returns in the form of pollution." For him, this *return from the utopian future* (of production reified as pollution) "is thus the calamity of bourgeois thought."[58] Moreover, it is a matter of a *zero degree* of separation between this "calamity" & the "prestige commodity of revolution itself" returned from the dustbin as the model of its own interminable recycling, from entropy to phantasmatic *re-production*. Bernard Stiegler's *Negenthropocene* is a case in point; historicism & an appeal to the "ethics" of counter-modernity (manual "work" versus "proletarianisation") merely restores the potential of catastrophe to be an engine of abstract spectacular production. Stiegler says: "The Anthropocene is an 'Entropocene,' that is, a period in which entropy is produced on a massive scale, thanks precisely to the fact that what has been liquidated & automated is knowledge, *so that in fact it is no longer knowledge at all*, but rather a set of *closed systems*, that is, *entropic systems*."[59]

Stiegler proposes *epistemic catastrophism* as *counter-agency*, and within this quasi-Foucauldian, anti-positivist positivism, "knowledge," liquidated as "big data," may still be reconstituted as an "open system" that "includes a capacity for dis-automatisation that produces negentropy.[60] In his 1968 response to the Paris Epistemological Circle, Foucault argued that "knowledge cannot be analysed in terms of knowledge; nor can positivity in terms of rationality; nor can the discursive formulation in terms of science. And one cannot ask that their description be equivalent to a history of knowledge, a genesis of rationality, or the epistemology of science."[61] For Stiegler, the phantasm of an epistemic totality is brought into direct collision with the event of a global cybernetic system enlarged to the dimensions of an all-encompassing futurity whose production is no longer history but entropy. In this equation, a generalised Accelerationism & Neganthropoetics are ostensibly equivalent, with each premised upon the counter-futurity of capitalism's self-supersession, & with each desiring to re-inscribe a mode of historical materialism where catastrophe isn't transcended but assumes the status of both agency & transcendental signified. If nothing else, it renders the paradoxical insistence that the Anthropocene is, *in any case*, "unsustainable."

"If there is to be a future," Stiegler argues, "& not just a becoming, the value of tomorrow will lie in the constitutive negentropy of the economy-to-come of the Neganthropocene." This economy would be produced by the "forming & setting-to-work" of "motor affects" distinct from "dis-affected calculation, which in the twenty-first century *becomes algorithmic*" (as if it hadn't been all along).[62] It is a matter of the "hermeneutic investment" of what Stiegler terms *traces*, of "differentiating from the new anti-political economy in & through a neganthropological différance whose operation *must* effect bifurcations – *after the default*."[63] United by a metaphysics of *default*, Negentropology & Accelerationism each objectify "revolutionary thought" as catastrophic agency – catastrophe as teleology. This dualistic movement parallels the internal *algorithmic* dynamics of the commodity in terms of simultaneous desiring-production & consumptive-waste, excess & pseudo-negation. *Sustainability* becomes a code word for a perpetual-motion machine operated, on the one hand, by a hyper-speculative futurism, & on the other, by a diachronically self-substituting present of "alternative" world scenarios. In the former, the Anthropocene is not only a *fait accompli* but an instrument of emancipation; in the latter, emancipation can only arise from its amelioration; in both, it's a question of *which* Anthropocene (negative or otherwise) is to be preferred & in what ways the Anthropocene might constitute a technology of *de facto* re-evolution. The problem is the relation of this "technology" (an *instrument* of an implied historical subject) to an ideologically predetermined set of outcomes (neganthropocene, total communism, etc.) that are valorised by an appeal to the geological-real (a reification of *hypercommodified excess*).[64]

In his 2016 "theory for the Anthropocene," *Molecular Red*, McKenzie Wark disputes the idea that the Anthropocene can be reduced to a geological *symptom* of collective human agency, insisting it can only be understood as a *situation* to which theory must respond by firstly engaging with its different "classes" of organisation.[65] For Wark, any theory of the Anthropocene is fraught with uncertainties, such as those stemming from the need to critique prior assumptions about the character of the "collective agency" that allegedly symptomatizes the Anthropocene. The primary uncertainty, however, resides in the assumption that such an agency can (continue to) be called capitalism, or that the quasi-revolutionary thought directed at its subversion, negation or transcendence should (or can) be made to resemble the thought of May 1968 or its latter-day cognates (e.g., the Anti-Nuclear movement, the Anti-Globalisation movement, the Occupy movement, the Anti-Austerity movement & so on, all in one way or another repeating the *incomplete project* of "1968").

When this isn't simply trivial, it has the air of *passéisme*, belatedly informed by a recognition that the "prestige commodity" of May 1968 already, & from its inception, bore (however unwittingly) the mark of *counter-revolutionary spectacle* behind which the desiring-production of Wheeler's cybernetic "universal revolution" could be detected beneath that mass of sentiment that its opponents swaddled themselves in. The critical impetus of 1968's *abortiveness* lies here, permeating (& determining) the entire project that led to *Anti-Oedipus*, & via the autonomist movement, persisting in that radical ambivalence upon which the various Accelerationist dichotomies have succeeded in erecting themselves. The question remains: How is the abortiveness of the specific "revolutionary idea" encapsulated in "1968" (immanent, spontaneous, foreclosed) to be reconciled to this *other revolution*? Can this (symbiotic) counterpart, contradiction, or subject be "internalised" in the *machinic surplus value* of its very representation?

From Revolution to Phantasmatic Re-Production. Well may it be said that LES RÉCOUPÉRATEURS SONT PARMI NOUS![66] While forms of abortiveness, however, appear bound to the (avant-gardist) dilemma of "third phase" revolutionary normalisation from within or expropriation from without (i.e., "revolutionary ideas" that are "permitted" by the Corporate-State Apparatus as long as they have no consequences beyond their commodifiability), it remains to be thought about on the same plane of immanence as revolutionary thought (rather than a Guattarian *external synthesis*). This doesn't occur at the point where revolution succumbs to algorithmic capture. The social algorithm of revolutionary desire is its *genetic inscription*, & the historical materialist trajectory of revolutionary failure cedes to a stochastic materialism of re-evolutionary "metabolic rift." Metabolic rift refers to ecological-crisis tendencies under capitalism, an idea Wark develops partly from Marx ("the irreparable rift in the independent processes of social metabolism"[67]), but mostly via the science fiction of Andrei Platonov & Alexander Bogdanov's *tektology*, to describe a mechanics of "redistribution without return" that underlies the production of the Anthropocene. The idea is a counterpoint to the general course of "capitalist critique" after 1968. Yet, where the Anthropocene stands as a kind of ideal, universalising horizon of post-'68 "abortivist" thought of the various belated Accelerationist & Negentropological types, for Wark, it points to a rift in the planetary code that implicates the logic of "revolutionary agency."

Since 1751, Wark notes, 400 billion tonnes of carbon have been released into the Earth's atmosphere while an estimated 1400 billion tonnes trapped under melting Arctic ice threaten to percolate up from newly formed lakes – a process already begun & visible from space. This radical redistribution of carbon isn't merely a symptom of a *world-out-of-balance* & a consequence of unregulated "anthropogenesis" that needs to be *aborted* in order to conserve a status quo with "nature." It is a systemic re-organisation whose base material character is brought into view through the disappearance of the Rousseauesque human/nature dichotomy. In a synthesis that recalls the anthropotechnics of La Metrie,[68] Platonov is enlisted in service of the idea that "nature is actually labour … it is already working on itself in its poverty" & thus "joins a human poverty to that of nature, human nature meets nature's labour, of which it is a metonymic part, not a metaphoric double." This line of argument broadly accords with the contemporary synergetics of Buckminster Fuller, the cybernetics of Norbert Wiener, & the mind-ecologies of Gregory Bateson in the West. In synthesising this approach with the idea of metabolic rift, the agent/catalyst relation is subverted in such a way that the classic Marxist base-superstructure schema is redrawn with carbon as the base & the Anthropocene as a superstructure. Ambivalent in its *form* to anything that might be called human design, the accelerated redistribution of carbon produces a "surplus, over & above life" as "the production of the means of existence."[69] Wark once more points to a transcendental *technē*. The question that arises here is how "life" can in any way continue to be distinguished from technicity in general.

Wark's interpretation extrapolates Debord's criterion of revolution (i.e., *knowledge converted into power*) by positing revolution in terms of a metaphysics of technology & a mechanistical pragmatics. By drawing out the proto-cybernetics of Bogdanov's "equivalence of experimental knowledge," Wark attempts to dissociate the idea of revolutionary agency from the social rationality of class/caste while retaining a technological binarism tacitly bound to those epistemological hierarchies that constantly threaten to return in a proliferation of machines & schemas. (Recall Deleuze & Guattari's *A Thousand Plateaus*, which might easily be read as a forecast of late-stage proliferation in the military-entertainment complex, cyberwarfare, dronology, mass automated surveillance, data aggregation & other parasitic-aggressive forms of contemporary "social media" & the politics of "World Order.") The drive to epistemological totalisation represented as the horizon of a "universal" cybernetics, on the other hand, seeks to reprise the movement of history as a calculus of ever-increasingly circumscribed probabilities. Between the two is a contest over what we might call the possibility of the possible: a "poetics" of stochastic materialism *constituted by the inherent ambivalences of binary/algorithmic logic* by which the ideological determinations of the epistemic control system are susceptible to non-causal perturbation. The implication is that an Anthropocenic metabolic rift describes that agency of "experimental knowledge" commensurate with the "critique" of a World System of cyber-capitalism. The question that remains is whether or not such an experimental knowledge may also constitute a (non-anthropic, revolutionary) agency in & of itself.

The conversion of experimental knowledge into *a countervailing and subversive force* (to globalisation's epistemic totality) is a radical lability with fluctuations that have become disordered by the normed coordinates of historical antagonism. It isn't a relation to the future horizon of an *End of the Present in its interminable, post-historical "phase"* (the abortion of the World as the abortion of "capitalism"). Nor is it *feedback through a history of accelerated industrialisation* that has, in any event, *already* characterised State Socialism's historical attempts to negate Western hegemony. This radical liability is less a war-machine than an entropy-machine, recalling (before Deleuze & Guattari) Blanqui's poetics of cyclic redundancy & the "eventful irruption of the possible within the real."[70] It is, in other words, a force of a dissipation internal to modernity as phantasmagoric repetition & revalorisation, encountered – as Marx says – in the epochal illusion of an "End" ("the dictatorship of the fait accompli").[71] Yet for the Anthropocene to be considered the latest ("ultimate") term in the signifying chain of modernity's self-contradictions – thereby superseding the Nazi *Todeslager* as the defining image of "rationalist" excess – we would have to duplicate the idea that "universal revolution," like universal history, "has no theoretical armature. Its method is additive, it musters a mass of data to fill the homogenous, empty time."[72] This would be equivalent to absolving its entire ideological system of any strategic operation without recognising that strategy is the logistical discourse *par excellence* of what Freud called repetition automation. The error has always been in the refusal to grasp universal history as an always-already *terminal* farce, from Ricardo's "iron-clad laws" to *The Triumph of the Will*, the "Eternal Soviet" & the neo-liberal "End of History."

But if the role of revolution is to produce this phantasm *in the real* & to repeat, as Foucault says, "the universal event in its extreme point of singularity," then what is this revolution if not "the event that befalls the phantasm & the phantasmatic repetition of the absent event"[73] (i.e., of history grieving its own recurrent disappearance)? This is the supposedly contradictory path that the "problem" of revolutionary thought – which represents (in its enactment) a *rupture with history* – has paved by drawing from capitalism the resources for its critique & ultimately its negation. In the convergence of a certain teleology upon the Anthropocene as the emergent "autonomous agent" of world-transformative-thought (in place of a "subject of history" & finally in place of history) – does such a topology not represent *in extremis* precisely that encounter between the phantasm & event to which "1968" bore only as much resemblance as a prehistoric child's toy? And does it not belie some catastrophic symptom *avant la lettre* of an imminent (& terminal) "technological singularity" in favor of a rupture-of-antecedence in the re-evolutionary form (universalised into a general condition) of the *im*-possible?

Prague, September 2018

10

DISPATCHES FROM THE EVENT HORIZON

Ce n'est pas la technique qui represent
le vrai danger pour la civilisation,
c'est l'énertie des structures.

Beguiled by the idea that a multiple-scenario universe means "alternative real-ities" that can be tuned in or out as a matter of convenience (or as a solution to whatever local or global crisis they choose to evoke), the mutant children of Buckminster Fuller & Ayn Rand have bequeathed social & ecological practices deeply at variance with their objectivist, progressivist & emancipatory claims. In this uncanny region between "Spaceship Earth" & *Atlas Shrugged*, there is no such thing as *immaterial labour*; every action is aggregated into the production of the Real, whether curated or elective, occult or flagrantly commodified. In so doing, the quasi-adversarial structure of this collectivity of fractured viewpoints accords with a principle of dynamic maximisation that William Blake deemed "enough or too much." The question that confronts us here is: How is it pos-sible to *anticipate* that ideal mode of operation – that advantageous balance between contending forces – of a World System contiguous with the so-called "dominion of Man"?

From the *Epic of Gilgamesh* to the Greek city state, Malthus & our contem-porary cybersphere, the concept of a natural "homeostatic" order has evolved into entirely unforeseen formulations. Where the "Eridu Genesis" evokes the prototypical Great Flood to correct human excess, the City State evokes a *technē politikē* (colonisation). Malthusianism, in turn, conjures built-in eugenic mechanisms in the balance between population & productivity that devolve to corporate-colonial exploitation & morph into redistributive autopoeitic *machines for living* (as in Ted Nelson's xanalogy & Lebbeus Woods' fusions of the Le Corbusian "Radiant City" & nomadism). It's sobering to consider that, when Aristotle sought to define sustainable population growth in the *Politics*, the size of the average Greek city state was 3-4,000 inhabitants, with Athens & Sparta representing the exception at approximately 10,000 apiece. By the advent of the Industrial Revolution, the city state was obviously no longer the political unit to account for growth. Nonetheless, mercantilism & the emerging predominance of corporate entities in political & economic life in Britain & elsewhere would continue to draw on the city state as a model for human resource management.

Patching Holes in the Escape Pod. In the early 1800s, one of the so-called fathers of British socialism, Robert Owen, proposed a reorganisation of the State on the principle of the semi-autonomous industrial polis. The Scottish mill town of New Lanark, which Owen managed, served as the paradigm. New Lanark housed a permanent workforce of approximately 1,200. Owen envisaged a national grid of some 400 similar entities, interspersed by agricultural zones, supporting a UK population of some 5.5 million people. By simple multiplication, these numbers would today represent an industrial polis of merely 14,000 against a total current UK population of 66 million. Unadorned comparisons of this kind expose the need to factor in those economies of scale consistent with two-&-a-half centuries of urban industrialisation; they also raise questions about the *political* sustainability of a socioeconomic system driven by an undisguised tendency towards obsolescence. With an increased efficiency in core production through automation that is matched to an inflationary growth of consumption, there still occurs a significant contraction in the industrial labour force against a rapid expansion of the general population.

Here arises the basic paradox of any constructed mercantile social system exposed to increasingly globalised economic pressures – what Moldbug calls Patchwork – as soon as it is evoked as an alternative model to a global socioeconomic system productive of climate-catastrophe & no-futurism. In Moldbug's formulation, this alternative amounts to a system of elective apartheid, "a global spiderweb of tens, even hundreds, of thousands of sovereign & independent mini-countries, each governed by its own joint-stock corporation."[1] This antithesis of a welfare state questions whether such a system is technically viable (or even desirable) once the social problem of human obsolescence is addressed (e.g., by broad-based consumer credit, service industries, etc.). But the real question is: If, through analogous "distributed systems" of communication & control, cybernetics radically evolves the mechanisms of population growth as conceived by Aristotle, producing what, on the face of it, appears to be the conditions for widespread "emancipation" from onerous labour, does it provide a political idea of what this growth is *for*?

If cybernetics purports to re-engineer the limits of collective human action by altering the ratios of environmental self-sustainability, this movement is nevertheless "compensated for" by the seemingly irrational tendency of free market capitalism to generate ever-increasing amounts of waste. The incongruity between efficiency & profit-incentive has grown to such dimensions as to define an entire globally-evolved system of entropy, one which threatens an immanent "homeostatic" readjustment on a planetary scale while, in a monstrous iteration of the commodity fetish, assuming the characteristics of an autonomous agency. Like the approaching "technological singularity" with which its evolution appears symbiotic, such a global system of entropy more & more acquires the character of a phenomenon independent of human control. This cybernetic doppelgänger has become detached from any *technē politikē* capable of halting (let alone regulating) its excesses. It appears to be driven by an inherent catastrophism. This, at least, might be described as the *conservationist* viewpoint – alarmed, if not by the environmental consequences, then by consequences that maintain a liberal-humanist status quo. From a broadly *accelerationist* perspective, this movement belongs to a globally-transformative, revolutionary force that heralds the "society to come." In anticipation of the latter, numerous templates have been proposed (e.g., Moldbug's joint-stock patchwork feudalism to open-source eco-social platforming,[2] distributed crypto-cybernetic systems of non-government, & full luxury communism). The price appears modest: the formal perfection of a "sixth mass extinction," the End-of-Life-as-we-know-it, the End-of-the-World even, or simply the End-of-Humanity & (who knows?) the beginning of a next evolutionary phase.

What does not feature in this prognosis is the End of the Corporate-State Apparatus, which is holographically propagated under the guise of an Ayn Rand ego-franchise of so-called voluntarist libertarianism.

Politically, the cybernetic revolution left no alternatives on the table. What we call the global order is a full-spectrum capitalist technocracy whose market harmonisation belies a system of exploitative & grossly unequal social & environmental relations. The technocracy hides behind the false dichotomies of democracy & totalitarianism. These dichotomies have more in common with each other than their ruling classes have with the mass of their populations or than their consumptive social systems have with the environment's capacity to support them. Such naked irreconcilables have contributed to a return to political resistance on the margins of the "permitted,"[3] spanning the Black Bloc & the CyberGuerrilla Column to populist "anti-movements" like Extinction Rebellion & the Gilets Jaunes. But by their representation (or non-representation in the political imaginary), these forms of resistance are always made to entail a paradox in terms of the desire to subvert the Corporate State while simultaneously resurrecting (if only by the formality of protest) the idea of a benevolent welfare state (called upon to compassionately self-supersede or reform). On the one hand, it is an abolition or an opting-out; on the other, it is a procedural reconstitution. Subversion, in any case, is always an operation from "within" a relation to the Law.

The real character of this paradox can be gauged by examining the logistical obstacles that the cybernetic revolution has placed in the path of autonomous political action.[4] Yet the political task posed by the Anthropocene can too easily be obfuscated by sheer statistics, magnifying the convulsions of that Great Anonymous, as Victor Hugo wrote, which is always found "in human crises & in social births."[5] If such a debilitating movement is a *fait accompli*, it simultaneously evokes the statistical complexities solely accessible to cybernetic understanding.

We can see how such a situation might appear emancipative within the frame of reference of a humanist project that imagines it has succeeded in transcending its worldly conditions by means of pure *technē*.

But in speaking this way, can we even know, first of all, what the Anthropocene is?

If we accede in the idea that the Anthropocene defines a *geological* epoch materially inscribed as the historical accumulation of technology defined against the history of industrialisation, we make it appear as if the agent of the present crisis (i.e., the *crisis of the present*) isn't the ideological system that produced it. Instead, it becomes some calamitous non-human agency that can only be appeased, if not brought under the yoke. A *Götterdämmerung* marks the great revolutionary event of "our" time. We must either succeed in overthrowing the planetary gods or sacrifice ourselves to them – whether it be the revolt against the "World" or against capitalism. Like all false choices, these too are ideologically inscribed. They mask the movement of capital as both the technological transcendence of *this* world & the promise of the one *to come*. In the contest between neoliberalism & its discontents, capital has come to designate both the "concrete form" of this crisis & its only possible "negation." The return of the geologic "real" (now named the Anthropocene) is nothing less than capital's reification as a *planetary agency* that inscribes a global destiny of its own as inexorable as plate tectonics. This is neoliberalism's masterful *fait accompli*.

The End Always Comes Before its Time. The problem of the Anthropocene is the problem of the *fait accompli*: the *logic capture of an entire world* in all its "alternative" scenarios. Here the Anthropocene approximates a singularity – the singularity of history, we might say – or as Hegel & Marx (ventriloquised by Fukuyama) would say, the End of History. Jena in 1807, Paris in 1848, the Fall of the Berlin Wall in 1989 were all premature signals,[6] but the point is surely moot since, in positing itself as such an End, this *fait accompli* always arrives "before its time" & will be the last thing anyone remembers. It marks the return of the proverbial repressed from beyond the event horizon: the uncanny doppelgänger of a "universal anachronism." *Time out of joint.* Like that endlessly extruded present of "post-ideology" that neoliberalism *still* pretends to be, the anachronism inhabits our World View like a vertically-integrated crisis balanced on a pinhead. The tipping point is right there in a Future that doesn't exist but already happened & must be deferred at any cost. "Beyond" lies the unpresentable, the impossible, that most ideal of all Possible Worlds to which the word "Future" corresponds solely to the extent that it represents an *end* to the spectral existence of history & an *end* to a certain political *possibility* of history.[7] This neo-evangelist mesmerism by *ultimate ends* goes beyond mere Hegelian "theory" & "bewitches" the teleology of power. Henceforth power's hegemony becomes *destined* to be what must necessarily *befall* every possible present to come (as though it were an emissary of this Non-Future). It also becomes the *manifestation* of non-futurity (its "being," so to speak, as if to distinguish from its "signifier").

In the final instance, however, this most extraordinary *fait accompli* – the singularity of the World refracted through the supposed *manifestation* & *transcendence* of its own End ("world without," etc.) – reveals nothing other than the spectacle of power (history) converging with its ideal image (technicity). In this cosmic micro-drama, the supervening spectre of capital, a "production of phantasms" & a "phantasmatic mode of production,"[8] returns not *in place of the Real* (its transcendental signified) but *as the production of the Real "as such."* Yet its anachrony means that this movement of totalisation describes a feedback loop, an interminable circuit of sign-substitution in which the Return of the Real is "suspended" like a premonition – the premonition of the "as such." Call it a metaphor-of-metaphor, irreducible along the vector of its algorithmic freefall. Event horizon. Blackhole metaphysics. History & World, sign & concept all converge in this "ideal" (because unpresentable) anachronism of which capital nevertheless produces an "image."[9] In its desire to inhabit the "as such," we might begin to imagine that capital *produces* this irreducibility as both "sameness within self-difference" & "sameness as the non-identical."[10] Capital is the *persistence* of this irreducibility in spite of the appearance of an insistent dialecticism that causes it to assume the form of a *return* "in the Real."

Groundwork for Zero Gravity. Let's suppose that this *irreducibility* signifies in the Anthropocene *both* the failure of capital's totalising movement *to accomplish itself* & the contrary (marked by this *failure*).

The "return of the Real" in the form of a *fait accompli* consequently acquires the form of a *return of the Impossible* (capital's impossible "ideality" reified as the "future impossibility" of the World). We might say that capital returns *in its "pure" form* in the Anthropocene. In this sense, both the Impossible & the End-of-Capitalism consists not, as Žižek suggests, in a conceptual failure to *imagine a world without capitalism*, but the contrary: in capital's own failure to *ideally produce itself* (the dream of communism). What appears in this formulation to be somehow revelatory is that the logic of capital is vested in this fundamental incommensurability as a *dynamic interval* & a source of every operation of power, value & information whose desire to internalise by a paradoxical reification (under the sign of an absolute self-sufficiency) causes it to resemble the insuperable *alienation* of the Freudian *Ego-Ideal*. In the *Grundrisse*, Marx correctly surmises that this alienation is the inauguration & the constitutive condition of the "individual."[11] Its movement "isn't something that happens to a transcendental subject: it produces a subject."[12]

This is why we must guard ourselves against the kind of thinking that would reduce the problem of the Anthropocene (& of capital in general) to one of "concrete situations" versus "mere abstractions."

In producing a subject alongside the representation of an Ego-Ideal, the logic of capital disseminates in a broadly isomorphic movement that gives rise to what we might call, somewhat ironically, the *consciousness of the Real.* This "consciousness" constitutes ideology. Not one ideology or another (capitalism, socialism, communism, etc.),[13] nor any privileged ideology above all others (in the presumptive form of an ideology-of-ideology like Judeo-Christian Islam), but the possibility of a system of signification. It disseminates in this way because capital is ambivalent with regard to supposed "ideological content" & is concerned solely with the leveraging of value; its structures have evolved accordingly & in such complex multiplicity that they can only be described as universal. This universality must somehow be reconciled with the perception of capital as monolithic, a vision of "globalisation" fixated upon an image of One World: the convergence of all possibility upon a singular End. If such a convergence only *appears* to be mediated by the so-called Anthropocene, however, it is because the "consciousness of the Real" to which the logic of capital gives rise is *not* the reflection of an Ego-Ideal. To this anthropomorphism, too, it remains fundamentally ambivalent since it "itself" is not a *reflection of* but a generalised *reflection-effect.* Virtually nothing separates this consciousness from technicity.

The Weird & the Global. What, then, is this Anthropocene in which a consciousness of the Real manifests *technologically*?

Quantum research has arrived at the somewhat belated supposition that reality is *information*, which it qualifies by adding that information is in turn *produced by consciousness* (i.e., by some form of observational event, some mechanism or valency productive of a determinate state from a superposition of probabilities). Translated into the social realm, an analogy may be established via Žižekian parallax whereby "an 'epistemological' shift in the subject's point of view always reflects an 'ontological' shift in the object itself."[14]

If we ask "What is the state of the World?" it appears we are posing both a theoretical question & a question about the Earth's material condition. One might appear political, the other geological (or even cosmological), yet both are addressed first of all to their own descriptive systems; & the "World" to which these systems correspond is co-dependent & ideological, although not in the concerted sense of a mass hallucination, in the purely doctrinal sense of a "world view," or even an epistemology. If ideology is the consciousness of the Real, it is so in a manner that is profoundly uncanny with regard to conventional notions of what constitutes "reality." This is because the "symbolic order" that corresponds with consciousness is *emergent*[15] & not determined by what we imagine a "rational" causality to be.

Should we posit the Anthropocene, therefore, as the *negative consciousness* of a Non-Future that represents its own failed transcendence? As a consciousness that doesn't correspond to an objective correlative of human agency or to any type of *emancipation* from "capitalist subjectivity," but rather its inscription as the "thought of the impossible"? What would the subject of such a thought be?

If the limits of the World are those of ideology, then there is nothing *abstract* about ideological operations. By the same token, the work of *abstraction* defines the real. When we ask "What is *the* state of the World?" we are asking about the state of the descriptive system, which is our frame of reference. In other words, we are asking about the relation of subjectivity to consciousness. Ideology isn't some kind of subject*ivism* that projects onto the World. As the (non)correlation of subjectivity & consciousness, the World describes a mobile semiosphere, a *poiēsis*, whose holographic "surface of sense" may be said to affect what has been called "global weirding."[16] This "weirding" is a *patchwork* of discrete valences producing a composite *image of reality* that remains uncanny with relation to "itself." It "is" the event horizon of all information pertaining to a World that does not *appear* as "the World," which, as Wittgenstein says, is *everything that is the case* – not (only) as it is perceived, but as it consists in its "possibility."

Global weirding isn't a glitch in the World. It's the mode of operation of a World *that has become impossible*. What is *glitched* is the relationship between the way these operations signify & the ideological character of the descriptive systems applied to them. The World, after all, in either its possibility or impossibility, is *emergent information* & not some transcendental entity.[17]

One of the disconcerting features of ideology is that, rather than describe a deleuzoguattarian *delirium*, it describes the *constitutive condition* of any descriptive system. What Lacan calls the symbolic order is precisely such a contiguity with that "fundamental fantasy" of experience which, in Freud, elides with reason. Consequently, an unwelcome thesis emerges: in place of the Blakean "eternal contraries," the "irreconcilable antagonisms" of class conflict, & the dialectical supersessions of history & technology, there is only a *smeared-out* topology of superpositions. These so-called Possible Worlds are brought into being or abolished under the critical mass of consciousness. They are fundamentally irreconcilable to anything more "Real," more *totalisable*, than their own status as information.

From Revolution to *Ricorso*. When we speak of "the World," then, we are speaking of a global patchwork of "delocalised" subsystems[18] in which "other worlds" end all the time. But is that enough to affect a politics beyond vague appeals to terms like "salvage," "sustainability," survival" & "supersession"?

By themselves, such patchworks do not perform a demystification of the "ideological construction" of the global any more than a pixelated universe represents a disillusionment of "smooth space." Patchwork, like pixelation, makes the perception of smoothness *possible*. It does so by defining a minimum interval or minimum difference from which the "fabric of the World" is comprised. This is how "alienated subjectivity" constitutes the minimum political *unit*, not because it is in any way more *fundamental* than, say, the commodity, but because the logic & structure of commodification originates in it, just as the logic & structure of the *social* originates in it. That both of these possibilities occur simultaneously goes some way towards accounting for the inherent "weirdness" of the political that permits classical market capitalism to give rise to global neoliberalism & the thought of its transcendental recapitulation into world socialism. This is not the same thing, however, as the concerted effects of "weirding" produced *by* such ideological antagonism.[19]

Such *weirdness* nowhere permeates contemporary political discourse more than on the question of the Anthropocene. Here, the movement of history, as Marx notoriously conceived it, has strayed beyond the tragic & farcical into the domain of the sublime, which is encapsulated in the title of Servigne, Stevens & Chapelle's recent critique of globalisation, *Un autre fin du monde est* possible,[20] a quasi-Situationist détournement of those optimistic 1968 slogans about alternative futures *without capitalism*. This isn't quite the same thing as McKenzie Wark's reflection (vis-à-vis Rosa Luxembourg) that "it used to be 'socialism or barbarism' ... Now it's 'barbarism or barbarism.'"[21] In one form or another, the End-of-the-World has always served as a teleological reference point. *Barbarism à la mode*.

But if the recurrence of this trope in the present owes a specific historical debt to a European "civilising" project, it's mostly due to the considerable resources it directed towards constructing an idea of One World that, to paraphrase Hegel, would be seen everywhere & always reflected.[22] An image of the sublime would thus be destined, like so much Romantic poetry, to be sabotaged by its own worst metaphor: the pathetic fallacy of transcendent "Man." Discontented with what it saw, it became desirous of *alternative worlds*, *alternative civilisations*, *alternative natures* (all to its own specifications, of course).The entire project of western humanism can be regarded as an education in rational barbarism, wresting the End-of-the-World from the grip of "irrational gods" via compulsory mass industrialisation. There is nothing at all *uncanny* about the present "world crisis." It is the business of humanism to endow every crisis of its own making with an all-too-familiar productivist, materialist vector,[23] thereby providing the occasion for its next magical act of transcendence. Call it the eternal return of the Posthuman. As Lautréamont might have said, the End-of-the-World is necessary – progress implies it.

Prague, January 2019

11

TRANS/MORPHIC

All of the writing of Jorge Luis Borges, an inveterate hoaxer & forger, is both an investigation & parody of monadic thought & of its various cognates in the realms of mysticism, psychology, allegorical history & the literary sciences. Monadism is a system of generic totalities in a crucial relation to the operations of randomness (or overdetermination) & the "always-already" internally bifurcated nature of singularities. Borges' 1949 collection of short fiction, *El Aleph*, is the most explicit pursuit of this project, announced already in the book's title, which refers to a point in space & time that contains all space & all time simultaneously. About one-third of the way from the end of the collection, two texts stand out in a complementary or symbiotic relation to each other & to the question of the monad: "El Zahir" & "La escritura del dios" (i.e., "The Writing of the God"). The former includes a description of a prison cell in Mysore State, India, "on whose floor, walls & vaulted ceiling a Moslem fakir had designed (in fantastic colours, which time, rather than erasing, refined) of an infinite tiger. It was a tiger composed of many tigers, in the most dizzying of ways; it was criss-crossed with tigers, striped with tigers & included seas & Himalayas & armies that resembled tigers. The painter had died many years before, in that same cell."[1] "La escritura del dios" centres on the figure of an actual tiger (a jaguar) incarcerated in an actual prison cell, which it shares across a partition with an Aztec priest named Tzinacán. Tzinacán is a victim of Alvarado, a conquistador who devotes his remaining days to deciphering the pattern on the wild cat's fur. Alvarado "foresee[s] that at the end of time many disasters & calamities would befall … [A legendary god] had written a magical phrase, capable of warding off those evils. He wrote it in such a way that it would pass down to the farthest generations, & remain untouched by fate." Tzinacán believes that the god's phrase is encoded in plain view within the tiger's stripes. In an accomplishment rivalling the greatest feats of literary insanity, Tzinacán claims to have deciphered the phrase:

> It is a formula of fourteen random (apparently random) words, & all I would have to do to become omnipotent is speak it aloud. Speaking it would make this stone prison disappear, allow the day to enter my night, make me young, make me immortal, make the jaguar destroy Alvarado,

bury the sacred blade in Spanish breasts, rebuild the Pyramid, rebuild the empire. Forty syllables, fourteen words, & I, Tzinacán, would rule the lands once ruled by Moctezuma. But I know that I shall never speak those words, because I no longer remember Tzinacán.[2]

Absolute Language. Borges' tiger is "really" a kind of genome, a *matrix* of potential significations existing in a morphogenetic spacetime continuum with the *divine archetype*, the *first permutation*, the recursive tiger of all tigers. Inscribed in its form is the index of creation, or at least a talisman against disaster & calamity, the word of words, etc., etc.:

> I reflected that in the language of a god every word would speak that infinite concatenation of events, & not implicitly, but explicitly, & not linearly but instantaneously ... A god, I reflected, must speak but a single word, & in that word there must be absolute plenitude. No word uttered by a god could be less than the universe, or briefer than the sum of time. The ambitions & poverty of human words — all, world, universe – are but shadows of simulacra of that Word which is the equivalent of a language & all that can be comprehended within a language.[3]

The force of this absolute language, however, remains a mere hypothesis, a *potentiality* within the (actual) world. Each of its words nevertheless corresponds to (or *is no less than*) the world, but in its concatenation resides an impossible excess: *more* than the world, *more* than the sum of time. *At the same time*, this potential is described by Borges' protagonist as, in addition, encompassing the *antithesis* of the world, which is an instrument of its *uncreation*, of transposition or transcription into a parallel universe of contrary states of affairs (the Anti-Conquista). Each unworld equates to one among a series of shadowy simulacra, of *language* & "all that can be comprehended within a language." All this is rendered moot because, among other things, Tzinacán has acquired the indifference of godhead upon discovering the divine xenotext's secret formula of "fourteen random (apparently random) words."

Is it for the sake of a self-propagating stratagem that an absolute language *encompassing* the totality of space & time assumes the *appearance* of randomness? Is such a stratagem construed as an afterthought? Is it a counter-measure against those already foreseen "dissenters & calamities" that must necessarily accompany the disaster of the end of time? Is this the descent of the apparently infinite into teleology? Insofar as this language constitutes its own message, its addressee can be none other than teleology, standing in relation to an ideal doppelgänger: the *post*man to the divine *pen*man, to borrow a Joycean formulation. Is not Tzinacán more than simply a priest or reader of heavenly signs? Is he not the god in its embodied, dialectical progress towards self-consciousness, just as the posthumous author of "El Zahir" is the creator of this same divinity, like some negentropic *demon* producing signifying multiplicities from an arbitrary & otherwise undifferentiated state of solitary incarceration? "Little by little," Borges writes, "a man comes to resemble the shape of his destiny; a man is, in the long run, his circumstances."[4] Are a tiger's stripes legible in the sense that they are *like a language* & therefore bear the appearance of being susceptible to a hermeneutic (other than that masqueraded by insanity)? This is not the question.

Consider Wittgenstein's famous dicta: "If a lion could speak we could not understand it" & "The limits of my language are the limits of my world."[5] It might seem a simple reprise of these dicta to suggest that, in comprehending the anagogic character of the tiger by the morphogenesis of its stripes, that the author of "El Zahir" & Tzinacán the Aztec priest have each been translated beyond themselves to *another world.* What concerns us here, however, among the metaphors of agency & worldfulness, is the mechanism & *prior possibility* of this morphogenesis *as such.*

Turing Patterns. In theoretical biology, a tiger's stripes are sometimes referred to as a "Turing pattern." The attribution derives from a 1952 paper by Alan Turing on "The Chemical Basis of Morphogenesis."[6] Turing discusses the mechanism by which a complex system of structures or patterns may emerge from otherwise homogenous states due to spontaneously occurring instability in the homogenous equilibrium. The "material" of these homogenous states are "morphogens," a term intended to convey the idea of a form-producer. "It is not intended to have any very exact meaning, but is simply the kind of substance concerned in this theory."[7] A morphogen is analogous to those "intermediate particles" (e.g., gluons, photons & bosons) that carry a force – in this case, the *force* of morphogenesis or form-production, although Turing doesn't speak of them that way. This touches upon the question of the *medium* of sense (e.g., the production of language as an action *not* metaphysically determined). Between Borges' two stories, morphogenesis is the author (i.e., the form-producer) of the divine iteration, the *logos,* whose teleology it is. There is no ultimate external element, no *eidos* to which the system refers for its meaning that doesn't already belong to the *mythos* of its self-propagation. The text's ontogenesis derives not from any stable point of reference, of identity; it emerges from no point of being or becoming that isn't already a *perturbation* on the basis of its (intermediate) materiality. As the Song dynasty philosopher Zhuang Zhou once wrote: "All the creatures of this world have dimensions that cannot be calculated."

For Borges, the question hinges upon the trope of creation *ab nihil*: the divine action of producing the world/word as if from "nothing." What gives rise to the potential of a morphogen to produce morphogenesis if not morphogenesis? To ask, therefore, if language is a Turing pattern isn't to equate a 14-word permutation code with a tiger's stripes, but to examine the shared possibility of each to present the appearance of an ordered structure produced out of random interactions of matter. But just as matter possesses intermediate characteristics that, only under specific observational conditions, coincide with any determinate *thingness* & remain a function of probability, so too do Turing's morphogens remain a *theoretical substance* that could just as readily be designated by the term *différance* (Derrida)[8] or *infrathin* (Duchamp).[9] In effect, a "difference minimum" would result from the passing of a random, near-uniform, or equilibrium state into a nonequilibrium state, from ambivalence to *ambiviolence* (Joyce).[10] This "difference minimum" haunts Borges' narrators: it doesn't so much escape or evade a hermeneutics as it constitutes a paradoxical impetus & the phantasm of an object. In psychoanalysis, this is the mark of the polymorphously perverse, which is the movement (*vers*) that engenders form-production, both *in tension with* & *as a function of* the entropic tendency to "normalisation" (i.e., equilibrium).

Mythopoetics. In "El Zahir," the titular figure is a polymorphous fetish object, a *signifier* & an *enablement of a signifying relation* between an apparently random, shapeless impulse & the assumption of a (teleological) form. For Freud, the object exists between the libido or sexual drives & some provisional or phantasmatic object to which it appears to have a *non-essential* relation that isn't predetermined by a "biological function." Borges writes:

> In Buenos Aires the Zahir is a common twenty-centavo coin into which a razor or letter opener has scratched the letters NT & the number 2; the date stamped on the face is 1929. (In Gujarat, at the end of the eighteenth century, the Zahir was a tiger; in Java it was a blind man in the Surakarta mosque, stoned by the faithful; in Persia, an astrolabe that Nadir Shah ordered thrown into the sea; in the prisons of Mahdi, in 1892, a small sailor's compass, wrapped in a shred of cloth from a turban, that Rudolf Karlvon Slatin touched; in the synagogue in Córdoba, according to Zotenberg, a vein in the marble of one of the twelve hundred pillars; in the ghetto in Tetuán, the bottom of a well.)[11]

This ambivalence in the transmigrations of the zahir inevitably gives rise to speculations about divinity (a metaphor of totality) or schizophrenia (the tendency, in the coinage of Klaus Conrad, to *apophenia*: the *false* perception of relations between otherwise unconnected phenomena). The zahir is the proverbial god-particle that produces formal connections across space & time in an increasingly universal array. We are duly informed by Borges' narrator that, "[i]n Arabic, 'zahir' means visible, manifest, evident; in that sense, it is one of the ninety-nine names of God; in Muslim countries, the masses use the word for 'beings or things which have the terrible power to be unforgettable, & whose image eventually drives people mad.'" In short, the zahir is the outward aspect of the infinite, whose apprehension is, *ipso facto*, the paradigm of madness. It encompasses what, in quantum physics, is often referred to as the observer paradox, which supposes that an object's "reality" (i.e., its objectness) is determined by the act of observation. Otherwise "it" exists solely in the "formlessness" of a probability field or superposition in which a "particle" may be in an arbitrary number of "discrete" positions simultaneously. This superposition is unobservable, & by causing it to collapse into a *single* discrete position, observation can thus be understood as *form-production*: a superposition *is not a physical object*.

Borges relates this back to the question of language – to representation & unrepresentability, & to the *poetic* function of the signifier in its potential for morphogenesis drawn from an underwriting *ambivalence*. In the logic of Russell & Whitehead, Borges transposes *exceptions* to the system of linguistic meaning (i.e., all forms of ambiguity) into the centre of that system as what orientates & determines its operations. ("In the rhetorical figure known as *oxymoron*, the adjective applied to a noun seems to contradict that noun. Thus, Gnostics spoke of the 'dark light' & alchemists, of a 'black sun.'"[12]) While this contributes to a certain aesthetics of irreality in Borges' writing, the point is that these "rhetorical" effects are not an aberration in the signifying economy but marks of its precondition. As a *mode of production*, Borges reiterates, reality "itself" is abstract, like money, signifying a relation to some future state where a debt of meaning falls due ("money is future time"[13]). It appears to operate by a kind of magical insurance against its own finitude. "El Zahir" ends with the speculation that "perhaps behind the coin is God"[14] – the totality of space & time, absolute "value," etc., etc., etc. It's not by chance that, in addition, *zahir* bears an uncanny resemblance to the word *az-zahr*, the Arabic term for *dice* & one of the possible etymologies of *hasard*, or the "apparently random." Recall that well-known line from Mallarmé: "Un coup de dés jamais n'abolira le hasard" ("A throw of dice will never abolish chance").

Hysteresis. In quantum mechanics, reality is observer-dependent, and observed states are future-determined in a recursively continuous fashion. This apparent retrocausation (sometimes referred to as two-state-vector formalism) raises important questions about classical time-symmetry & the unidirectional character of entropy, which recent experimental results in quantum thermodynamics (& not merely Borgesian fictions) have shown cannot be treated as an absolute concept.[15] In the 1890s, James Alfred Ewing coined the term *hysteresis* to describe the behaviour of certain systems (e.g., magnetic fields) whose states exhibit dependence upon the system's history. Hysteresis has been associated with irreversible thermodynamic processes. Derived etymologically from ὑστέρησις ("deficiency, lagging behind"), Ewing's term nevertheless evokes a condition of anachrony in which a certain historical "time-lag" points to feedback from states seemingly *yet to be arrived at*. Such anachrony demands that the idea of "history" is separated from a simple linearity. Causation is not vested in a succession of events or even retroactively inscribed; rather, it is a concatenation, a *discontinuous change* of state (i.e., history as montage). Thus we have the constellated "identity" of the zahir, whose recurrence in Borges' story marks an itinerary of superpositions, & whose causal echoes resound bidirectionally so that, in a violation of the statistical mantra, correlation implies causation. "A man," as Borges writes, "comes to resemble the shape of his destiny." And what is this "man," after all, but a certain concatenation of events defining a paranoiac system *in which meaning will always find its language*. Lacan calls it the *"thing* that thinks": "Implicitly, modern man thinks that everything which has happened in the universe since its origin came about so as to converge on this thing which thinks ... which is this privileged vantage-point called consciousness."[16]

In *Critique of Cynical Reason*, Sloterdijk casts the sovereignty of humanistic reason, a paradigm of the negative that, as if by default, is at the epicentre of the phenomenal universe: "the sovereignty of minds," he states, "is always false."[17] At best, it constitutes a set of "psychosomatic coordinates of pain & pleasure."[18] Yet a *false binary* (a "cynical" negation-of-negation) erupts between the figure of the sovereign & the primordial subject. By an implicit movement of algorithmic ramification & truth/falsity, this binary is designed to exclude from its "critique" the possibility that, as Artaud puts it, "thought is a secretion of matter."[19] The question of the subject always pertains to the question of history, & no deconstruction of the one can proceed without a deconstruction of the other. This *thing that thinks* by a process of *secretion* can only be posed as the unpresentable "meaning" expressed by language or thought – not "thought" conceived in any humanistic sense, but as in Borges' formulation, the sheer concatenation of space & time. Wittgenstein says that we cannot comprehend it. But "we" are *comprehended by it*. Similarly, the Turing patterns in the tiger's stripes should not be regarded as the *object* of a hermeneutics. They are the mode of production of a *form of lability* that negates the *subject as such*. In "The Writing of the God," Tzinacán ceases to be Tzinacán precisely when "he" enters a state of ambivalence.

Alien Entities. Within the framework of a humanism, the "thing that thinks" is destined to retain the status of a fetish. So the question of a morphogenesis in which matter is *spontaneously* entroped, giving rise to a generalised *autopoiēsis*, can only remain a *mystification*. Like paranoia, fetishism re-centres the world in the subject; *everything* is potentially a representative of its desire or of its regard. What is erased in fetishism is, according to Rancière, "the structural implication that founds the distance of the thing from itself, a distance which is precisely the site at which the economic relations are at play."[20] The *autonomy* of these relations remains in question, since in Rancière's formulation, as in Sloterdijk's, this *distancing* is an historical (or pseudo-evolutionary/teleological) movement. Consequently, Rancière is compelled to state: "What *passes into* the thing is not the essence of subjectivity but a relation."[21] The *thing* is always & in all respects the *receptacle* of a *subjective relation*, even as we speak of its existence *in the absence of a subject*. Thus, while "it is not a subject which is separated from itself, whose predicates pass into an alien entity," it is still "a form which becomes alien to the relation that it supports &, in becoming alien to it, *becomes a thing* & leads to the *materialisation of relations.*"[22]

In Rancière's critique, this *secretion of subjectivity* is bound up with a Marxian/ Hegelian terminology of *alienation, reification* & the (fetishistic) *self-valorisation of capital.* It's never simply a "matter" of inverting that single-point perspective whereby the human observer has come to be regarded as "catalyst of the universe" (Artaud).[23] To travel out through the eye, into the world – certain mental forces are supposed to be exercised upon *matter* according to that spectrum of phenomena called *action.* Such metaphysics has always presupposed a master discourse of the human avatar, a privileged agent of that fiat economy derived from & animated by the heavenly logos. This is its archetypal *economic relation*, the substance of its "economimesis" (Derrida).[24] A necessary probability within purely stochastic processes, its materialist counterpart fixes upon the implication of the *human* within a universal teleology, such as the humanist approximation of the Fermi paradox (vis-à-vis the Drake equation, which sets a high probability for the existence of extraterrestrial life despite a complete lack of evidence for any such existence). Still, both the work of probability & the task of observation can be accomplished without the intercession of any human agent whatsoever. This is the irony of Drake's extraterrestrial hypothesis. While quantum has long determined that *observation* is an action detached from any subjectivity, however, its implications need also to be extended to an understanding of hysteresis as well as "history" & "historical materialism." The precarity of the "human" as an ideological category lies in the assault upon its self-privileging purview on the *soi-disant* universal condition, in its tenuous claims over "intelligence," & in the substance of its "reality."

Resonance. In the quantum view of reality, there is no objective *durée*. There is only a non-unitary, non-local concatenation of observational events or *phenomena*,[25] marking an itinerary between episodes of superpositional "collapse" & reversion to superposition, "the apparent vanishing of particles in one place at one time – & their reappearance in other times & places."[26] This itinerary is prospectively & retrospectively subject to (its own) causal influence.[27] There is only an appearance of *durée*, of historical continuity or time-evolution, under conditions of attenuated observation (a quantum Zeno effect). Combined with quantum Darwinism – the idea that observed quantum states are "selected" on a principle of statistical viability (even if this selection is unpredictable beyond a certain probability) – what is commonly thought of as the historical-real in fact describes something like a Turing Pattern or morphogenesis whose constituents (morphogens) remain *provisional*. Borges' analogy between the tiger's stripes & an "apparently random" 14-word permutation code raises the prospect that "history" is a matrix or probabilistic space-time generator. (The number 14 is a recurring figure in Borges, a kind of categorical maximum, just as there are, e.g., fourteen possible Bravais lattices[28] that fill three-dimensional space). The *apparent* randomness of the encoded words "mirrors" the *imaginary* relation to the pattern of the jaguar on which the "divine script" mirrors the symbolic function of this imago. Each possible itinerary or permutation would thus *determine* a possible world as well as the universe that constitutes that world in all of its potential spatial & temporal configurations. In this sense, each morphogen is a Cantorian set of *other* possible morphogens (words/worlds) in a recursive genesis that phenomenalises the "real," as if out of a distributed lattice or Turing pattern of superposition & collapse.[29] These morphogenetic pathways don't describe but *affect* a hysteresis, which can be viewed as the frequency or internal resonance that transmits the pathology of its *form*. This reflexive itinerary can be construed as "thought" secreted by matter that retains its secret, an enigmatic cipher that admits only of an "apparently random" key in which the idea & possibility of presentation annihilates itself. In its ineffability, something recognises itself, constitutes itself in an impossible act of recognition as the self-similarity of a spontaneous (i.e., autocatalytic), indeterminate & unpredictable event. For this "living paradox," *the same* will always-already have "broken apart."

Prague, September 2020

12

XENOTEXT

Life: The Perfect Malware. Rotating once every seven hours, the spectral Cg-type object resembles, as the spacecraft approaches it, a dark kilometre-wide diamond-in-the-rough. In 2015, the Minor Planet Centre designated it "162173 Ryūgū" in reference to a Japanese fable about a magical underwater dragon's palace. In the fable, the palace is a time-machine, & inside the walls, one day it corresponds to a century in the outside world. The object rotating in space is also a time-machine: an asteroid of the Apollo group, designated as "potentially hazardous," meaning its 474-day passage around the sun transects Earth's orbit. There is the possibility that one day in the future the two will collide.

On the monitors at JAXA mission control,[1] Ryūgū spins slowly along its vertical axis in digital timelapse. The camera tracks it from a distance of 400 kilometres to a final approach of 20, the image resolving into a sudden sharp focus. A prominent crater stands out of the asteroid's equator; it appears something has landed there before. The spacecraft, Hayabusa2, powered by ion thrusters, completes its approach on 27 June 2018. Its mission is to collect multiple sub-surface mineral samples & return them to Earth by the year 2020. A Reuters news bulletin marking the occasion recycles the standard PR line: "Asteroids are believed to have formed at the dawn of the solar system & scientists say Ryūgū may contain organic matter that may have contributed to life on Earth." It may also, as if *incidentally*, present a viable opportunity for future asteroid mining.

Two scenarios, then: on the one hand, a time-machine possibly bearing secrets of celestial human origins; on the other, a potentially resource-rich stepping-stone to a hyper-Anthropocenic, space-faring future.

"Life," @christianbok tweeted three days later, "is the perfect malware for infecting the computations of matter." It could easily have meant that the "search for life" is an ideal alibi for extending semiocapitalism's horizons into outer space, or simply that capital (& only nominally "space technology") is already *alien life*. It's a matter of no small significance to such speculations that travelling aboard the Hayabusa2 on its mission to Ryūgū – among an array of cameras, sampling devices, impactors, landers & rovers – is a digital payload incorporating Christian Bök's *The Xenotext*. *American Scientist* described the outcome of this 15-year project as a combination of "poetry, cryptography &

bioengineering." *Engadget* blog (alluding to Blaise Cendrars' 1913 simultanéiste masterpiece) called it "prose at the end of the universe."

The Xenotext isn't the first cultural artefact to have journeyed off-world. In 1972 & 1973, at the behest of Carl Sagan, the Pioneer 10 & 11 space probes were fitted with gold-anodized aluminium plaques featuring nude male & female human figures & symbolic diagrams designed to communicate information about the spacecraft's origin. In 1977, Voyagers 1 & 2 each carried a gold-plated phonograph record containing 116 images & a variety of natural sounds (surf, wind, thunder & animals) as well as recordings of Bach, Mozart, Beethoven, Stravinsky, & Chuck Berry. These items were selected to provide a picture of the diversity of life & culture on Earth for any extraterrestrial disc-jockeys who might one day find them. In 1982, 154 op-art serigraphs by Viktor Vasarely were sent aboard the Soviet space station Salyut 7, but later returned to Earth to be auctioned in aid of UNESCO.

Referred to as a "poetic cipher, gene X-P13," *The Xenotext*'s DNA code is programmed to generate "Protein 13." The bacterium cell responds to this protein by causing the bacterium to fluoresce red (via a fluorophore tag) while transcribing the inserted DNA into a sequence of amino-acids. The structure of this sequence is readable by Bök's "Xenocode" as the counterpart of the original verse entitled "Eurydice."

POET (DNA ENCODED TEXT)	GERM (RNA ENCODED TEXT)
any style of life	the faery is rosy
is prim	of glow
oh stay	in fate
my lyre	we rely
with wily ploys	moan more grief
moan the riff	with any loss
the riff	any loss
of any tune aloud	is the achy trick
moan now my fate	with him we stay
in fate	oh stay
we rely	my lyre
my myth	we wean
now is the word	him of any milk
the word of life	any milk is rosy

What sets Bök's *The Xenotext* apart is its ambivalent status as *artefact*; neither aesthetic commodity nor message-to-the-cosmos in any straightforward sense, it represents an *autopoiēsis* founded in biological cybernetics – an attempt, as Bök says, at a "living poetry." Its medium is the stuff of evolution. Bök goes beyond Masura Tomita's inscription of Einstein's formula $e = mc^2$ into bacterial DNA (2007) & genome-privateer Craig Venter's coding of three short texts (by Robert Oppenheimer, Richard Feynman & James Joyce, respectively, along with a code table comprising the entire alphabet & punctuation, the names of 46 contributing scientists & an email address) into a synthetic single-celled organism. At its core, *The Xenotext* project is an attempt to initiate a coherent tropological process in which the inscribed texts serve an immediate biological function. So far, it has only been accomplished in the laboratory. Its task is to translate what Bök describes as a 14-line sonnet "about language & genetics" entitled "Orpheus." He uses a programming language called Python, a substitution code & chemical alphabet that converts into a functional DNA sequence implanted into the genome of Deinococcus radiodurans, a polyextremophile bacterium notable for its resistance to radiation.

In order to accomplish the task put forth in "Eurydice," Bök "arbitrarily assigned a letter of the alphabet to each of 26 codons (the nucleotide triplets that form the basic units of genetic code) that he'd chosen from a possible 64." He then generated word-lists that "indicated which words could be substituted for each other within a given code set," producing "a basic vocabulary for each potential cipher." Thereafter, these ciphers – approximately 7 trillion of them – were tested to determine optimal functionality & coherence, resulting in the approximately 120-word Xenocode ("ANY-THE 112").

```
ALPHABET: a b c d e f g h i j k l m n o p q r s t u v w x y z
XENOCODE: t v u k y s p n o x d r w h i g z l f a c b m j e q
```

ANY-THE 112 cipher in which Bök composed *The Xenotext* "sonnets."

The texts themselves were composed with additional constraints simultaneously: the plaintext ("Orpheus") & ciphertext ("Eurydice") should be syntactically coherent & "act in dialogue with each other, while also commenting on the subjects of bioengineering & mortality."[2] What complicates this arrangement is that the plaintext & cyphertext are not merely coded versions of one another. They are *complementary*, immanent to the code. As Darren Wershler outlined in a 2012 article, "The Xenotext Experiment, So Far":

> Transcription is much like a newspaper cryptogram, except that instead of one set of letters being gibberish & the other being meaningful, both sets are meaningful, because there is a *codependent* biochemical relationship between any preliminary DNA sequence & its resultant RNA sequence (which creates the string of amino acids in the protein), Bök's two poems must also be *codependent* in order for his project to work. He is therefore always writing two poems at the same time – poems that are mutual ciphers of each other. There are 7 trillion, 905 billion, 853 million, 580 thousand, 6 hundred & 25 (7,905,853,580,625) ways to pair up all of the letters in the alphabet so that they mutually refer to each other. All Bök has to do is find one of these ciphers that works in such a manner that when he writes a poem using one of the letters in the pair, it produces a second poem using the other letter.[3]

The process of enzyme transcription that Bök's code initiates is ongoing &, at least in principle, capable of replicating itself indefinitely without mutation. Far beyond the event-horizon of Hyabusa2's sample-return mission, it encompasses a hypothetical timeframe that would, in all probability, exceed that of the life-sustaining capacity of Earth. Indeed, Deinococcus radiodurans was specifically selected for its potential not only to accommodate Bök's "alien" DNA code, but to survive in the vacuum of space with the possibility of transmitting *The Xenotext* to distant points in the galaxy far beyond the temporal horizon of life on Earth. Bök describes it as, "in effect, aspires to a life-form" that "becomes not only a durable archive for storing a poem, but also as an operant machine for writing a poem – one that can persist on the planet until the sun itself explodes."[4] Or off-world, in interstellar space, generating future "semantic" content for an ever-expanding void, by the dimming light of heavens that it alone may remain to witness gradually turning black.

Logos Cast upon the Void. Bök's *The Xenotext* represents an attempt at both a radical *literalising* of the poetic & a radical *conceptualism*. It's a kind of sur-plus-effect of the idea of "history," inscribed within the sign of an absolute erasure of context: the proverbial "logos" cast upon the void; the detached remainder of an impossible authorisation. If conceptualism – a mode of art that "works with meaning" (à la Joseph Kosuth) – thereby seeks to question "the inherent values" of culture & society by challenging "the traditional status of the art object,"[5] *The Xenotext* becomes a self-avowed attempt to subvert aesthetic categorisation by challenging categorical thoughtvia the taxonomic order of cultural epistemology & social meaning under a humanist purview both defined & contested by previous art/literary movements. But how far does Bök's anti-aesthetic of "alienation" actually go beyond the anthropocentric perspectivesof symbolic capital & of autonomous agency?[6] Is the gesture towards a certain posthuman "idea," while simultaneously affecting a conceptualist "machine to make *art*" (Sol LeWitt)[7] within a formal system for a synthesis of *art & life*, as sufficient as it is made to seem?

a treasury	a tapestry	a threnody
it amasses	it affirms	it arouses
via twists	via tropes	via tempos
knit among	that atoms	odic grief
runic gaps	along clad	using calm
almost all	string can	lament and
regalia to	encrypt an	erotica to
ornament a	alphabet a	disquiet a
thought as	formula to	pageant as
lacing can	uplift all	utmost awe
mimic gold	adept airs	might avow
cast alloy	long cries	epic glory
set aglint	set adrift	set alight
at auroras	at abysses	at arcadia
a tapestry	a threnody	a treasury

"The March of the Nucleotides" from Book 1 of *The Xenotext*.

If *The Xenotext*'s procedural poetics falls between a bioengineered "origin" of future life & an indeterminate/open-ended posthuman "surplus-production" of semiocapital, Bök nevertheless contends that *The Xenotext* is "not simply a code that governs the development of an organism & the maintenance of its function" since "the genome can now become a vector for heretofore unimagined modes of artistic innovation & cultural expression."[8] Which is also to say, of *ideology*. Herein lies the more radical dilemma of *The Xenotext* experiment: the purchase (however provisional) of ideology upon the *idea* of a future & its *operative materiality*, far beyond the assumed horizon of ideology's *global* reach. Yet this possibility arises in a strictly *technopoetic* function. Notably, Bök's own thinking is marked less by a clear conception of a technopoetics than by a desire to renovate an historical concept of the avant-garde. "Postmodern life," he observed in a 2007 interview with Kenneth Goldsmith,

> has utterly recoded the avant-garde demand for radical newness. Innovation in art no longer differs from the kind of manufactured obsolescence that has come to justify advertisements for "improved" products; nevertheless, we have to find a new way to contribute by generating a "surprise" (a term that almost conforms to the cybernetic definition of "information"). The future of poetry may no longer reside in the standard lyricism of emotional anecdotes, but in other exploratory procedures, some of which may seem entirely unpoetic, because they work not by expressing subjective thoughts, but by exploiting unthinking machines, by colonizing unfamiliar lexicons, or by simulating unliterary artforms.[9]

"Life" isn't the privileged referent here that it seems. We are confronted with a poetic operation that constitutes an ambivalent translational zone between life "itself" & non-life, language ("living speech") & matter. This is what *Tiqqun*, in 2001, referred to as the "Cybernetic Hypothesis": "a political hypothesis, a new fable" that has "definitively supplanted the liberal hypothesis. Contrary to the latter, it proposes to conceive biological, physical, & social behaviours as something integrally programmed & re-programmable."[10] Bök refers to *The Xenotext* as a bioart project, a *poetry of record* of the Anthropocene. For him, cyberneticisation opens the possibility for *de-romanticising* the social function of avant-gardism & the value of the manufacture of *surprise*, which is no longer just an aesthetic novelty, but something of much more profound consequence. There is a clear distinction to be made between the implicit humanism of *Tiqqun*'s stance (& that of much post-1968 cultural criticism) & Bök's engagement with an avant-gardism both cognisant of & prepared to exploit the "cybernetic hypothesis" that, for political theorists like Harvey Wheeler, already constituted a "universal revolution" in 1968.[11]

In "Aleatory Writing: Notes Towards a Poetics of Chance" (2006), Bök notes: "Modern writers who deploy an aleatory strategy in their work may appear to do little more than *emulate* the random excess of irrational liberation, when in fact they confirm that, within language, such random excess is itself a sovereign necessity, an overriding requisite, which reveals the coincidental, if not conspiratory, order of words set free from the need to mean."[12] Bök relates such post-literary strategies, "a hybrid fusion of science & poetics,"[13] to an encounter between literary experimentalism & phenomena like Markov chains, quantum indeterminacy & stochastic systems of "information," resulting in a species of *alien lettrisme* that encompasses DNA & protein as *textual constraints* & as *media*. Claude Shannon & Warren Weaver called this the "asymptote of intelligibility."[14] The implications are no less ideological than they are empirical: it describes not a *conceptualism* (an "alien" *logos* subsisting like a "harmless parasite, inside the cell of another life-form" ultimately indistinguishable from "language"[15]) so much as a *data aggregate* or "critical mass" of signifiability. This asymptote of intelligibility points to the status of *The Xentotext* as an entropological feedback system that projects a cannibalised posthumanism (in holograph) of a *Homo Xenopoeticus*.

Autonomy, then, is an epiphenomenon – "an emergent result," as Katherine Hayles puts it, "of all the technological couplings, communications, energy flows, & material affordances that are deeply integrated with computational media."[16] But it is necessary to grasp how *transcription* here gives formal "expression" to the meaning of *possibility*, which is neither transcendental nor immanent, but a stochastic operation. Bök's DNA coding is an abstraction & recombination of terms. It does not *precede* the a-causal "codependency" of transcription that Merleau-Ponty called "differences *without* terms"[17] & Derrida called "*différance*."[18] Hence Bök's apparently straightforward proposition for engineering "a primitive bacterium so that it becomes a durable *archive* for *storing* a poem and a usable *machine* for *writing* a poem"[19] likewise produces the problem that it is a *poiēsis* & not a vehicle (or a "machine"[20]) acting *upon* the "poem" as an abstract entity. This is where the materialism of Bök's *The Xenotext* experiment runs against a theoretical limit in the assumption that "language" is an external agency, an operating system supervening in the otherwise autonomous operations of "writing" (i.e., transcription). Bök:

> [E]ven though language *may attempt to regulate the ephemeral interplay between the errancy of the arbitrary letter & the grammar of its mandatory syntax*, the act of writing nevertheless finds itself traversed, inevitably & invariably, by the entropic dyslalia of chance-driven phenomena (mistakes, blunders, ruptures, hiatuses, glitches, etc.) – forces of both semiotic atomization & semantic dissipation, threatening always to relegate language to a dissonant continuum of chaos & noise.[21]

But language *is* this field of "chaos & noise" constitutive of the seven trillion possible substitution ciphers from which the constraints of *The Xenotext* experiment "caused" the 120-word Xenocode ("ANY-THE 112") to be "selected." It is also constitutive of the evolutionary processes resulting in the given characteristics of Deinococcus radiodurans, its cell structures, & the transcriptive operations that underlie all of "life." This generalised semiotics (autopoetic & codependent) doesn't equate to some sort of "portentous cryptogram" beyond which lies a hidden "concept" or even a "human design." Again, Bök:

> Borges in "The Library of Babel" imagines a hellish archive of books – a macrocosmic columbarium, whose infinite chambers provide an exhaustive repository for all the permutations & combinations of the alphabet. Inside this endless library (where a single, random volume might consist of nothing but the letters MCY, perversely reiterated on every page), nonsensical texts so drastically outnumber any intelligible books that a coherent phrase, like "0 time thy pyramids," must seem tantamount to a wondrous mishap: "for one reasonable line [...] there are leagues of insensate cacophony"; hence, "[t]he impious assert that absurdities are the norm in the Library & that anything reasonable [...] is an almost miraculous exception." Such an allegory inverts the dominant norms of semantic value in order to suggest that meaningful statements constitute only the tiniest, fractional subset of an even greater, linguistic matrix. Such a repressed nightmare already haunts the work of literary scholars, who confront the oppressive totality of literature with the nagging concern that each book might have arisen of its own accord, not from the expressed sentiment of a unique author, but from the automated procedure of a formal system – a fatal order, in which even the most unlikely sequence of letters, *dhcmrlchtdj,* might yet convey a message in the form of a portentous cryptogram.[22]

Alien Wor(l)ds. Such portentousness always evokes the existence of an occult meaning that, by a paranoiac iteration, assumes the form of a "message" presenting its addressee with the spectacle of its withdrawal behind an endless promise. It is the secret promise of teleology, of the *concept* governing history as the "meaning of Being." This portentous cryptogram is nothing less than the *logos* of Homo Sapiens. *The Xenotext* represents the "metonymic dwarf"[23] of this portentous cryptogram; as Derrida infers, "its own finitude [appears] at the very moment when its limits seem to disappear, when it ceases to be self-assured, contained, & guaranteed by the infinite signified which seemed to exceed it."[24] Adrift "in the threat of limitlessness," *The Xenotext* rehearses the Platonic theatre of paternalistic dread issuing from the *crisis of writing* as allegorised in the *Phaedrus*. The limitless *dérive* opened to the logos in the guise of a supplemental "writing" – which exemplifies "mnemotechnique & the power of forgetting"[25] – threatens to *exceed any supervening context*. This radical inflation is arrested only by the "finitude" of writing. Derrida reformulates it in his critique of Plato (via the semiology of Saussure) as a "becoming-space of time & the becoming-time of space."[26] In other words, it is the finitude inscribed in difference.

The Xenotext is an analogue to Pak Chung Wong's "data-preservation problem of apocalyptic magnitude, using genome encryption in extremophile bacteria."[27] In a posthuman future, the problem *signifies* obsolescence & self-supersession, with "human data" amounting to redundant genetics; yet its operations miti-gate an *apocalyptic* view of history that can only be defined, paradoxically, by a posthumous *living-on* (bacterial genome as Noah's Ark) in the significations of "dead language." Here *The Xenotext* represents a certain *ambivalence* in which the apparently contradictory forms of living archive & mausoleum coincide. "DNA," Bök writes, "might permit us to preserve our cultural heritage against planetary disasters," citing Wong to the effect that "organisms [...] on Earth for hundreds of millions of years represent excellent candidates for protecting critical information for future generations."[28] A preservational imperative that likewise gives birth (by way of a certain ambivalence) to "a man of the future," in the words of André Leroi-Gourhan, who will "no longer be a 'man'" but rather a "toothless humanity that would exist in a prone position using what limbs it had left to push buttons with."[29]

But this preservational imperative, vested in the "alien words" of Deino-coccus radiodurans, contradicts the technogenesis it seeks to enlist, relying on a wholly *artificial* instrumental limit that is implicitly imposed upon it (e.g., the analogy between the instrumentality of Hayabusa2 & *The Xenotext* as both experimental organism & remote "space-probe"). It would be simple enough to imagine such an organic probe linked to some "human" future-present by quantum entanglement as a prosthesis for the exploration of space & *time* (a "lived experience," as Derrida says, "neither *in* the world, nor in 'another world'"[30]). Where genetic transcription becomes indistinguishable from a certain "cybernetic programme," evolutionary *semblance* (man *of the future*) would be a piece of corresponding code, a *poetics* of an imaginary idea (the human, the alien, "any style of life") that would *preserve only its erasure*. ("In the last instance, the difference between the signified & signifier *is nothing*," says Derrida.[31]) It's not the concept (of man) that is communicated through the movement of transcription, but transcription that produces the concept.

Enciphered in its logic, the "content" of Bök's conceptualism entails the human idea acting *in the gap between art & life* even as it is disguised in the autonomous operations of an abstract materiality. It implies that, even in a universe where humanity may be theoretically absent, a certain *human idea* will never cease its claims of paternity over those forms of "autonomous agency" that persist as if *in place of it*, whether in the guise of *autopoiēsis* or metaphysic. As Lacan suggested in his 1954 seminar on a materialist definition of consciousness, this is what could be called the *posthumous* counterpart of that panoptic illusionism of seeing-oneself-seeing. Lacan constructs a scenario similar to Bök's, with the distinction that he describes a world from which *all living beings* have vanished.

In the scenario, a photographic mechanism remains standing on a tripod at the edge of a lake, focused on the image of a mountain reflected there. The camera is set to operate automatically, recording whatever is framed through its viewfinder. Lacan explains:

> Once again, we're dealing with a mirror. What is left in the mirror? The rays which return to the mirror make us locate in an imaginary space the object which moreover is somewhere in reality. The real object isn't the object that you see in the mirror. So here there's a phenomenon of consciousness as such. That at any rate is what I would like you to accept, so that I can tell you a little apologue to aid your reflection.
>
> Suppose all men have disappeared from the world. I say *men* on account of the high value which you attribute to consciousness. That is already enough to raise the question – *What is left in the mirror?* But let us take it to the point of supposing that all living beings have disappeared. There are only waterfalls & springs left – lightning & thunder too. The image in the mirror, the image in the lake – do they still exist?[32]

Doubtless analogies can be drawn between the camera's production of a "perception" & the bacteria's production of a "poem" (i.e., the production, by way of transcription, of a *reading* that is also a *writing*). Does this reflexive theatre constitute *agency*? The "image," the "text" – *do they still exist?* This question haunts Bök's project. In its implied universalism, it calls attention to a crisis of self-supersession in the rationality that has so far appeared to govern its "experimental" programme. It evokes the spectre of an End-of-History in the manner of an "historico-metaphysical epoch," as Derrida says, finally determining "as language the totality of its problematic horizon."[33] With each iteration, *The Xenotext*, an index of pure repeatability, *erases* the conceptual domain of historicity by re-inscribing it as *technopoiēsis* (history *as writing*).

In this relation of an "*autonomous*" *excess* of the symbolic function, we can properly speak of a poetics of *The Xenotext* experiment, but not as the post-humanist kitsch of Bök's aestheticised glowing bacterium. This poetics is the intelligenic DNA of a *poiēsis without content*. As in Beckett, there is an appeal to an *autopoiēsis* in which writing (*différance*) is reduced to a degree zero, the pure repetition-compulsion of a signifying materiality conceived as "something of nothing": the epigenetic code as *objet petit a* onto which this "nothing" is transcribed. Yet if Derrida's notion that writing can never *in any case* be subsumed "under the category of the subject,"[34] then the alienism of *The Xenotext* is immanent to writing/transcription. The self-serenading of a mutant bacteria in space becomes an exotic *exemplum* of *astrocapitalist poetics*[35] whose message-in-a-bottle – like Carl Sagan's Voyager records or microplastics in the Mariana Trench – is ultimately *designed*, in the absence of any God, to infect the universe with an indelible *human* absence. Read against *The Xenotext*'s radical technicity, what Bök really offers, by way of the red-herring of "the poem," is an autocritique of *a* conceptualism *that mystifies itself* as a "means of art to construct a 'system' of … internally coherent signs."[36] By means of a remote proxy agent of signifying-dissipation, a residual humanism nonetheless persists within this system of signs through its attempt to *produce the "real."*

Krakow, October 2018

NOTES

CATASTROPHE PRAXIS

1. Slavoj Žižek, *Pandemic!: COVID-19 Shakes the World* (Verso, 2020).
2. Giorgio Agamben, "L'invenzione de un'epidemia," *Quodlibet* (24 February 2020): Web.
3. Giorgio Agamben, "Requiem per gli studenti" (23 May 2020): Web.
4. Pierre Bourdieu, *The Rules of Art*, trans. Susan Emanuel (Stanford University Press, 1996): 292.
5. "Advice on the Use of Masks in the Community, during Home Care & in Health Care Settings in the Context of the Novel Coronavirus (2019-nCoV) Outbreak," World Health Organization (29 January 2009): Web.
6. Zuzana Holečková, "Modernism after Modernity," Unpublished Paper.
7. The corporate state is inaugurated as a guarantor of the *mercantile contract*; the welfare state is inaugurated to provide for the maintenance of the mercantile subject, which it calls the *social contract*.
8. See Theodor Holm Nelson, "Xanalogical Structure, Needed Now More Than Ever: Parallel Documents, Deep Links to Content, Deep Versioning & Deep Re-USE," *ACM Computing Surveys* 31.2 (1999): Web.
9. David Krakauer, Nils Bertschinger, Eckehard Olbrich, et al., "The Information Theory of Individuality," *Theory of Biosciences* 139.2 (2020): 209-23.
10. Emphasis added. "Chaque parole échangée, chaque ligne imprimée établissent une communication entre les deux interlocuteurs, rendant étale un niveau qui se caractérisait auparavant par un écart d'information, donc une organisation plus grande. Plutôt qu'anthropologie, il faudrait écrire 'entropologie' le nom d'une discipline vouée à étudier dans ses manifestations les plus hautes ce processus de désintégration." Claude Lévi-Strauss, *Tristes tropiques* (Plon, 1955): 496; in English, trans. John Russell (Hutchinson & Company, 1961): 413-14.
11. Entropology, in Lévi-Strauss' terms, is a critique of anthropology that rests on the prediction of the ultimate thermodynamic levelling of all culture.
12. Claude Shannon, "A Mathematical Theory of Communication," *Bell System Technical Journal* 27 (July/October 1948): 379-423.
13. Jacques Derrida, "Structure, Sign & Play in the Discourse of the Human Sciences," *Writing & Difference*, trans. Alan Bass (Routledge, 1978): 292.

14. Derrida, "Structure, Sign & Play in the Discourse of the Human Sciences," 151-52.

15. Jacques Rancière, "The Concept of Critique & the Critique of Political Economy," *Reading Capital: The Complete Edition*, trans. Ben Brewster & David Fernbach (Verso, 2015): 160.

16. Rancière, "The Concept of Critique," 159.

17. Rancière, "The Concept of Critique," 159-60.

18. Krakauer et al., "The Information Theory of Individuality," passim.

19. See Bernard Stiegler, "Escaping the Anthropocene," Talk at Durham University (January 2015): Web.

20. See Léon de Mattis, "Epidemic Crisis & Crisis of Capital," *Non* (14 April 2020): Web.

21. See Michelet: "I define the Revolution: the advent of the Law, the resurrection of Right, & the reaction of Justice." *History of the French Revolution*, ed. G. Wright (Chicago University Press, 1967): 17.

22. See Ahmed Almheiri, Netta Engelhardt, et al., "The Entropy of Bulk Quantum Fields & the Entanglement Wedge of an Evaporating Black Hole," *High Energy Physics-Theory* (4 November 2019): Web; cf. Kaonan Micadei, John P.S. Peterson, Alexandre M. Souza, et al., "Reversing the Direction of HeatFlow using Quantum Correlations," *Nature Communications* 10.2456 (2019): Web.

APRÈS LE FUTUR … SIX PROPOSITIONS ON THE ENDS OF MODERNITY

1. Irmgard Emmelhainz, "Self-Destruction as Insurrection, or, How to Lift Earth Above All That Has Died?" *e-flux* 87 (December 2017): Web.

2. Walter Benjamin, "Theses on the Philosophy of History," *Illuminations*, trans. Harry Zohn (Schoken, 1968): 255.

3. Jürgen Habermas, "Modernity – An Incomplete Project," *The Anti-Aesthetic: Essays in Postmodern Culture*, ed. Hal Foster (The New Press, 1983).

4. Francis Fukuyama, *The End of History & the Last Man* (The Free Press, 1992).

5. Emmelhainz, "Self-Destruction as Insurrection."

6. McKenzie Wark, "Late Holocene Style," *Alienist* 4 (2018): 14-19.

7. Interior Ministry, *Principles of Anarchitecture* (Alienist, 2019): 15.

8. Jean-François Lyotard, *The Postmodern Condition: A Report on Knowledge*, trans. Geoff Bennington & Brian Massumi (Manchester University Press, 1991): 81.

9. Theodor Adorno, "Cultural Criticism & Society," *Prisms*, trans. Samuel & Sherry Weber (MIT Press, 1967): 19.

10. See Walter Benjamin, "The Work of Art in the Age of Mechanical Reproduction," *Illuminations*, trans. Harry Zohn (Fontana, 1995): 242. "This is evidently the consummation of *l'art pour l'art*. Mankind, which in Homer's time was an object of contemplation for the Olympian gods, now is one for

itself. Its self-alienation has reached such a degree that it can experience its own destruction as an aesthetic pleasure of the first degree."

11. Wark, "Late Holocene Style," 17.
12. Antonio Negri, *Insurgencies: Constituent Power & the Modern State*, trans. Maurizia Boscagli (University of Minnesota Press, 1999): 334.
13. Negri, *Insurgencies*, 335.
14. Negri, *Insurgencies*, 334.
15. Cf. Negri, *Insurgencies*, 335.
16. Lyotard, *The Postmodern Condition*, 81.
17. Guy Debord, "Theses on the Situationist International & Its Time," *The Real Split in the International*, trans. John McHale (Pluto, 2003): 23.
18. Debord, "Theses on the Situationist International & Its Time," 24.
19. Lyotard, *The Postmodern Condition*, 81.

THE POSTHUMAN ABSTRACT

1. See Jeremy Bentham, *The Panopticon Writings*, ed. Miran Bozovic (Verso, 1995).
2. Hubristically, from the point-of-view that the Anthropocene confirms humanity's mastery over the "nature."
3. Francis Fukuyama, *The End of History & the Last Man* (Hamish Hamilton, 1992).
4. Francis Fukuyama, *Our Posthuman Future: Consequences of the Biotechnological Revolution* (Picador, 2002).
5. Fukuyama, *Our Posthuman Future*, xii.
6. Jean Baudrillard, *Utopia Deferred*, trans. Stuart Kendall (Semiotext(e), 2006): 260.
7. Germán Sierra, "Deep Media Fiction," *Numéro Cinq* VII.1 (January 2016): Web.
8. Sierra, "Deep Media Fiction."
9. Baudrillard, *Utopia Deferred*, 94.
10. Baudrillard, *Utopia Deferred*, 96.
11. Manuel De Landa, *War in the Age of Intelligent Machines* (Zone, 1991): 2.
12. Cf. Jacques Lacan, "A Materialist Definition of the Phenomenon of Consciousness," *The Seminar of Jacques Lacan: Book II – The Ego in Freud's Theory & in the Technique of Psychoanalysis (1954-1955)*, trans. S. Tomaselli (Cambridge University Press, 1988): 43.
13. Mikhail Prokopenko & David M. Budden, "Is Humanity Just a Phase in Robotic Evolution?" *World Economic Forum* (September 2015): Web.
14. Gregory Bateson, "Conscious Purpose versus Nature," *Steps to an Ecology of Mind* (Paladin, 1973).
15. Prokopenko & Budden, "Is Humanity Just a Phase in Robotic Evolution?"
16. Jacques Derrida, *Dissemination*, trans. Barbara Johnson (Johns Hopkins University Press, 1981): 90.

17. Bernard Stiegler, *The Neganthropocene*, trans. & ed. Daniel Ross (Open Humanities Press, 2018): 52.
18. Jacques Lacan, *The Four Fundamental Concepts of Psychoanalysis*, ed. Jacques-Alain Miller, trans. Alan Sheridan (The Hogarth Press, 1977): 54.
19. Alfred McCoy, "The Decline & Fall of the American Empire," *The Nation* (6 December 2010): Web.
20. Karl Marx, *Outlines of the Critique of Political Economy*, trans. Martin Nicolaus (Penguin, 1973): 690-91.
21. James Joyce, "The Sisters," *Dubliners* (Viking Press, 1967): 1.
22. Slavoj Žižek, *Absolute Recoil: Towards a New Foundation of Dialectical Materialism* (Verso, 2014): 404.
23. Ignacio Torrent, "Totalising Actors in the Anthropocene: UN Peacebuilding & the Civil Society in the Magic Mountain," Paper at the London Conference in Critical Thought, University of Westminster, 29 June 2018.

ENTROPOLOGY

1. Liaisons, "The Evil to Come," *The New Inquiry* (23 April 2019): Web.
2. Jean-Luc Nancy, "Changing of the World," trans. Steven Miller, *A Finite Thinking*, ed. Simon Sparks (Stanford University Press, 2003): 22.
3. Nancy, "Changing of the World," 31.
4. Nancy, "Changing of the World," 6.
5. Nancy, "Changing of the World," 30.
6. Peter Sloterdijk, "The Anthropocene: A Process-State on the Edge of Geohistory?" trans. Anne-Sophie Springer, *Art in the Anthropocene: Encounters Among Aesthetics, Politics, Environments & Epistemologies*, eds. Heather Davis & Etienne Turpin (Open Humanities Press, 2015): 327.
7. Sloterdijk, "The Anthropocene," 329-30.
8. Sloterdijk, "The Anthropocene," 334.
9. See chapter 15 of Karl Marx, *Capital*, vol. III, ed. Friedrich Engels (International Publishers, 1967).
10. Vincent Garton, "Accelerate Marx," *Cyclonotrope* (7 March 2017): Web.
11. Primož Krašovec, "Alien Capital," trans. Miha Šuštar, *Vast Abrupt* (July 2018): Web.
12. Marx, *Capital*, vol. III, 259.
13. Krašovec, "Alien Capital."
14. Sloterdijk, "The Anthropocene," 338.
15. Georges Bataille, "The Use Value of D.A.F. de Sade," *Visions of Excess*, trans. Allan Stoekl (University of Minnesota Press, 1985): 99.
16. Sloterdijk, "The Anthropocene," 335.
17. The book was written in Paris but not translated into French until 1929.
18. Albert Goldbeter, "Dissipative Structures in Biological Systems: Bistability, Oscillations, Spatial Patterns & Waves," *Philosophical Transactions of the*

Royal Society: Mathematical, Physical & Engineering Sciences 376.2124 (June 2018): Web.

19. Marx, in the 1844 *Economic & Philosophical Manuscripts*, famously states that "nature is man's inorganic body." Here, however, the *transformation of nature* isn't accomplished by human labour, but is an *a priori condition* of generalised technicity (alienation): the inorganicity of nature in which the human is thus *embodied*. It's in this sense that Marx's formulation needs to be understood.

20. Vladimir Vernadsky, *The Biosphere*, trans. David Langmuir & Mark McMenamin (Springer, 1998): 56-57.

21. Vernadsky, *The Biosphere*, 143.

22. Vladimir Vernadsky, *Geochemstry & the Biosphere*, ed. Frank B. Salisbury (Synergetic Press, 2007): 185.

23. Vladimir Vernadsky, "The Transition from the Biosphere to the Noösphere," trans. William Jones, *21st Century* (Spring/Summer 2012): 27-28.

24. Erwin Schrödinger, *What Is Life? The Physical Aspect of the Living Cell* (Cambridge University Press, 1944).

25. Léon Brillouin, "The Negentropy Principle of Information," *Journal of Applied Physics* 24 (1953): 1152-63.

26. Schrödinger, *What Is Life?*, 68-69.

27. Schrödinger, *What Is Life?*, 69.

28. Schrödinger, *What Is Life?*, 70.

29. Schrödinger, *What Is Life?*, 73.

30. Qtd. in Sloterdijk, "The Anthropocene," 329.

31. Marx, *Capital*, vol. III, 195ff. Marx refers to "social metabolism" – the term "metabolic rift" itself was coined by John Bellamy Foster, *Marx's Ecology: Materialism & Nature* (Monthly Review Press, 2000).

32. Bernard Stiegler, "Dreams & Nightmares: Beyond the Anthropocene Era," trans. Daniel Ross, *Alienocene: The Journal of the First Outernational* (June 2019): 9.

33. Jacques Derrida, "Freud & the Scene of Writing," *Writing & Difference*, trans. Alan Bass (Routledge, 1978): 203.

34. Stiegler, "Dreams & Nightmares," 6.

35. Stiegler, "Dreams & Nightmares," 1.

36. Stiegler, "Dreams & Nightmares," 23.

37. Louis Althusser, "The Object of Capital," *Reading Capital: The Complete Edition*, trans. Ben Brewster & David Fernbach (Verso, 2015): 337.

38. The question here is one already posed by Derrida: "Under what conditions, then, could one *mark*, for a philosopheme in general, a *limit*, a margin that it could not infinitely reappropriate, *conceive* as its own, in advance engendering & interning the process of its expropriation (Hegel again, always), proceeding to its inversion by itself?" Derrida, "Tympan," *Margins of Philosophy*, trans. Alan Bass (University of Chicago Press, 1982): xiv.

39. Stiegler, "Dreams & Nightmares," 10.
40. See Jacques Derrida, "Différance," *Margins of Philosophy*, 1-28.
41. Stiegler, "Dreams & Nightmares," 11.
42. Stiegler, "Dreams & Nightmares," 23. Emphasis added.
43. Stiegler, "Dreams & Nightmares," 23.
44. Stiegler, "Dreams & Nightmares," 23.
45. Stiegler, "Dreams & Nightmares," 21.
46. Derrida, "Freud & the Scene of Writing," passim.
47. The dialectical movement of Anthropos/Neganthropos is both instrumental & finite (premised upon a sequence of ends, of unsustainable epochs) & totalising (it seeks to account for the transcendence of the epochal as such). The "end of the finitude of man," as Derrida says, "the unity of the finite & the infinite, the finite as the surpassing of the self – these essential themes of Hegel's are to be recognised at the end of the Anthropology when consciousness is finally designated as the 'infinite relation to self.'" Derrida, "The End of Man," *Margins of Philosophy*, 121.
48. Stiegler, "Dreams & Nightmares," 23.
49. See Jacques Derrida, "The Law of Genre," *Acts of Literature*, ed. Derek Attridge (Routledge, 1992): 221-52.
50. See both the *Grundrisse* & chapter 13 of *Capital*, vol. III – the principles of the 2nd law of thermodynamics were stated by Kelvin (1851) & Claussius (1854) virtually contemporaneously.
51. Derrida, "Différance," *Margins of Philosophy*, passim.
52. The expression "capitalist abstraction" is pleonastic, since capitalism *is* abstraction, evolved into a *system of self-propagation*.
53. Benjamin Noys, "Accelerationism as Will & Representation," *The Future of the New: Artistic Innovation in Times of Social Acceleration* (Valz/Antennae, 2018): Web.
54. Stiegler, "Dreams & Nightmares," 24. Here Stiegler equates an "economy of entropy" with "libidinal economy" by appeal to a certain Freudian language that should cause us to recall Derrida's injunction that the "difference between the pleasure principle & the reality principle, for example, is not uniquely, or primarily, a distinction, an exteriority, but rather the original possibility, within life, of the detour, of deferral (*Aufschub*) & the original possibility of the economy of death." Derrida, "Freud & the Scene of Writing," 198.
55. Qtd. in Natalie Wolchover, "A New Physics Theory of Life," *Quanta Magazine* (22 January 2014): Web. Emphasis added.
56. S. Sarkar & J.L. England, "Sufficient Physical Conditions for Self-Replication," *Physical Review E* 100 (2019): Abstract.
57. Jeremy L. England, "Statistical Physics of Self-Replication," *The Journal of Chemical Physics* 139 (2013).
58. Reza Negarestani, "Unidentified Gliding Object: The Day the Earth Was Unmoored," *Šum* 11 (2019): 1653.

59. What is called evolution may thus be understood not as a process of "selection" (among competing forms) but of "resonant adaptation" (*différance*), comparable to the semiological (Saussurian) principle of *differences without terms*. See Maurice Merleau-Ponty, "Indirect Language & the Voices of Silence," *Signs*, trans. Richard C. McCleary (Northwestern University Press, 1964): 39. "What we have learnt from Saussure is that, taken singly, signs do not signify anything, & that each one of them does not so much express a meaning as mark a divergence of meaning between itself & other signs. Since the same can be said of all signs, we may conclude that language is made of differences without terms; or more exactly, that the terms of language are engendered only by the differences which appear among them."

60. Cf. J.M. Horowitz, K. Zhou & J.L. England, "Minimum Energetic Cost to Maintain a Target Nonequilibrium State," *Physical Review E* 95 (2017).

61. Althusser, "The Object of Capital," 349.

62. Buckminster Fuller, *Synergetics: The Geometry of Thinking* (Macmillan, 1975).

63. Cf. Derrida, "Freud & the Scene of Writing," 202.

64. Althusser, "The Object of Capital," 344.

65. Benjamin Bratton, *The Terraforming* (Strelka, 2019): Web. Emphasis added.

66. Karl Marx, *Outlines of the Critique of Political Economy*, trans. Martin Nicolaus (Penguin, 1973): 106-07.

67. Roc Jiménez de Cisneros, "The Accelerationist Vertigo (II): Interview with Robin Mackay," *CCCB Lab* (5 November 2014): Web.

68. Marx, *Grundrisse*, 706. "Nature builds no machines, no locomotives, railways, electric telegraphs, self-acting mules, etc. These are products of human industry, natural material transformed into organs of the human will over nature, or of human participation in nature. They are organs of the human brain, created by the human hand; the power of knowledge, objectified. The development of fixed capital indicates to what degree general social knowledge has become a direct force of production, & to what degree, hence, the conditions of the process of social life itself have come under the control of the general intellect & been transformed in accordance with it; to what degree the powers of social production have been produced, not only in the form of knowledge, but also as immediate organs of social practice, of the real life process."

69. Matteo Pasquinelli, "On the Origins of Marx's General Intellect," *Radical Philosophy* 2.6 (Winter 2019): 43.

70. See Charles Babbage, *On the Economy of Machinery & Manufactures* (Charles Knight, 1832).

71. Pasquinelli, "On the Origins of Marx's General Intellect," 47.

72. Pasquinelli, "On the Origins of Marx's General Intellect," 46-47.

73. Marx, *Capital*, vol. III, 179.

74. Pasquinelli, "On the Origins of Marx's General Intellect," 47.

75. Pasquinelli, "On the Origins of Marx's General Intellect," 47. Emphasis added; see Karl Marx, *Capital: A Critique of Political Economy,* vol. I, trans. Ben Fowkes (Penguin Books, 1990): 496.

76. Just as global debt economics is ramified in the self-transcending myth of the post-Anthropocene.

77. Jacques Derrida, "From Restricted to General Economy: A Hegelianism without Reserve," *Writing & Difference*, 271.

78. Qtd. in Derrida, "From Restricted to General Economy," 270. Emphasis added.

79. Derrida, "From Restricted to General Economy," 272.

80. Jacques Derrida, "Economimesis," trans. R. Klein, *Diacritics* 11.2 (Summer 1981): 4.

81. "It is also in this sense that the contemporary biologist speaks of writing & *programme* in relation to the most elementary processes of information within the living cell. And finally, whether it has essential limits or not, the entire field covered by the cybernetic *programme* will be the field of writing. If the theory of cybernetics is by itself to oust all metaphysical concepts – including the concepts of soul, of life, of value, of choice, of memory – which until recently served to separate the machine from man, it must conserve the notion of writing, trace, *grammē*, or grapheme, until its own historico-metaphysical character is also exposed." Jacques Derrida, *Of Grammatology*, trans. Gayatri Spivak (Johns Hopkins University Press, 1976): 9.

82. Sigmund Freud, "Beyond the Pleasure Principle," *The Standard Edition of the Complete Psychological Works of Sigmund Freud* [SE], trans. James Strachey (Hogarth Press & the Institute of Psychoanalysis, 1954): XVIII.28.

83. Freud, "The Uncanny," *SE* XVII.6.

84. Derrida, "Economimesis," 6.

85. Derrida, "From Restricted to General Economy," 251.

86. Freud, "Why War?," Letter to Albert Einstein, September 1932, *SE* XXII.211.

87. Derrida, "Economimesis," 4.

88. Derrida, "Economimesis," 9.

THE TERATOLOGISTS

1. "TNT Considered as 'Storm Killer,'" *Morning News,* Delaware (11 October 1961): 17.

2. "Nuclear Bombs Planned to Break Up Hurricanes," *Newark Advocate* (11 October 1961): 1.

3. Jack W. Reed, "Some Speculations on the Effects of Nuclear Explosions on Hurricanes," *Proceedings of the Second Plowshare Symposium, May 13-15, 1959, San Francisco, California, Part V: Scientific Uses of Nuclear Explosives* (Lawrence Radiation Laboratory, 1959): 78ff.

4. Reed, "Some Speculations," 78-79.

5. Carl Sagan, "Planetary Engineering on Mars," *Icarus* 20.4 (1973): 513.

6. Carl Sagan, "The Planet Venus," *Science* 133.3456 (1961): 849-58.
7. Robert H. Haynes, "Ecce Ecopoiesis: Playing God on Mars," *Moral Expertise: Studies in Practical & Professional Ethics*, ed. Don MacNiven (Routledge, 1990): 161-63.
8. James Lovelock & Michael Allaby, *The Greening of Mars* (St. Martins Press, 1984).
9. See Michio Kaku, *The Future of Humanity: Terraforming Mars, Interstellar Travel, Immortality & Our Destiny Beyond Earth* (Doubleday, 2018).
10. See Loren MuGrush, "Elon Musk Elaborates on His Proposal to Nuke Mars," *The Verge* (2 October 2015): Web.
11. Anthony C. Muscatello & Michael G. Houts, "Surplus Weapons-Grade Plutonium: A Resource for Exploring & Terraforming Mars," Los Alamos National Laboratory (July 1996): Web.
12. *The Castle of Fu Manchu*, dir. Jess Franco (1969).
13. Samuel Johnson, *The History of Rasselas, Prince of Abissinia* (W. Baynes & Son, 1824): 494.
14. See Myron Sharaf, *Fury on Earth: A Biography of Wilhelm Reich* (St. Martins Press, 1983): 379-80.
15. On hyperstition (a portmanteau of hyper + superstition referring to "fictional entities" that "function causally to bring about their own reality"), see Nick Land, *Fanged Noumena: Collected Writings 1987-2007* (Urbanomic, 2011): 554ff.
16. See Daniel A. Vallero, *Biomedical Ethics & Decision-Making in Biomedical & Biosystem Engineering* (Academic Press, 2007): 73.
17. Oliver Morton, *The Planet Remade: How Geoengineering Could Change the World* (Princeton University Press, 2015): 312ff.
18. Qtd. in Morton, *The Planet Remade*, 313.
19. Qtd. in Morton, *The Planet Remade*, 313.
20. *United States Congressional Record* 118. 26 (24 February 1974): 4475.
21. Gregory Bateson, "Conscious Purpose versus Nature," *Steps to an Ecology of Mind* (Paladin, 1973): 405.
22. Buckminster Fuller, *Operating Manual for Spaceship Earth* (Lars Muller, 1968): 104. See also Buckminster Fuller, *Synergetics: The Geometry of Thinking* (Macmillan, 1975).
23. Benjamin H. Bratton, "Cloud Megastructures & Platform Utopias," *Entr'acte: Performing Publics, Pervasive Media, & Architecture,* ed. Jordan Geiger (Palgrave, 2015): 35.
24. Benjamin H. Bratton, "Strelka 2020: New Programme Presentation," (27 August 2020): Web.
25. *2010: The Odyssey Continues*, dir. Peter Hyams (1984).

ALTERNATIVE THREE

1. Scott Heron, *A New Black Poet: Small Talk at 125th & Lenox* (Flying Dutchman Records, 1970).
2. Other than Armstrong, Aldrin & Collins themselves – & even then, the question is moot – though now we have Damien Chazelle's Armstrong biopic, *First Man* (2018), a lens through which to witness the fictional re-enactment of this "spectacle of witness."
3. Jean Baudrillard, *La guerre du golfe n'a pas eu lieu* (Galilée, 1991).
4. Tom Wolfe, "One Giant Leap Nowhere," *New York Times* (18 July 2009).
5. Paul Virilio, *City of Panic*, trans. Julie Rose (Berg, 2007): 141-42.
6. Jean Baudrillard, "Two Essays," trans. Arthur B. Evans, *Science Fiction Studies* 18.55 (November 1991): Web.
7. See Philip K. Dick, *The Simulacra* (Ace Books, 1964).
8. Baudrillard, "Two Essays."
9. Baudrillard, "Two Essays."
10. Francois Laruelle, *Tétralogos* (Le Cerf, 2019): 112.
11. Terrance Blake, "Laruelle & Radical Science Fiction," *ResearchGate.com* (October 2019): Web.
12. Darko Suvin sought to define science fiction as a "literary genre whose necessary & sufficient conditions are the presence & interaction of estrangement & cognition, & whose main formal device is an imaginative framework alternative to the author's empirical environment." See Peter Nicholls, "Darko Suvin," *The Encyclopaedia of Science Fiction* (25 March 2019): Web.
13. Blake, "Laruelle & Radical Science Fiction." "One could summarise Laruelle's complete formula for science fiction: hard science, space opera, human destiny from dystopia to utopia."
14. Jacques Lacan, "The Subversion of the Subject & the Dialectic of Desire in the Freudian Unconscious," *Écrits*, trans. Bruce Fink (Norton, 2006): 671ff.
15. Jacques Lacan, "Seminar on 'The Purloined Letter,'" *Écrits*, trans. Bruce Fink (Norton, 2006): 7.
16. Steven Shaviro, *No Speed Limit: Three Essays on Accelerationism* (Continuum, 2015): Web.
17. Mark Fisher, *Ghosts of My Life: Writings on Depression, Hauntology & Lost Futures* (Zero Books, 2014).
18. Baudrillard, "Two Essays."
19. See Jacques Lacan, *Le séminaire VIII: Le transfert, 1960-61*, ed. Jacques-Alain Miller (Seuil, 1991): 127.
20. Lacan, "Seminar on 'The Purloined Letter,'" 7.
21. The question of fiction's epistemological status has evoked a great deal of debate. Strong positions have been taken against supposed forms of cultural relativism; the differences between science & the arts are allowed to become obscured in the name of a generalised discourse of "alternative

facts." Against this relativistic standpoint, it is argued that the use of fiction & hypothesis obey strict rules from the point of view of finality & justification, which forbid us to consider fiction & hypothesis as equivalent. We may see, however, that a so-called "equivalence of fictions" is not the same as recognising an equivalence of discursive structures (to rephrase Wittgenstein, there is no "scientific language," there is only language as such; for a proposition to be possible at all, it must be possible across discourse, *without exception*. It is for precisely this reason that an environment of "alternative facts" is able to operate at all).

22. Jacques Derrida, "Economimesis," trans. R. Klein, *Diacritics* 11.2 (Summer 1981): 2-25.
23. These ideas echo those of Charcot, Breuer & Freud concerning hysteria in which psychosomatic illness is recognised as indistinguishable from "conventional" illness.
24. Karl Popper, *The Logic of Scientific Discovery* (Hutchinson & Co., 1959).
25. Hugo Gernsback, "Baron Münchhausen's New Scientific Adventures: Thought Transmission on Mars," *Electrical Experimenter* 3.9 (January 1916): 475.
26. In the twentieth century, with the increased prevalence of new information, communication technologies & mass-mechanised warfare, many writers no longer viewed "science fiction" as a domain of literary utopianism, but rather a *state of affairs* reflecting a technocratised reality. We might think of George Orwell's *1984*, Karel Čapek's *R.U.R.* (*Rossum's Universal Robots*), or even Fred M. Wilcox's 1956 film *Forbidden Planet* in which Shakespeare's Caliban reappears in the form of a robotic "id monster" (reason's nemesis). During the 1920s & 30s, the rise of fascism exploited a widespread form of technological irrationalism & utopianism, sustained by a massive project of pseudo-scientific propaganda. In reaction, during the period following WW2, we encounter increasingly radical elements in "science fictional" writing, as seen in the works of novelists like Anthony Burgess (*A Clockwork Orange*) & behavioural scientists like José Delgado (*Towards a Psychocivilised Society*). These works respond in conflicting ways to the belief that social ills, including the abuse of science represented by the Nazi holocaust, may be remedied by means of *new* forms of ethics, education & social engineering.
27. Hugo Gernsback, "Science Fiction versus Science Faction," *Wonder Stories Quarterly* 2.1 (Autumn 1930).
28. Derrida, "Economimesis," 5.
29. Jacques Derrida, "Le facteur de la vérité," *The Post Card: From Socrates to Freud & Beyond*, trans. Alan Bass (Chicago University Press, 1987): 436.
30. Jacques Lacan, "The Youth of Gide, or the Letter & Desire," *Écrits*, 625. Translation modified. See Derrida, "Le facteur de la vérité," 467.
31. Derrida, "Le facteur de la vérité," 467-68.
32. J.G. Ballard, "Fictions of All Kinds," *#Accelerate#: The Accelerationist Reader*, eds. Robin Mackay & Armen Avanessian (Urbanomic, 2014): 237-38.

33. And, presumably, Ariosto's *Orlando Furioso* & Cyrano de Bergerac's *Voyage de la terre à la lune*, among others. See Vladimir Nabokov, *Strong Opinions* (Vintage, 1973).

34. See Bertrand Russell, "We Don't Want to Be Happy," *The New Leader* (11 March 1932).

35. In this respect, Ballard argues, however contentiously, that the "compassion, imagination, lucidity & vision of H.G. Wells & his successors (e.g., Huxley), & above all their grasp of the real identity of the twentieth century, dwarf the alienated & introverted fantasies of James Joyce, Eliot & the writers of the so-called Modern Movement, a nineteenth-century offshoot of bourgeois rejection." Ballard, "Fictions of All Kinds," 237.

36. Baudrillard, "Two Essays."

37. Qtd. in Derrida, "Le facteur de la vérité," 467.

38. Michel de Montaigne, "Of the Cannibals," *Essays*, trans. John Florio (Edward Blount, 1603): 258.

39. Lacan, "Seminar on 'The Purloined Letter,'" 11.

40. This may be driven by the entry of China, Japan, India, Israel & privateers like Virgin Galactic & SpaceX. There have been an increasing number of revivals of Wernher von Braun's space colonisation project, from Robert Zubrin's Mars Direct – the inspiration behind Brian De Palma's *Mission to Mars* (2000) & Ridley Scott's *The Martian* (2015) – to Elon Musk's SpaceX, which in 2018 successfully launched a test payload aboard the Falcon Heavy rocket comprising a Tesla Roadster, with a stereo playing David Bowie's "Space Oddity" on a loop & a digital copy of Isaac Asimov's 1950s *Foundation* saga encoded on a data crystal.

41. J.G. Ballard, "Memories of the Space Age," *The Penguin Book of Modern British Short Stories*, ed. Malcolm Bradbury (Penguin, 1988): 237.

42. Baudrillard, "Two Essays."

43. Cybernetics & Future Science Institute.

44. William Gibson, *Pattern Recognition* (Berkeley Books, 2003): 59.

45. Through "science," however, we have become accustomed to certainties that are both timeless & tolerant of contradiction. These certainties possess the adaptive qualities of "fiction," & we may indeed treat them as forms of discourse into which the unknown & the indeterminate are constantly assimilated. In this sense, "science fiction" might describe a mode of being *with* possibility. It points to the way literature describes a "philosophy of life" – a means of understanding what it is we are constantly on the verge of becoming.

46. D. Harlan Wilson, "Experiments in Postcapitalism: On Dempow Torishima's *Sisyphean*," *Los Angeles Review of Books* (3 August 2019): Web.

47. Wilson, "Experiments in Postcapitalism."

48. Carl Sagan et al., *Murmurs of Earth: The Voyager Interstellar Record* (Random House, 1978): 42.

49. Aaron Swartz, "Guerilla Open Access Manifesto" (2008): Web.

50. Baudrillard, "Two Essays."
51. Bernard Stiegler, "Hermeneutics, Heuristics & Paideia in the Digital Episteme," Talk at University of California-Berkeley, October 2013.
52. Ballard, "Memories of the Space Age," 237-38.
53. See Jacques Lacan, "Le point de capiton," *Le séminaire III: Les psychoses, 1955-56*, ed. Jacques-Alain Miller (Seuil, 1981): 296ff.
54. Science may contradict ideology (as systems of meaning) *in certain respects*, but it cannot critique it.

THE END-OF-THE-WORLD IS NECESSARY – PROGRESS IMPLIES IT

1. Often neglected in Plato's drama is the seizure, under the guise of emancipation, i.e., the *means of producing* the experience of reality (truth) as "representation."

2. We are expected to believe – whenever some oppositional movement or another arises in the face of rampant commodification, globalisation, austerity, corruption – that even the invitation to imagine such a state of affairs must really be a provocation or manoeuvre, a tactic designed to induce a kind of paranoia: that to demand the "impossible" must be madness. By the same token, we have learnt through bitter experience the language of agents provocateurs. Present day infiltration & counterintelligence operations against environmentalists, women's rights & peace activists, animal rights activists, collectivists & hackers – like LulzSec, Greenpeace, Animal Liberation Front, Climate Camp, Reclaim the Streets, Antifa – find their immediate antecedents in the practices of clandestine Cold War stay-behind operations like "Gladio," which actively pursued violent escalation among political dissidents from the 1960s onwards, falsely implicating left-wing groups in terrorist actions & discrediting movements opposed to the expansion of free market economics. These operations occurred in tandem with military & economic terrorism directed at left-wing governments in the Persian Gulf, South East Asia, Latin America & Sub-Saharan Africa, including a series of coups & assassinations in Nicaragua, El Salvador, Grenada, Chile, Guatemala, Congo, Biafra, Lesotho, Iran & elsewhere. In the period since the end of the Cold War (& the so-called "End of Ideology"), a form of paranoia has persisted whose indefinite entanglement with itself risks engendering monsters far more terrible than any conspiracy. (During the last four decades in Britain alone, undercover police infiltrated over one thousand political groups.) Today, nothing seems to be more commonplace.

3. Jacques Derrida, *The Truth in Painting*, trans. Geoffrey Bennington & Ian McLeod (Chicago University Press, 1987): 17.

4. The curve described by the "Lorenz Factor" may be said to correspond to an increment of *resistance* built into spatio-temporality & brought into view by *acceleration*. It marks the inertial event-horizon whose traversal

requires an infinite investment of energy & "represents" the impossible, the condition under which the vector of "representation" implodes.

5. The teleology of this no-futurism isn't *negated* by this radical ambivalence in which the supersession of the human is (paradoxically) its own precondition. It is constituted by the ambivalence as a kind of magical, negentropic hyper-commodity (the unpresentable "transcendental signified" that postulates the entire movement of History is no-thing but the recursive interval of signifying-substitution "itself," iterability "itself").

6. Nick Land, "A Quick & Dirty Introduction to Accelerationism," *Jacobite* (May 2017): Web.

7. We are confronted here with a movement that, in its deconstructive involutions, describes teleology as an effect of recursivity (the "strange attractor" phenomenon) or decoherence (e.g., spontaneous wave-function collapse in the quantum field), rather than any kind of latent purposiveness – a teleology, in other words, of random or pseudo-random events whose "transcendentalism" is a vectoral rate-of-change, an acceleration. It would appear to occupy a position of lability between gravitational contraction & cosmic expansion – teleology as cosmological horizon: the limit of the coherence of matter, of light (& therefore of the *imaginary*, a "teleology" whose superluminal transcendence is the realm of *mythic unpresentability*). At what point does a discussion of teleology point to a breakdown not only of "sense" but of any kind of signifying materiality (the sign distended to such an extent that iteration ceases to be possible, the exponential limit of *différance*, a semiological "Lorenz factor")? But the sign (as "Saussurian algorithm"), like the vector, is the structural (pre)condition of its own teleology. The sign is the unit of signifying-substitution (self-supersession & recursion); the vector is the unit of spacetime directionality.

8. Primož Krašovec, "Alien Capital," trans. Miha Šuštar, *Vast Abrupt* (July 2018): Web.

9. Herbert Marcuse, *One-Dimensional Man* (Beacon Press, 1964): 151.

RE-EVOLUTIONARY ABORT

1. Guy Debord, "Theses on the Situationist International & Its Time," *The Real Split in the International*, trans. John McHale (Pluto, 2003): §47, 63.

2. Debord, "Theses on the Situationist International & Its Time," §47, 63-64. Emphasis added.

3. Debord, "Theses on the Situationist International & Its Time," §43, 60.

4. Debord, "Theses on the Situationist International & Its Time," §46, 62.

5. "Le rôle de l'avant-garde culturelle, l'Internationale situationniste (IS), sur les slogans et la thermodynamique de Mai 68 est évident et pourtant difficile à établir tant la posture de père spirituel s'accorde mal avec l'esprit du mouvement." Emmanuelle Loyer, *Mai 68 dans le texte* (Éditions Complexe, 2008): 34.

6. Gilles Deleuze & Félix Guattari, "Capitalism: A Very Special Delirium," *Chaosophy: Texts & Interviews, 1972-1977*, trans. David L. Sweet, Jarred Becker & Taylor Adams (Semiotext(e), 2009): 41.
7. Deleuze & Guattari, "Capitalism: A Very Special Delirium," 42. Emphasis added.
8. Deleuze & Guattari, "Capitalism: A Very Special Delirium," 46.
9. Guattari, "Desire Is Power, Power Is Desire," *Chaosophy*, 282.
10. Deleuze & Guattari, "Capitalism: A Very Special Delirium," 36.
11. Deleuze & Guattari, "Capitalism: A Very Special Delirium," 58.
12. Mustapha Khayati, "De la misère en milieu étudiant, considérée sous ses aspects économique, politique, psychologique, sexuel et notamment intellectuel et de quelque moyens pour y remédier," (UNEF, 1966).
13. Michel Foucault, *Surveiller et punir: Naissance de la prison* (Gallimard, 1975).
14. Theodor Adorno & Max Horkheimer, *Dialectic of Enlightenment*, trans. Edmund Jephcott (Continuum, 1972).
15. Alvin Toffler, *Future Shock* (Penguin, 1970).
16. Mikhail Bakunin, "The Policy of the International," *From Out of the Dustbin: Bakunin's Basic Writings, 1869-1871*, trans. Robert M. Cutler (Ardis, 1985): 97.
17. Deleuze & Guattari, "Capitalism: A Very Special Delirium," 45.
18. Harvey Wheeler, *Democracy in a Revolutionary Era* (The Centre for the Study of Democratic Institutions, 1968): 14.
19. Wheeler, *Democracy in a Revolutionary Era*, 6.
20. Wheeler, *Democracy in a Revolutionary Era*, 124-25.
21. Wheeler, *Democracy in a Revolutionary Era*, 104-05.
22. Originally intended to be pejorative, this term was coined in 1962 by Donald Brennan. See Donald Brennan, "Strategic Alternatives: I," *New York Times* (24 May 1971): 31. "[A] Mutually Assured Destruction posture as a goal is, almost literally, mad."
23. See Herman Kahn, *On Thermonuclear War* (Princeton University Press, 1960).
24. See Vernor Vinge, "The Coming Technological Singularity: How to Survive in the Post-Human Era," *Whole Earth Review* 81 (Winter 1993).
25. A term most associated with Eugene F. Stoermer & Paul J. Crutzon, who adopted it in 2000 as an epochal geological designator of uniquely human impact upon the planetary ecosystem, including anthropogenic climate change. See Crutzen & Stoermer, "The 'Anthropocene,'" *Global Change Newsletter* 41 (2000): 17.
26. See Roy Ascot, "The Psibernetic Arch," *Telematic Embrace: Visionary Theories of Art, Technology & Consciousness*, ed. Edward A. Shanken (University of California Press, 2003): 163.
27. Gilles Deleuze, "Preface for the Italian Edition of *A Thousand Plateaus*," *Two Regimes of Madness: Texts & Interviews 1975-1995*, trans. A. Hodge & M. Taormina, ed. D. Lapoujade (Semiotext(e), 2006): 308.
28. Félix Guattari, "Deleuze & Guattari Fight Back," *Desert Islands & Other Texts: 1953-1974*, trans. Michael Taormina (Semiotext(e), 2004): 216.

29. Deleuze & Guattari, "May '68 Did Not Take Place," *Two Regimes of Madness,* 233. Emphasis added.
30. Deleuze & Guattari, "May '68 Did Not Take Place," 234.
31. Deleuze, "Preface for the Italian Edition of *A Thousand Plateaus*," 309. See Deleuze & Guattari, *Anti-Oedipus: Capitalism & Schizophrenia*, trans. R. Hurley, M. Seem & H.R. Lane (Viking, 1977).
32. Deleuze, "Dead Psychoanalysis: Analyse," *Dialogues II*, trans. Hugh Tomlinson & Barbara Habberjam (Continuum, 2006): 66.
33. Deleuze, "Dead Psychoanalysis," 58.
34. Deleuze, "Preface for the Italian Edition of *A Thousand Plateaus*," 309.
35. Guattari, "Deleuze & Guattari Fight Back," 216.
36. Guattari, "Deleuze & Guattari Fight Back," 216-17.
37. Guattari, "Deleuze & Guattari Fight Back," 217.
38. James Joyce, *Finnegans Wake* (Faber, 1941): 218:02.
39. Deleuze, "On the Superiority of Anglo-American Literature," *Dialogues II*, 38.
40. Deleuze, "Dead Psychoanalysis," 86.
41. Gilles Deleuze & Michel Foucault, "Intellectuals & Power," *Desert Islands*, 206.
42. Michel Foucault, "Nietzsche, Freud, Marx," *Essential Works of Michel Foucault, Vol. 2: Aesthetics, Method & Epistemology*, ed. James D. Faubion (The New Press, 1998): 274.
43. Deleuze, "Dead Psychoanalysis," 86. Emphasis added.
44. What Merleau-Ponty characterised as "differences without terms." See Maurice Merleau-Ponty, "Indirect Language & the Voices of Silence," *Signs*, trans. Richard C. McCleary (Northwestern University Press, 1964): 39.
45. Deleuze, "How Do We Recognise Structuralism?" *Dialogues II*, 175.
46. Deleuze, "Capitalism & Schizophrenia," *Desert Islands*, 232.
47. Deleuze, "Capitalism & Schizophrenia," 232.
48. Deleuze, "Dead Psychoanalysis," 58.
49. For an overview of Accelerationism & some of the legacies of Deleuze & Guattari, see Benjamin Noys, *Malign Velocities: Accelerationism & Capitalism* (Zero Books, 2014).
50. See Jean-François Lyotard, *The Postmodern Condition: A Report on Knowledge*, trans. Geoff Bennington & Brian Massumi (Manchester University Press, 1991).
51. Debord, "Theses on the Situationist International & Its Time," §14-15, 20-21.
52. Debord, "Theses on the Situationist International & Its Time," §15, 22.
53. Debord, "Theses on the Situationist International & Its Time," §16, 24.
54. Debord, "Theses on the Situationist International & Its Time," §37, 53.
55. Deleuze & Guattari, "Capitalism: A Very Special Delirium," 43.
56. Debord, "Theses on the Situationist International & Its Time," §35, 46.
57. Debord, "Theses on the Situationist International & Its Time," §16, 23.
58. Debord, "Theses on the Situationist International & Its Time," §16, 23-24.

59. Bernard Stiegler, *The Neganthropocene*, trans. & ed. Daniel Ross (Open Humanities Press, 2018): 51.

60. Stiegler, *The Neganthropocene*, 52.

61. Foucault, "On the Archaeology of the Sciences," *Essential Works of Michel Foucault: Volume 2*, 325.

62. Stiegler, *The Neganthropocene*, 52-53. Emphasis added.

63. Stiegler, *The Neganthropocene*, 267.

64. Like every collapse into singularity, the Anthropocene has inaugurated itself through a breakdown of the laws of physical semantics, thus giving rise to an ever-increasing number of "explanatory theories" concerned solely with its denial (i.e., pseudo-critical noise).

65. McKenzie Wark, *Molecular Red: Theory for the Anthropocene* (Verso, 2016).

66. Comité Enragés/Situationist International Placard, 1968. Gérard Berréby & Raoul Vaneigem, *Rien n'est finit, tout commence* (Alia, 2014): 281.

67. Karl Marx, *Capital*, vol. III, trans. Ben Fowkes (Vintage, 1981): 949. The term "metabolic rift" was coined by John Bellamy Foster in *Marx's Ecology: Materialism & Nature* (Monthly Review Press, 2000).

68. See Julian Offray de La Metrie, *L'homme machine* (1747).

69. McKenzie Wark, "Molecular Red in Nine Minutes (Responding to Maria Chehonaskih)," *Public Seminar* (29 September 2015): Web.

70. Daniel Bensaïd & Michael Löwy, "Auguste Blanqui, Heretical Communist," trans. Philippe Le Goff, *Radical Philosophy* 185 (May/June 2014): 35. Cf Auguste Blanqui, *Eternity by the Stars*, trans. Frank Chouraqui (Contra Mundum, 2013): 40.

71. Bensaïd & Löwy, "Auguste Blanqui, Heretical Communist," 40.

72. Walter Benjamin, "Theses on the Philosophy of History," *Illuminations*, trans. Harry Zohn (Schocken, 1968): 262.

73. Foucault, "Theatrum Philosophorum," *Essential Works of Michel Foucault*, vol. 2, 353.

DISPATCHES FROM THE EVENT-HORIZON

1. Mencius Moldbug (aka Curtis Yarvin), "Patchwork: A Positive Vision (Part 1)," *GitHub* (13 November 2008): Web.

2. Michael James, "Global Wyrding & Deeply Adaptive Patchworking," *Synthetic Zero* (8 November 2018): Web.

3. Corresponding to this return of resistance is a certain return of the repressed, which might otherwise be stated as a return of the "Real" – both in the political & psychoanalytic sense.

4. Take Britain's largest sustained experiment in "alternative living," the Eel Pie Island commune located in the Thames at Twickenham (London) that dates from the 1960s, current population 100, only marginally less than the 130 recorded at the community's height. By comparison, Freetown

Christiania in Copenhagen sustains a resident population of 900. (The models of sustainability that these communities represent differ & need to be compared with the urban environments from which they are annexed (e.g., Metropolitan London has a population of 14 million over an area of 1,572 km^2 – Eel Pie Island is .036 km^2 – while Copenhagen's population is roughly 600,000 over 88.25 km^2, with Christiania just over .07 km^2, densities amounting to 8,900/km^2 & 6,800/km^2 respectively. Consider both of these in relation to that paradigm of vertically-integrated, globally-decentred neo-liberalism: Amazon, whose UK workforce is distributed around the country in a series of logistical hubs redolent of Owen's semi-autonomous microstates & currently totals just 27,500 in an industry that, in 2017 alone, accounted for 586.3 billion of GDP & spans the datasets of a global demographic in the billions. Meanwhile, according to conventional manufacturing statistics, the UK is presently ranked eighth largest globally by output. New technology & "smart factories" mean that this output corresponds to a domestic work-force of only 2.6 million against national unemployment figures of 1.49 million or 4.5%. None of these structures – communal, corporate, statist – is self-sufficient: their autonomy rests solely (& somewhat paradoxically) on comprising integral units in what amounts to a multidimensional global "patchwork." It's no surprise, either, that the island of Britain produces only 50% of the foodstuffs it annually consumes, purchased at the expense of its strategic advantage in manufacturing; a £40.7 billion deficit means its economy will never of its own accord be "in balance." These figures offer no real augury of coming events when arrayed before the spectre of the Anthropocene against whose immanent derangements of the World Order neither fiscal policy nor "technological solutions" appear likely to be mitigation strategies for the Corporate-State Apparatus, the ecosystem at large, or the mass of humanity. Given that the scenario is one of NO EXIT, the outcomes are more likely to be infrastructural collapse, resource wars, mass eugenics, famine, epidemic & other apocalyptic niceties, not some proactive conversion of the Corporate State to debt reduction, environmental responsibility & sustainable communitarianism. Such a thing isn't even possible with populations reaching 512.7 million in the EU, 325.7 million in the US, 264 million in Indonesia, 209 million in Brazil, 144.5 million in Russia, not to mention the 1.34 billion in India & the 1.386 billion in China, etc., etc., etc.).

5. Victor Hugo, *Les Misérables* (1903).
6. See Francis Fukuyama, *The End of History & the Last Man* (London: Hamish Hamilton, 1992): xii & following.
7. Jacques Derrida, *Spectres of Marx*, trans. Peggy Kamuf (London: Routledge, 1994): 100.
8. Derrida, *Spectres of Marx*, 97; cf. Guy Debord, *Société du Spectacle* (1967) & Jean Baudrillard, *Simulacres et Simulation* (1981).

9. "Every concept is necessarily & essentially inscribed in a chain or a system, within which it refers to another & to other concepts, by the systematic play of differences. Such a play – *différance* – is no longer simply a concept, but the possibility of conceptuality, of the conceptual system & process in general." Jacques Derrida, "The Voice that Keeps Silence," *Speech & Phenomena, & Other Essays on Husserl's Theory of Signs*, trans. David Alison (Northwestern University Press, 1973): 140.

10. Derrida, "The Voice that Keeps Silence," 82.

11. Karl Marx, *Outlines of the Critique of Political Economy*, trans. Martin Nicolaus (Penguin, 1973): 693.

12. Derrida, "The Voice that Keeps Silence," 82.

13. Capital is to capitalism as DNA is to gene editing.

14. Slavoj Žižek, *Living in the End Times* (Verso, 2010): 244.

15. That is to say, it possesses properties unaccounted for by either its parts or its causality.

16. James, "Global Wyrding & Deeply Adaptive Patchworking." "[C]omplex, multi-faceted, networked, & nonlinear changes & disruptions have been collectively & broadly described in many journalist circles as 'global weirding' since the mid-2000s." See also Mark Fisher, *The Weird & the Eerie* (Repeater, 2016).

17. The potential of the uncanny to disturb *systemically* is a symptom of the system that operates cybernetically by *breaking down*. The so-called weird isn't a mode of *subverting* the system of Capital but its operational norm. If we take the apparent "weirdness" of Hunter S. Thompson's gonzo journalism, for instance, it isn't "fake news" & it isn't a parody; it's a form of direct reporting of the predominant Capitalist Realism of the times. The contemporary Chinese literary genre *chaohuan* (i.e., "ultra-unrealism") is similarly an example of how this situation is misrecognised. It isn't the world of hypercapitalism that's somehow become "ultra-unreal." Quite the contrary. It's those cultural & political discourses bound to certain historical representations of themselves that persist in misconstruing their relationship. These are the "ideological social forms" that produce this experience of ultra-unrealism.

18. Ognyan Oreshkov, qtd. in Philippe Guérin & Časlav Brukner, "Observer-Dependent Locality of Quantum Events," *arXiv* (31 October 2018): 2.

19. In his notes on engineering a corporate anti-society of the future, Moldbug has this to say: "Patchwork is something new. It will not feel like the past. It will feel like the future. The past – that is, the democratic past – will feel increasingly grey, weird, & scary" ("Patchwork: A Positive Vision [Part 1]"). But this is par for the course. "Democracy" has always provoked fear in such visionary egoists of corporate statism ("all exit & no voice"), just like the workers' movements, the civil rights movements, the women's liberation movements – anything at all that entailed collective political representation against the abstract prerogatives of the marketplace. Yet emancipation speaks with a forked tongue. As Margaret Thatcher once declared: "There's

no such thing as society. There are individual men & women & there are families. And no government can do anything except through the people, & people must look after themselves first" (Thatcher, Interview with *Woman's Own* [31 October 1987]: 8-10). This remark was later clarified in a statement to the *Sunday Times* (10 July 1988): 45. Here, Thatcher adds: "[S]ociety as such does not exist except as a concept. Society is made up of people. It is people who have duties & beliefs & resolve. It is people who get things done." Yet it is precisely the *weirdness* of such advertisements for the obsolescence of government that serves to legitimise their appeal to the emancipation of the self-interested individual, while simultaneously excluding the individual from the function of governance. (*Détournement*, as Debord was pleased to observe, tends in rapid order to the lowest ideological denominator.)

20. Pablo Servigne, Raphaël Stevens & Gautier Chapelle, *Un autre fin du monde est possible* (Seuil, 2018).
21. Victor L. Shammas & Tomas B. Holen, "Leaving the Twenty-First Century: A Conversation with McKenzie Wark," *Continental Thought & Theory* 2.3 (December 2018): 297-328, 299.
22. G.W.F. Hegel, *Phenomenology of Spirit*, trans. A.V. Miller (Oxford University Press, 1978): 14. Cf. Martin Heidegger, "The Question Concerning Technology," *Basic Writings: From Being & Time (1927) to The Task of Thinking (1964)*, ed. David Farrell Krell (Routledge, 1993): 308.
23. From Revelation to *ricorso* to self-supersession.

TRANS/MORPHIC

1. Jorge Luis Borges, *Collected Fictions*, trans. Andrew Hurley (Penguin, 1999): 242.
2. Borges, *Collected Fictions*, 253.
3. Borges, *Collected Fictions*, 252.
4. Borges, *Collected Fictions*, 253.
5. Ludwig Wittgenstein, *Tractatus Logico-Philosophicus*, ed. C.K. Ogden (Routledge & Kegan Paul, 1922): 5.6.
6. Alan Turing, "The Chemical Basis of Morphogenesis," *Philosophical Transactions of the Royal Society of London, Series B, Biological Sciences* 237.641 (1952): 37-72.
7. Turing, "The Chemical Basis of Morphogenesis," 38.
8. Jacques Derrida, "Différance," *Margins of Philosophy*, trans. Alan Bass (Chicago University Press, 1982).
9. "The possible, implying the becoming – the passage from one to the other takes place in the infra-thin." Marcel Duchamp, *Notes*, trans. Paul Matisse (G.K. Hall, 1983).
10. James Joyce, *Finnegans Wake* (Faber, 1939): 518.02.

11. Borges, *Collected Fictions*, 242.
12. Borges, *Collected Fictions*, 244.
13. Borges, *Collected Fictions*, 248.
14. Borges, *Collected Fictions*, 251.
15. See, e.g., Katia Moskvitch, "Quantum Correlations Reverse Thermodynamic Arrow of Time," *Quanta* (2 April 2018): Web.
16. Jacques Lacan, "A Materialist Definition of the Phenomenon of Consciousness," *The Seminar of Jacques Lacan: Book II – The Ego in Freud's Theory & in the Technique of Psychoanalysis (1954-1955),* trans. S. Tomaselli (Cambridge University Press, 1988): 48.
17. Peter Sloterdijk, *Critique of Cynical Reason*, trans. Michael Eldred (University of Minnesota Press, 1988): xxxiii.
18. Sloterdijk, *Critique of Cynical Reason*, xxxiii.
19. Antonin Artaud, *Oeuvres Complètes* (Gallimard, 1956): VIII.192.
20. Jacques Rancière, *Reading Capital: The Complete Edition*, trans. Ben Brewster & David Fernbach (Verso, 2015): 160.
21. Rancière, *Reading Capital*, 159.
22. Rancière, *Reading Capital*, 159-60.
23. Antonin Artaud, "What I Came to Mexico to Do," *Selected Writings*, ed. Susan Sontag (FSG, 1976): 374.
24. Jacques Derrida, "Economimesis," trans. R. Klein, *Diacritics* 11.2 (Summer 1981): 2-25.
25. It is meaningless to speak of observable or unobservable phenomena: a phenomenon is produced by observation.
26. Philip Ball, "Quantum Physics May Be Even Spookier Than You Think," *Scientific American* (21 May 2018): Web.
27. See, e.g., the concept of the *delayed-choice quantum eraser* in Yoon-Ho Kin et al., "A Delayed 'Choice' Quantum Eraser," *Physical Review Letters* 84.1 (2000): 1-5.
28. Corresponding to the 14 possible configurations into which atoms can be arranged in crystals: triclinic (1), monoclinic (2), orthorhombic (4), tetragonal (2), hexagonal (2), cubic (3).
29. Their mirror-correlation might also be regarded as a mode of bistability, between episodes of suprathreshold perturbation (bifurcations & transmissions from one stable attractor to another).

XENOTEXT

1. Japanese Aerospace Exploration Agency (Tokyo).
2. Barbara Auclino & Dianne Timblin, "The Making of a Xenotext," *American Scientist* (22 June 2016): Web.
3. Darren Wershler, "The Xenotext Experiment, So Far," *Canadian Journal of Communication* 37.1 (2012): 50. Emphasis added.

4. Christian Bök, "The Xenotext Works," *Poetry* (April 2011).
5. Tony Godfrey, *Conceptual Art* (Phaidon, 1998): 4.
6. See Primož Krašovec, "Alien Capital," trans. Miha Šuštar, *Vast Abrupt* (n.d.): Web.
7. Sol LeWitt, "Paragraphs on Conceptual Art," *Artforum* (1967): Web.
8. Christian Bök, *The Xenotext Experiment* (ubu Editions, 2007): 4.
9. Christian Bök & Kenneth Goldsmith, "The Xenotext Experiment: An Interview with Christian Bök," *Postmodern Culture* (28 July 2007): Web.
10. "The Cybernetic Hypothesis," *Tiqqun* (2001): Web.
11. Harvey Wheeler, *Democracy in a Revolutionary Era* (The Centre for the Study of Democratic Institutions, 1968): 14.
12. Christian Bök, "Aleatory Writing: Notes Towards a Poetics of Chance," *Public 33 Errata* (2006): 26. Emphasis added.
13. Bök, *The Xenotext Experiment*, 7.
14. As, i.e., the defining contour of "language." See Claude Shannon & Warren Weaver, *The Mathematical Theory of Communication* (University of Illinois Press, 1963): 43.
15. Bök, *The Xenotext Experiment*, 4.
16. N. Katherine Hayles, "Literary Texts as Cognitive Assemblages: The Case of Electronic Literature," *Top of FormBottom of FormElectronic Book Review* (2018): Web.
17. Maurice Merleau-Ponty, "Indirect Language & the Voices of Silence," *Signs*, trans. Richard C. McCleary (Northwestern University Press, 1964): 39.
18. Jacques Derrida, "Différance," *Margins of Philosophy*, trans. Alan Bass (Chicago University Press, 1982).
19. Bök, *The Xenotext Experiment*, 4. Emphasis added.
20. See Paul Davies, "Do We Have to Spell It Out," *New Scientist* 2459 (7 August 2004): 30-31.
21. Bök, "Aleatory Writings," 26. Emphasis added.
22. Bök, "Aleatory Writings," 25.
23. Jacques Derrida, "Two Words for Joyce," *Post-Structuralist Joyce: Essays from the French*, eds. Derek Attridge & Daniel Ferrer (Cambridge University Press, 1984): 148.
24. Derrida, *Of Grammatology*, 6.
25. Derrida, *Of Grammatology*, 24.
26. Derrida, *Of Grammatology*, 68.
27. Bök, "Aleatory Writings," 3.
28. Bök, "Aleatory Writings," 3. See Wong, Pak Chung, et al., "Organic Data Memory Using the DNA Approach," *Communications of the ACM* 46.1 (January 2003): 95-98.
29. André Leroi-Gourhan, *Le geste et la parole* (1965), qtd. in Derrida, *Of Grammatology*, 85.
30. Derrida, *Of Grammatology*, 65.

31. Derrida, *Of Grammatology*, 23.

32. Jacques Lacan, "A Materialist Definition of the Phenomenon of Consciousness," *The Seminar of Jacques Lacan: Book II – The Ego in Freud's Theory & in the Technique of Psychoanalysis (1954-1955)*, trans. S. Tomaselli (Cambridge University Press, 1988): 46. Lacan's engagement with cybernetics, & his treatment of the status of the thing in Freud ("A Materialist Definition of the Phenomenon of Consciousness," "Homeostasis & Insistence," "Freud, Hegel & the Machine," "The Circuit") is conspicuous for the way it eschews any easy gesture of transcendence in the category of humanism in approaching a definition of consciousness not seated in the "I" of Cartesian subjectivity. Instead, Lacan posits an antecedent subjective condition of an apparently paradoxical post-human/ism, i.e., the positing of a post-human/ism as the condition for any human/ism by which subjectivity is grasped as an operation or set of operations – in short, we might say, a *poiēsis*. This is an inversion of the classical dichotomy of *technē* & *poiēses* as well as a thinking anew of a techno-poetic foundation of subjectivity that is techno insofar as subjectivity always involves a logic of prosthesis & is aim-orientated, poetic in the sense that subjectivity is tropic.

33. Derrida, *Of Grammatology*, 6.

34. Derrida, *Of Grammatology*, 68.

35. See Joshua Schuster, "On Reading Christian Bök's 'The Xenotext Book 1' Ten Thousand Years Later," *Jacket 2* (February 2016): Web.

36. Jacques Rancière, "Documentary Fiction: Chris Marker & the Fiction of Memory," *Blackout* (2018): Web.

ENTROPOLOGY

LOUIS ARMAND is the author of *Videology, The Organ-Grinder's Monkey, Literate Technologies, Technē, Event-States, & Incendiary Devices*. Other publications include the collage-hybrid *Glitchhead*; the novels *The Garden, Vampyr, & The Combinations*; & the poetry collections *East Broadway Rundown* and *Monument* (with John Kinsella). Armand directs the Centre for Critical & Cultural Theory at Charles University, Prague.

www.ingramcontent.com/pod-product-compliance
Lightning Source LLC
Chambersburg PA
CBHW070836100426
42813CB00003B/639